Shortcuts in
QUANTIATIVE APTITUDE

for Competitive Exams

- **Corporate Office :** 45, 2nd Floor, Maharishi Dayanand Marg, Corner Market, Malviya Nagar, New Delhi-110017
  Tel. : 011-49842349/49842350

DISHA PUBLICATION

ALL RIGHTS RESERVED

© Copyright Publisher

For further information about books from DISHA,

Log on to **www.dishapublication.com** or email to **info@dishapublication.com**

Index

Number System & Simplification

When two numbers are divided by a third number, leave the same remainder, then the difference of these two numbers is always perfectly divisible by third number.

1. **24345 and 33334 are divided by certain number of three digits and the remainder is the same in both the cases. Find the divisor and the remainder.**
   (a) 103, 6 (b) 809, 3 (c) 101, 4 (d) 109, 5

Sol. **(c)** Difference = 33334 − 24345 = 8989

Since, 8989 = 101 × 89

∴ 101 is the required 3 digit divisor

On dividing any of the given numbers by 101, we get 4 as remainder.

To find the greatest n digits number completely divisible by a divisor. Find the remainder by dividing greatest n digits number by the divisor.

Required number = (Greatest n digits number) − (Remainder)

2. **What is the largest number of 4 digits which is completely divisible by 18?**
   (a) 9990 (b) 9984 (c) 9992 (d) None of these

Sol. **(a)** Greatest four digits number = 9999

Divisor = 18

$$
\begin{array}{r|l}
18 & \underline{9999}\;(555 \\
   & \;\,90 \\
   \hline
   & \;\,99 \\
   & \;\,90 \\
   \hline
   & \;\,99 \\
   & \;\,90 \\
   \hline
   & \;\;\,9
\end{array}
$$

Remainder = 9

So, required number = 9999 − 9 = 9990

3. **What is the greatest odd number of 4-digits which is completely divisible by 17?**

    (a) 9996   (b) 9979   (c) 9981   (d) 9991

Sol. **(b)**   Greatest four digits number = 9999

          Divisor = 17

$$17 \,\big)\, \overset{9999}{85} \,\big(\, 588$$

```
17 | 9999  (588
   |   85
   | ----
   |  149
   |  136
   | ----
   |  139
   |  136
   | ----
   |    3
```

          Remainder = 3

          So, number = 9999 – 3 = 9996

          But, 9996 is even number, so subtract

          17 from 9996.

          Difference = 9996 – 17 = 9979.

          (Which is odd number)

          Hence, the required number is 9979

⊕ Shortcut Approach - 3

To find the least *n* digits number completely divisible by a divisor. Find the remainder by dividing least *n* digits number by the divisor.

Required number = (Least *n* digits number) + (Divisor – Remainder)

4 . **What is the smallest number of 4-digits which is completely divisible by 22?**

    (a) 1008   (b) 1010   (c) 1002   (d) 1012

Sol. **(d)**   The least four digit number = 1000

          Divisor = 22

```
22 | 1000  (45
   |   88
   | ----
   |  120
   |  110
   | ----
   |   10
```

          So, required number

          = 1000 + (22 – 10) = 1012

⊕ Shortcut Approach - 4

If sum and difference of two numbers are given, then
Product of the two numbers

$$= \frac{(\textbf{Sum + Difference}) \times (\textbf{Sum – Difference})}{4}$$

5. The product of two terms is 4640 and their difference is 22. Find the sum of their reciprocals.

(a) $\dfrac{14}{2025}$ (b) $\dfrac{69}{2320}$ (c) $\dfrac{19}{3941}$ (d) $\dfrac{11}{1347}$

Sol. (b) Let the numbers be x and y

$$\text{Product} = \left[\frac{(\text{Sum} + \text{Difference})(\text{Sum} - \text{Difference})}{4}\right]$$

$$4640 = \left[\frac{(\text{Sum} + 22)(\text{Sum} - 22)}{4}\right]$$

$$4640 = \left[\frac{(\text{Sum})^2 - (22)^2}{4}\right]$$

$$(\text{Sum})^2 = 4640 \times 4 + (22)^2$$
$$= 18560 + 484$$
$$\text{Sum} = (19044)^{1/2} = 138$$

$$\text{Now, } \frac{1}{x} + \frac{1}{y} = \frac{x+y}{xy} = \frac{\text{Sum}}{\text{Product}} = \frac{138}{4640} = \frac{69}{2320}$$

⊕ Shortcut Approach - 5

Sum of the digits of a given two digit number is S. When its digits are interchange their places, the number decreased by D. Then,

$$\text{Given number} = 5\left(S + \frac{D}{9}\right) + \frac{1}{2}\left(S - \frac{D}{9}\right)$$

6. Sum of the digits of a given 2–digit number is 12. When its digits interchange their places, the number decreases by 54. Find the number.

(a) 93   (b) 84   (c) 75   (d) 66

Sol. (a) Given number

$$= 5\left[S + \frac{D}{9}\right] + \frac{1}{2}\left[S - \frac{D}{9}\right]$$

$$= 5\left[12 + \frac{54}{9}\right] + \frac{1}{2}\left[12 - \frac{54}{9}\right]$$

$$= 5 \times 18 + \frac{1}{2} \times 6 = 93$$

⊕ Shortcut Approach - 6

Sum of the digits of a given two digit number is S. When its digits interchange their places, the number is increased by I. Then

$$\text{Given number} = 5\left(S - \frac{I}{9}\right) + \frac{1}{2}\left(S + \frac{I}{9}\right)$$

7. **Sum of the digits of a given 2-digit number is 13. When its digits interchange their places, the number increases by 9. Find the given number.**

    (a)   76   (b) 94   (c) 67   (d) 85

Sol. **(c)**   Given number

$$= 5\left(S - \frac{I}{9}\right) + \frac{1}{2}\left(S + \frac{I}{9}\right)$$

$$= 5\left(13 - \frac{9}{9}\right) + \frac{1}{2}\left(13 + \frac{9}{9}\right)$$

$$= 5 \times 12 + \frac{1}{2} \times 14$$

$$= 60 + 7 = 67$$

⊕ Shortcut Approach - 7

If difference between a two-digit number and the number obtained by interchanging the digits is given, then difference of the two digits of the two

$$\text{digits number} = \frac{\text{Difference in original and new number}}{9}$$

8. **If the difference between a two-digit number and the number obtained by interchanging digits is 36, then find the difference of the digits of the original number.**

    (a)   1   (b) 2   (c) 3   (d) 4

Sol. **(d)**   (Difference of the digits of the number)

$$= \frac{\left(\begin{array}{c}\text{Difference of original}\\ \text{and new number}\end{array}\right)}{9}$$

$$= \frac{36}{9} = 4$$

If ratio of the sum and the difference of two numbers is $a : b$, then

Ratio of the two numbers $= \dfrac{a+b}{a-b}$

9. **Ratio of the sum and difference of two numbers is 9 : 1. Find the ratio of these two numbers.**

    (a) 5 : 4   (b) 9 : 5   (c) 2 : 1   (d) 3 : 2

Sol. **(a)** Ratio of the two numbers $= \left(\dfrac{a+b}{a-b}\right)$

$$= \left(\dfrac{9+1}{9-1}\right) = \dfrac{10}{8} = 5 : 4$$

(i) $(a^n + b^n)$ is divisible by $(a + b)$ when n is odd

(ii) $(a^n - b^n)$ is divisible by both $(a + b)$ and $(a - b)$ when n is even

(iii) $(a^n - b^n)$ is divisible by only $(a - b)$ when n is odd

10. **If $(67^{67} + 67)$ is dividing by 68, the remainder is :**

    (a) 61   (b) 67   (c) 63   (d) 66

Sol. **(d)** $\because (x^n + y^n)$ is divisible by

      $(x + y)$ when n is odd

      So, $((67^{67} + 1^{67}) + 66)$

        $(67^{67} + 1^{67})$ is divisible by 68,

      Hence remainder is 66.

When $(x^n + k)$ is divided by $(x - 1)$,

(a)   Remainder $= 1 + k$; if $k < (x - 1)$

(b)   Remainder $= 1 +$ (Remainder obtained when

             k is divided by $x - 1$); if $k > x - 1$

11. **Find the remainder on dividing $(9^{16} + 6)$ by 8.**

    (a) 5   (b) 7   (c) 2   (d) 3

Sol. **(b)** Here $k = 6$ and $x - 1 = 8$

      $\therefore$ $k < (x - 1)$

      So, Remainder $= 1 + k = 1 + 6 = 7$

A number when divided by d_1 and d_2 successively, leaves the remainder r_1 and r_2 respectively. If the number is divided by $d_1 \times d_2$, then Remainder $= d_1 \times r_2 + r_1$

12. **A certain number when successively divided by 3 and 5 leaves remainder 1 and 2. What is the remainder if the same number be divided by 15?**
   (a) 7   (b) 8   (c) 9   (d) 10

Sol. **(a)**   Remainder $= (d_1 \times r_2 + r_1)$
$= (3 \times 2 + 1) = 7$

Shortcut Approach - 12

To find the number of zeros at the end of a product, write the product as prime factorisation like (in the prime factorise bases are different prime numbers and powers are natural numbers)

Product $= 2^m \times 5^n \times$ ......

Here m and n are natural numbers. Now you know that product of each pair of 2 and 5 gives a zero (0), therefore
The product has m zeros, if $m < n$ and
The product has n zeros, if $m > n$.
The product has m or n zeros, if $m = n$.

13. **Number of zeroes at the end in the product $1 \times 2 \times 3 \times 4 \times$ ...... $\times$ 25 is**
   (a) 5   (b) 6   (c) 10   (d) 25

Sol. **(b)**   Let $1 \times 2 \times 3 \times ... \times 25 = 2^x 5^y z$ where Z is the which is neither divisible by (2) nor by (5)
   5, 10, 15, 20, 25 are the multiplier of 5 where 25 has two multiples of 5. (i.e. : $5 \times 1 = 5, 5 \times 2 = 10, 5 \times 3 = 15, 5 \times 4 = 20, 5 \times 5 = 25$) So $y = 6$. It is clear that indices of 2 will be more than 5 means x > 6 means there will be maximum 6 pairs of 2×5. So their will be 6 zeros at the end of the given numbers.

14. **If $2 \times 4 \times 6 \times 8 \times 10 \times 12 \times$ .... $\times 60$ will be divisible by 10^n, then what can be the maximum value of n?**
   (a) 12   (b) 10   (c) 14   (d) 15

Sol. **(c)**   It is similar previous Question
   Here, total power on 5 will be $12 + 2 = 14$.

Shortcut Approach - 13

(a) Unit digit of any power of the numbers with unit digit 0, 1, 5 and 6 are respectively 0, 1, 5 and 6 i.e.
$$(\ldots \ldots 0)^n = (\ldots \ldots \ldots 0)$$
$$(\ldots \ldots \ldots 1)^n = (\ldots \ldots \ldots 1)$$
$$(\ldots \ldots \ldots 5)^n = (\ldots \ldots \ldots 5)$$
$$(\ldots \ldots \ldots 6)^n = (\ldots \ldots \ldots 6)$$

(b) If unit digit of any number is other than 0, 1, 5 and 6; then multiply its unit digit by itself least number of times till you get the unit digit as 1, 5 or 6.

Count the number of times you multiply the unit digit by itself.

Let's see

$(2)^4 = 16$ $(3)^4 = 81$

$(4)^2 = 16$ $(7)^4 = 2401$

$(8)^4 = 4096$ $(9)^2 = 81$

Therefore, if n is a natural number, then

Unit digit of $(2)^{4n} = 6$ Unit digit of $(3)^{4n} = 1$

Unit digit of $(4)^{2n} = 6$ Unit digit of $(7)^{4n} = 1$

Unit digit of $(9)^{2n} = 1$

(c)   Unit digit of a product $a \times b \times c \times$ ...... is the unit digit of the product of the unit digit of a, b, c, ...

Using the facts given above in section (a), (b) and (c), you can find the unit digit of any power of a number.

15.   **Find the unit digit of $(624)^{50}$.**

     (a)   9   (b) 6   (c) 4   (d) 3

Sol.   **(b)**   Digit at unit place in $624 = 4$

       Now, $(4)^{50} = (4)^{2 \times 25}$

       So, unit digit of $(4)^{2 \times 25} = 6$

       Hence, unit digit of $(624)^{50}$ is 6

Shortcut Approach - 14

If N is a composite number and $N = a^p \, b^q \, c^r$ ....where a, b, c are different prime numbers and p, q, r are natural numbers. Then

The number of divisors (factors) of N including 1 and the number N itself $= (p+1)(q+1)(r+1)$ ....

16.   **Find the different divisors of 37800, excluding unity.**

     (a)   95   (b) 94   (c) 93   (d) 92

Sol.   **(a)** $37800 = 2^3 \times 3^3 \times 5^2 \times 7^1$

       The number of divisors $= (p+1)(q+1)(r+1)$

       $= (3+1) \times (3+1) \times (2+1) \times (1+1) = 96$

       Therefore number of divisor, excluding unity

       $= 96 - 1 = 95$.

Shortcut Approach - 15

If the sum of squares of two numbers is x and the square of their difference is y, then the product of the two numbers

$$= \left(\frac{x-y}{2} \right)$$

Shortcut Approach - 16

Two different numbers when divided by the same divisor, leaves remainder x and y respectively and when their sum is divided by the same divisor, remainder is z. Then the divisor $= x + y - z$

17. **If two numbers are each divided by the same divisor, the remainders are respectively 3 and 4. If the sum of the numbers be divided by the same divisor, the remainder is 2. The divisor is :**
    (a) 9   (b) 7   (c) 5   (d) 3

Sol. (c) Divisor $= x + y - z$
$$= 3 + 4 - 2 = 5$$

Shortcut Approach - 17

If N be a composite number such that
$N = (x)^a \, (y)^b \, (z)^c \, ...;$ where $x, y, z, ...$ are different prime numbers, then sum of divisors or factors of

$$z = \frac{x^{a+1}-1}{x-1} \times \frac{y^{b+1}-1}{y-1} \times \frac{z^{c+1}-1}{z-1} \times ....$$

18. **Find the sum of the factors of 90.**
    (a) 214   (b) 234   (c) 224   (d) 226

Sol. (b) $(90) = [2 \times (3)^2 \times (5)]$
Hence, sum of divisor

$$z = \frac{\left(x^{(a+1)}-1\right)}{(x-1)} \times \frac{\left(y^{(b+1)}-1\right)}{(y-1)} \times \frac{\left(z^{(c+1)}-1\right)}{(z-1)} \times ....$$

$$z = \frac{2^2-1}{2-1} \times \frac{3^3-1}{3-1} \times \frac{5^2-1}{5-1} \quad \Rightarrow \quad \frac{4-1}{1} \times \frac{27-1}{2} \times \frac{24}{4}$$

$$= 3 \times 13 \times 6$$
$$= 234$$

Shortcut Approach - 18

If the product of the numbers is x and the sum of these two numbers is y, then the numbers are given by

The larger number $= \left(\dfrac{y + \sqrt{y^2 - 4x}}{2} \right)$ and

The smaller number $= \left(\dfrac{y - \sqrt{y^2 - 4x}}{2} \right)$

19. **If the sum of two numbers is 78 and their product is 1352, then find the larger number.**

   (a) 52   (b) 26   (c) 25   (d) 62

Sol. (a) Larger number

$$= \left\{ \dfrac{y + \sqrt{y^2 - 4x}}{2} \right\} = \left\{ \dfrac{78 + \sqrt{(78)^2 - 4 \times 1352}}{2} \right\}$$

$$= \dfrac{78 + 26}{2} = \dfrac{104}{2} = 52$$

Shortcut Approach - 19

If the product of two numbers is x and the difference between these two numbers is y, then the

Large number $= \dfrac{\sqrt{y^2 + 4x} + y}{2}$ and

Smaller number $= \dfrac{\sqrt{y^2 + 4x} - y}{2}$

20. **If the product of two numbers is 600 and their difference is 10, the find the smaller number.**

   (a) 30   (b) 20   (c) 10   (d) 40

Sol. (b) Smaller number $= \dfrac{\sqrt{y^2 + 4x} - y}{2}$

$$= \dfrac{\sqrt{(10)^2 + 4 \times 600} - 10}{2}$$

$$= \dfrac{\sqrt{2500} - 10}{2} = \dfrac{50 - 10}{2}$$

$$= 20.$$

Exercise

1. The digit in the unit's place of the number represented by $(7^{95} - 3^{58})$ is:
   (a) 0   (b) 4
   (c) 6   (d) 7

2. Find the remainder when
$$6^{6^{6^{6^{\cdot^{\cdot^{\cdot^{6^{66}}}}}}}} \quad (100 \text{ times}) \text{ divided}$$
   by 10?
   (a) 6   (b) 2
   (c) 4   (d) 8

3. If N is sum of factorials of all the prime numbers less than 100, find the last two digits of N
   (a) 48   (b) 58
   (c) 68   (d) 78

4. Find the last digit of $32^{32^{32}}$
   (a) 4   (b) 8
   (c) 6   (d) 2

5. Find the number of zeros at the end of the product $100! + 200!$
   (a) 24
   (b) 25
   (c) 49
   (d) None of these

6. Two numbers, when divided by 17, leaves remainder 13 and 11 respectively. If the sum of those two numbers is divided by 17, the remainder will be :
   (a) 13   (b) 11
   (c) 7   (d) 4

7. The last digit of the expression $4 + 9^2 + 4^3 + 9^4 + 4^5 + 9^6 + \ldots\ldots\ldots + 4^{99} + 9^{100}$ is :
   (a) 0
   (b) 3
   (c) 5
   (d) None of these

8. Find the number of zeros at the end of the product $1^5 \times 2^5 \times 3^5 \times \ldots\ldots\ldots \times 32^5$
   (a) 25   (b) 30
   (c) 32   (d) 35

9. Which of the following will not completely divide $(3^{41} + 7^{82})$?
   (a) 4   (b) 52
   (c) 17   (d) 26

10. Find the digit at the unit's place of
$$(377)^{59} \times (793)^{87} \times (578)^{129} \times (99)^{99}$$
   (a) 1   (b) 2
   (c) 7   (d) 9

11. A number which when divided by 32 leaves a remainder of 29. If this number is divided by 8 the remainder will be
   (a) 0   (b) 1
   (c) 5   (d) 3

12. If two numbers when divided by a certain divisor give remainder 35 and 30 respectively and when their sum is divided by the same divisor, the remainder is 20, then the divisor is
   (a) 40   (b) 45
   (c) 50   (d) 55

Hints & Solution

1. (b) Use Short Approach -13

2. (a) 6^n (where n is a natural number) will always leaves the remainder 6 when divide by 10.

3. (c) Since last two digits of all the factorials more than 9 is 00 hence required last two digits is given by
$2! + 3! + 5! + 7! = 2 + 6 + 120 + 5040 = 5168,$

4. (c) Use Short Approach -13

5. (a)

$$100! + 200!$$

$100!$ $200!$

5	100		5	200
5	20		5	40
	4		5	8
				1

$40 + 8 + 1 = 49$ trailing zeros in 200!

$20 + 4 = 24$ trailing zeros in 100!.

> If we add two numbers with 'm' trailing zeros and 'n' trailing zeros, the resultant number will end with 'm' zeros if (m < n) or 'n' zeros if (m > n).

Here, $24 < 49$

Hence 24 trailing zeros.

6. (c) Use Short Approach -16

7. (a)
4^{ODD} $\xrightarrow{\text{UNIT DIGIT}}$ 4

4^{EVEN} $\longrightarrow$ 6

9^{ODD} $\longrightarrow$ 9

9^{EVEN} $\longrightarrow$ 1

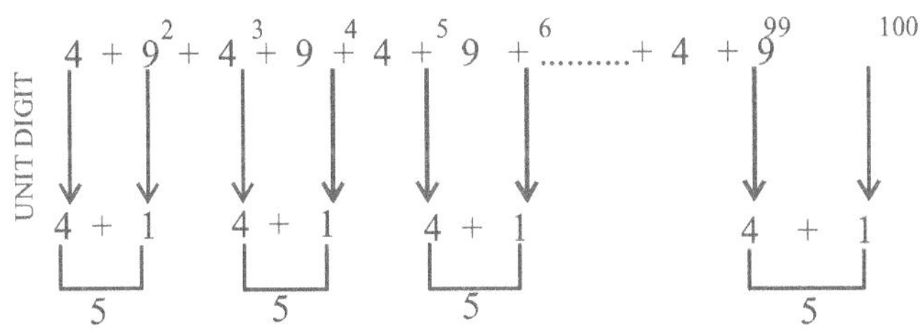

Sum of unit digits = (5 + 5 + 5 + ... 50 terms)

Hence, unit digit is 0.

8. (d) Use Short Approach -12

9. (c) $3^{41} + 7^{82} = 3^{41} + \left(7^2\right)^{41}$

$$= \underbrace{3^{41} + 49^{41}}$$
$$\downarrow$$
$$3 + 49 = 52$$

> Any number of the form '$A^n + B^n$' is always divisible by '$A + B$', if n is an odd number.

So, the given expression will be completely divisible by 52 and its factors, since 17 is not a factor of 52 .

10. (b) Use Short Approach -13

11. (c) Let this number be N then

$$N = 32 \times Q_1 + 29 \quad ...(1)$$

Again $N = 8 \times Q_2 + R ...(2)$

From (1) and (2)

$$32Q_1 + 29 = 8Q_2 + R$$

(where R is the remainder)

$$8Q_2 - 32Q_1 = 29 - R$$

$$8(Q_2 - 4Q_1) = 29 - R$$

$$\text{or}(Q_2 - 4Q_1) = \frac{29 - R}{8}$$

Since Q_1, Q_2, R are integers also $Q_2 - 4Q_1$ is an integer. Therefore $29 - R$ must be divisible by 8.

12. (b) Use Short Approach -16

HCF & LCM

For Finding HCF or GCD

To find the HCF of any number of given numbers, first find the difference between two nearest given numbers. Then find all factors (or divisors) of this difference. Highest factor which divides all the given numbers is the HCF.

1.   **Find the HCF of 132, 204 and 228.**
    (a)   24   (b) 12   (c) 36   (d) 48

Sol. **(b)**   Difference of two nearest numbers
        $= 228 - 204 = 24$
        All factors of $24 = 1, 2, 3, 4, 6, 8, 12, 24$
        Among all the factors of 24, only 12 is the highest factor which divides all of the three numbers 132, 204 and 228 completely
        $\therefore$ HCF of 132, 204 and $228 = 12$

2.   **Find the HCF of 1365, 1560 and 1755.**
    (a)   195   (b) 13   (c)   15   (d)   65

Sol. (a)   Difference of two nearest numbers $= 1560 - 1365$
                $= 195$
        All factors of $195 = 1, 3, 5, 13, 15, 39, 65, 195$
        Among all the factors, 195 is the highest factor that divides 1560, 1365 and 1755 completely.
        $\therefore$ Required HCF $= 195$

Using idea of co-prime, you can find the LCM by the following shortcut method:

LCM of 9, 10, 15 and 36 can be written directly as $9 \times 10 \times 2$.

The logical thinking that behind it is as follows:

Step (i): If you can see a set of 2 or more co-prime numbers in the set of numbers of which you are finding the LCM, write them down by multiply them.

In the above situation, since we see that 9 and 10 are co-prime to each other, we start off writing the LCM by writing 9×10 as the first step.

Step (ii): For each of the other numbers, consider what prime factor(s) of it is/are not present in the product (if factorised into primes) taken in step 1.

In case you see some prime factors of each of the other given numbers separately are not present in the product (if factorised into primes) taken in step 1, such prime factors will be multiplied in the product taken in step 1.

Prime factorisation of $9 \times 10 = 3 \times 3 \times 2 \times 5$

Prime factorisation of $15 = 3 \times 5$

Prime factorisation of $36 = 2 \times 2 \times 3 \times 3$

Here we see that both prime factors of 15 are present in the prime factorisation of 9×10 but one prime factor 2 of 36 is not present in the product taken in step 1. So to find the LCM of 9, 10, 15 and 36; we multiply the product taken in step 1 by 2.

Thus required product $= 9 \times 10 \times 2 = 180$

Step (iii): The work of finding the HCF may sometimes be simplified by the following devices:

(a) Any obvious factor which is common to both numbers may be removed before the rule is applied. Care should however be taken to multiply this factor into the HCF of the quotients.

(b) If one of the numbers has a prime factor not contained in the other, it may be rejected.

(c) At any stage of the work, any factor of the divisor not contained in the dividend may be rejected. This is because any factor which divides only one of the two cannot be a portion of the required HCF.

3. Find the LCM of 8, 15, 24 and 72.

  (a) 240 (b) 720 (c) 180 (d) 360

Sol. (d) Here, 8 and 15 are co-prime to each other.

Now, prime factorisation of $(8 \times 15) = 2 \times 2 \times 2 \times 3 \times 5$

Prime factorisation of $24 = 2 \times 2 \times 2 \times 3$

Prime factorisation of $72 = 2 \times 2 \times 2 \times 3 \times 3$

Here, all the prime factors of 24 are present in the prime factorisation of (8×15).

But one prime factor 3 among the factors of 72 is not present in that prime factorisation of (8×15).

$\therefore$ Required LCM $= (8 \times 15) \times 3 = 360$

Shortcut Approach - 3

The greatest number that will exactly divide x, y and z = HCF of x, y and z

4. Find the greatest possible length which can be used to measure exactly the lengths 7m, 3m 85 cm, 12m 95cm.

  (a) 35 cm (b) 45 cm (c) 1 m 15 cm (d) 90 cm

Sol. (a) $700 = 7 \times 5^2 \times 4$

$385 = 5 \times 7 \times 11$

$1295 = 5 \times 7 \times 37$

$HCF = 5 \times 7 = 35$

$\therefore$ Required length $= 35$ cm

5. **Which is the largest number which can exactly divide each of the numbers 264, 312 and 456?**

     (a) 26   (b) 24   (c) 28   (d) 32

Sol. (b) $264 = 2^3 \times 3 \times 11$

         $312 = 2^3 \times 3 \times 13$

         $456 = 2^3 \times 3 \times 19$

         $\text{HCF} = 2^3 \times 3 = 24$

         $\therefore$ Largest number $= 24$

Shortcut Approach - 4

Least number which is exactly divisible by x, y and z = LCM of x, y and z

6. **How many numbers are there between 4000 and 6000 which are exactly divisible by 32, 40, 48 and 60?**

     (a) 1   (b) 2   (c) 3   (d) 4

Sol. (d) $32 = 2^5$

         $40 = 2^3 \times 5$

         $48 = 2^4 \times 3$

         $60 = 2^2 \times 3 \times 5$

         $\therefore$ $\text{LCM} = 2^5 \times 3 \times 5 = 480$

         The numbers divisible by 480 between 4000 and 6000 are 4320, 4800, 5280 and 5760.

         $\therefore$ Required number of numbers $= 4$

7. **Find the least number which is exactly divisible by 12, 15, 90, 108, 135 and 150.**

     (a) 1500   (b) 3000   (c) 2700   (d) 2250

Sol. (c) $12 = 2^2 \times 3$

         $15 = 3 \times 5$

         $90 = 2 \times 3^2 \times 5$

         $108 = 2^2 \times 3^3$

         $135 = 3^3 \times 5$

         $150 = 5^2 \times 3 \times 2$

         $\therefore$ $\text{LCM} = 2^2 \times 3^3 \times 5^2 = 2700$

Shortcut Approach - 5

The greatest number that will divide x, y and z leaving remainders a, b and c respectively = HCF of $(x - a)$, $(y - b)$ and $(z - c)$

8. **Find the greatest number that divides 130, 305 and 245 leaving remainders 6, 9 and 17 respectively?**

     (a) 4   (b) 5   (c) 14   (d) 24

Sol. (a)   Required number = HCF of $(130 - 6)$, $(305 - 9)$ and

         $(245 - 17)$

         = HCF of 124, 296 and 228

$$124 = 2^2 \times 31$$
$$296 = 2^3 \times 37$$
$$228 = 2^2 \times 3 \times 19$$

$\therefore$ Required number (HCF) $= 2 \times 2 = 4$

9. **The numbers 400, 536 and 646; when divided by a number N, give the remainders of 22, 23 and 25 respectively. Find the greatest such number N.**

(a) 40   (b) 45   (c) 27   (d) 22

Sol. (c) Required number, N = HCF of $(400 - 22)$, $(536 - 23)$

and $(646 - 25)$

= HCF of 378, 513 and 621

$$378 = 3^3 \times 2 \times 7$$
$$513 = 3^3 \times 19$$
$$621 = 3^3 \times 23$$

$\therefore$ N (HCF) $= 3^3 = 27$

Shortcut Approach - 6

Greatest number that will divide x, y, z leaving the same remainder 'r' in each case

= HCF of $(x - r)$, $(y - r)$ and $(z - r)$

10. **What is the greatest that divides 13850 and 17030 leaves a remainder 17?**

(a) 477   (b) 159   (c) 107   (d) 87

Sol. (b) Greatest number = HCF of $(13850 - 17)$

and $(17030 - 17)$

= HCF of 13833 and 17013

$$
\begin{array}{r}
13833\overline{)17013}(1 \\
-13833 \\
\hline
3180\overline{)13833}(4 \\
-12720 \\
\hline
1113\overline{)3180}(2 \\
-2226 \\
\hline
954\overline{)1113}(1 \\
-954 \\
\hline
159\overline{)954}(6 \\
-954 \\
\hline
\times
\end{array}
$$

$\therefore$ Greatest number = 159

11. **What will be the greatest number that divides 1356, 1868 and 2764 leaving 12 as remainder in each case?**

    (a) 64   (b) 124   (c) 156   (d) 260

Sol. (a) Greatest number = HCF of $(1356 - 12)$, $(1868 - 12)$

    and $(2764 - 12)$

    = HCF of 1344, 1856 and 2752 = 64

    Hence, required number = 64

Shortcut Approach - 7

Least number which when divided by x, y and z leaves the same remainder 'r' in each case

= (LCM of x, y and z) + r

12. **The least number which when divided by 12, 16 and 18 leaves 5 as remainder in each case. Find the number.**

    (a) 139   (b) 149   (c) 159   (d) 169

Sol. (b) Here, $x = 12$, $y = 16$, $z = 18$, $r = 5$

    and, Required least number = (LCM of x, y and z)

    $+ r$ = (LCM of 12, 16, 18) + 5

$$
\begin{array}{c|c}
2 & 12, 16, 18 \\
\hline
2 & 6, 8, 9 \\
\hline
3 & 3, 4, 9 \\
\hline
 & 1, 4, 3
\end{array}
$$

    $\therefore$ LCM $= 2 \times 2 \times 3 \times 3 \times 4 = 144$

    Hence, required least number $= 144 + 5 = 149$

13. **What is the least number which when diminished by 7, is divisible by each one of 21, 28, 36 and 45?**

    (a) 1267   (b) 1157

    (c) 1077   (d) 1347

Sol. (a)

$$
\begin{array}{c|c}
2 & 21, 28, 36, 45 \\
\hline
2 & 21, 14, 18, 45 \\
\hline
3 & 21, 7, 9, 45 \\
\hline
3 & 7, 7, 3, 15 \\
\hline
7 & 7, 7, 1, 5 \\
\hline
5 & 1, 1, 1, 5 \\
\hline
 & 1, 1, 1, 1
\end{array}
$$

    $\therefore$ LCM $= 2 \times 2 \times 3 \times 3 \times 7 \times 5 = 1260$

    Hence, required number $= 1260 + 7 = 1267$

Shortcut Approach - 8

Greatest number that will divide x, y and z leaving the same remainder in each case (but remainder is not given)
$= $ HCF of $|x-y|$, $|y-z|$ and $|z-x|$.

14. **Find the largest number which divides 1305, 4665 and 6905 leaving same remainder in each case. Also, find the common remainder.**

   (a) 1210, 185   (b) 1120, 185

   (c) 1005, 175   (d) 1100, 175

Sol. **(b)** Here, $x = 1305$, $y = 4665$, $z = 6905$

       Now, $|x-y| = |1305 - 4665| = 3360$

             $|y-z| = |4665 - 6905| = 2240$

             $|z-x| = |6905 - 1305| = 5600$

       $\therefore$ Greatest number

       $= $ HCF of $|x-y|$, $|y-z|$ and $|z-x|$

       $= $ HCF of 3360, 2240 and 5600 $= 1120$

       Again, on dividing 1305 by 1120, we get remainder $= 185$.

       On dividing 4665 by 1120, we get remainder $= 185$.

       On dividing 6905 by 1120, we get remainder $= 185$.

       Hence, largest number $= 1120$

       and common remainder $= 185$

Shortcut Approach - 9

Least number which when divided by x, y and z leaves the remainder a, b and c respectively
$= ($LCM of x, y and $z) - k$, where $k = x - a = y - b = z - c$.

15. **What is the smallest positive integer which when divided by 4, 5, 8, 9 leaves remainder 3, 4, 7, 8 respectively?**

   (a) 119   (b) 319   (c) 359   (d) 719

Sol. **(c)** Here, $K = 4 - 3 = 5 - 4 = 8 - 7 = 9 - 8 = 1$

       $\therefore$ Required number $= ($LCM of 4, 5, 8 and 9$) - K$

       $= 360 - 1 = 359$

16. **What is the sum of the digits the least number which, when divided by 52, leaves 33 as remainder; when divided by 78, leaves 59 and when divided by 117, leaves 98 as reaminder?**

   (a) 17   (b) 18   (c) 19   (d) 21

Sol. **(a)** Here, $K = 52 - 33 = 78 - 59 = 117 - 98 = 19$

       $\therefore$ Required number $= ($LCM of 52, 78, 117$) - 19$

           $= 468 - 19 = 449$

       $\therefore$ Sum of the digits of the least number $= 4 + 4 + 9 = 17$

To find the *n*-digits greatest number divisible by *x*, *y* and *z*; follow the steps :

Step (i) : Find the LCM of *x*, *y* and *z*.

　　　　　Let LCM of *x*, *y* and *z* = *L*.

Step (ii) : Find the remainder by dividing *n*-digits greatest number by *L*. Let the remainder = *R*.

Step (iii) : Required number = (*n*-digits greatest number) – *R*.

17.　Find the greatest number of five digits which is completely divisible by 12, 16, 20, 24 and 28.

　　(a) 99120　　　　　　　　(b) 99908

　　(c) 99899　　　　　　　　(d) 99446

Sol. (a)　Greatest number of 5-digits = 99999

　　　　　LCM of 12, 16, 20, 24, 28, = 1680

　　　　　On dividing 99999 by 1680, we get 879 as remainder

$$
1680 \overline{\smash{)}\,99999\,} (59 \\
\underline{8400} \\
15999 \\
\underline{15120} \\
879
$$

　　　　　Hence, required number = 99999 – 879 = 99120

18.　Find the greatest number less than 900, which is divisible by 8, 12 and 28.

　　(a) 880　　(b) 800　　(c) 860　　(d) 840

Sol. (d)　LCM of 8, 12, 28 = 168

　　　　　On dividing 900 by 168, we get 60 as remainder.

　　　　　∴　Required number = 900 – 60 = 840

$$
168 \overline{\smash{)}\,900\,} (5 \\
\underline{840} \\
60
$$

To find the *n*-digits greatest number, which when divided by *x*, *y* and *z* leaves the same remainder *K* in each case; follow the steps:

Step (i) : Find the LCM of *x*, *y* and *z*.

　　　　　Let LCM *x*, *y* and *z* = *L*.

Step (ii) : Find the remainder by dividing n-digits greatest number by L.
Let the remainder $= R$.

Step (iii) : Required number $= (n\text{-digits greatest number}) - R + K$

19. Find the greatest number of 4 digits which when divided by 8, 9, 12 and 15 leaves 6 remainder in each case.

(a) 9980   (b) 9726   (c) 9920   (d) 9626

Sol. (b) Greatest number of 4-digits $= 9999$

LCM of 8, 9, 12, 15 $= 360$

On dividing 9999 by 360, we get 279 as remainder.

$\therefore$ Required number $= 9999 - 279 + 6 = 9726$

20. Find the largest number of 5 digits which when divided by 3, 5, 8, 12 leaves the same remainder 2 in each case.

(a) 99722   (b) 99958   (c) 99960   (d) 99962

Sol. (d) Largest number of 5-digits $= 99999$

LCM of 3, 5, 8 and 12 $= 120$

On dividing 99999 by 120, we get 39 as remainder

$\therefore$ Required number $= 99999 - 39 + 2 = 99962$

Shortcut Approach - 12

To find the smallest n-digits number divisible by x, y and z; follow the steps :

Step (i) : Find the LCM of x, y and z.
Let LCM of x, y and $z = L$.

Step (ii) : Find the remainder by dividing n-digits smallest number by L.
Let the remainder $= R$.

Step (iii) : Required number $= n\text{-digits smallest number} + (L - R)$

21. Find that smallest 6-digit number which when divided by 9, 12, 21 and 25 leaves no remainder

(a) 100005   (b) 100225 (c) 100800 (d) 100100

Sol. (c) Smallest 6-digits number $= 100000$

LCM of 9, 12, 21, 25 $= 6300$

On dividing 100000 by 6300, we get 5500 as remainder.

$\therefore$ Required number
$= 100000 + (6300 - 5500) = 100800$

Shortcut Approach - 13

To find smallest n-digits number which, when divided by x, y and z leaves K in each case; follow the steps :

Step (i) : Find the LCM of x, y and z.
Let LCM of x, y and $z = L$.

Step (ii) : Find the remainder by dividng n-digits smallest number by L.

Let the remainder $= R$.

Step (iii) : Required n-digits smallest number

$= n$-digits smallest number $+ (L - R) + K$.

22. Find the least possible 5-digit number, which when divided by 10, 12, 16 and 18 leaves remainder 27.

(a) 10107   (b) 10100   (c) 10027   (d) 10507

Sol. (a)   LCM of 10, 12, 16, 18 $= 720$

Smallest $5 -$ digit number $= 10000$

On dividing 10000 by 720, we get 640 as remainder.

$\therefore$ Required number $= 10000 + (720 - 640) + 27$

$= 10107$

⊕ Shortcut Approach -14

Least number which when divided by x_1, x_2 and x_3 leaves the remainder a_1, a_2 and a_3 respectively

$= (\text{LCM of } x_1, x_2, x_3) - (x_1 - a_1) \text{ or } (x_2 - a_2) \text{ or } (x_3 - a_3)$

Note that here, $x_1 - a_1 = x_2 - a_2 = x_3 - a_3$

23. Find that smallest number which when divided by 16, 24 and 30 leaves remainder as 6, 14 and 20 respectively.

(a) 116   (b) 224   (c) 300   (d) 230

Sol. (d) Here, $16 - 6 = 24 - 14 = 30 - 20 = 10$

$\therefore$ LCM of 16, 24 and 30 $= 240$

Hence, required number $= 240 - 10 = 230$

⊕ Shortcut Approach - 15

If product of two numbers and their HCF are given, then to find all possible pairs of numbers follow the steps :

Step- (i): Find the value of $\dfrac{\textbf{Product}}{\textbf{(HCF)}^2}$.

Step-(ii): Find the all possible pairs of co-prime numbers, whose product is equal to the value obtained in step-I.

Step-(iii): Multiply each number of the possible pairs obtained in step-II by HCF.

The new pairs obtained in this step is the required pairs.

24. Product of two numbers is 1440 and their HCF is 12. How many pairs of such numbers are possible?

(a) 2   (b) 3   (c) 1   (d) 4

Sol. (a) Step – (i) : $\dfrac{\text{Product}}{(\text{HCF})^2} = \dfrac{1440}{(12)^2} = 10$

Step – (ii) : All possible pairs of co–prime numbers

$= (1, 10)\,;\,(2, 5)$

$\therefore$ Only 2 pairs can be possible.

25. **The product of two whole numbers is 1500 and their HCF is 10. Find the numbers.**

(a) $(70, 80)$

(b) $(50, 38)$

(c) $(10, 150)$

(d) $(75, 20)$

Sol. (c) Step (i) : $\dfrac{\text{Product}}{(\text{HCF})^2} = \dfrac{1500}{(10)^2} = 15$

Step (ii) : All possible pairs of co–prime numbers

$= (1, 15)\,;\,(5, 3)$

Step (iii) : $(1 \times 10,\ 15 \times 10)$ and $(5 \times 10,\ 3 \times 10)$

Exercise

1. A hall is 13 metres 53 cm long and 8 metres 61 cm broad is to be paved with minimum number of square tiles. The number of tiles required is:
   (a) 123   (b) 77
   (c) 99   (d) 57

2. There are 4 numbers. The H.C.F. of each pair is 3 and the L.C.M. of all the 4 numbers is 116. What is the product of 4 numbers?
   (a) 9782   (b) 9396
   (c) 9224   (d) 9100

3. What will be the least number which when doubled will be excactly divisible by 12,18,21 and 30?
   (a) 196   (b) 630
   (c) 1260   (d) 2520

4. Four bells ring at an interval of 30 min, 1 hour, 1 hour 30 min and 1 hour 45 min. All bells started ring together at 12 noon. At what they will ring again?
   (a) 12 O' clock mid – night
   (b) 3 O' clock next morning
   (c) 6 O' clock next morning
   (d) 9 O' clock next morning

5. The largest number which will divide the numbers 104, 221 and 377 leaving the same remainder in each case is :
   (a) 56   (b) 13
   (c) 39
   (d) It does not exist

6. The sum of two numbers is 462 and their highest common factor is 22. What is the maximum number of pairs that satisfy these conditions ?
   (a) 1   (b) 3
   (c) 5   (d) 6

7. How many pairs of factors of number 7200 have HCF 20?
   (a) 10   (b) 44
   (c) 53   (d) 18

8. Find that number by which when 1050, 1250 and 1650 are divided respectively leaves 43, 31 and 7 as remainders.
   (a) 47   (b) 51
   (c) 53   (d) 57

9. The least number, which when divided by 2, 3, 4, 5 and 6, leaves in each case, a remainder 1, but when divided by 7 leaves no remainder. The number is
   (a) 121   (b) 181
   (c) 241   (d) 301

10. One pendulum ticks 57 times in 58 seconds and another 608 times in 609 seconds. If they started simultaneously, find the time after which they will tick together.
   (a) $\dfrac{211}{19}$ s   (b) $\dfrac{1217}{19}$ s
   (c) $\dfrac{1218}{19}$ s   (d) $\dfrac{1018}{19}$ s

11. If the product of the HCF and the LCM of 3 natural numbers p, q, r, equals pqr, then p, q, r must be :
   (a) such that $(p, q, r) = 1$
   (b) prime number
   (c) odd number
   (d) such that $(p, q) = (p, r) = 1$

12. Find the largest number of 5 digits which when divided by 3, 5, 8, 12 leaves the same remainder 2 in each case.
   (a) 99722   (b) 99958
   (c) 99960   (d) 99962

Hints & Solution

1. **(b)** Use Short Approach –2

2. **(b)** ∵ Product of 'n' numbers

= (HCF for each pair)^n × LCM of 'n' numbers

= $(3)^4 \times 116 = 9396$

3. **(b)** Use Short Approach - 4

4. **(d)** The L.C. M of 30, 60, 90 and 105 min = 1260 min = 21 hours means bells will ring next morning at 9' O Clock.

5. **(c)** Use short approach -8

6. **(d)** There are 6 such pairs :

$(22, 440), (44, 418), (88, 374), (110, 352)$

$(176, 286), (220, 242)$

7. **(c)** Since HCF of two numbers are 20 hence numbers must be in the form of 20a and 20b where a and b are co-prime to each other. 20a and 20b are factors of 7200 hence a and b must be a factor of $7200/20 = 360 = 2^3 3^2 5^1$

Now condition is that a, and b are co-prime to each other and they are factors of 7200.

From formula for total number of pairs

$= 1 + (p + q + r) + 2(pq + pr + qr) + 4pqr$ here $p = 3, q = 2$ and $r = 1$ hence

required number of such pairs are $1 + 6 + 22 + 24 = 53$

8. **(c)** Use short approach –5

9. **(d)** LCM (2, 3, 4, 5, 6) = 60

∴ Required number is of the form $60k + 1$

Least value of k for which $60k + 1$ is divisible by 7 is k = 5

∴ Required number = 60 × 5 + 1 = 301

10. **(c)** Time gap between two consecutive ticks

$\dfrac{58}{57}$ sec. and $\dfrac{609}{608}$ sec.

∴ Required time = LCM

of $\dfrac{58}{57}$ and $\dfrac{609}{608}$

$= \dfrac{\text{LCM of 58 and 609}}{\text{HCF of 57 and 608}} = \dfrac{1218}{19}$ sec

11. **(a)** It is possible only when there is no common factor among p, q and r. Hence, the HCF of p, q, r = 1

and the LCM of p, q, r = p.q.r

∴ (HCF × LCM) of p, q, r = 1 × p. q. r = pqr

12. **(d)** Use Short Approach –7

Fractions and Decimals

To compare two fractions $\dfrac{a}{b}$ and $\dfrac{c}{d}$, follow as

$$\dfrac{a}{b} \diagdown\!\!\!\!\!\diagup \dfrac{c}{d}$$

$ad \qquad\qquad bc$ [Write the product ad and bc on their numerator side a and c respectively]

If $ad > bc$, then $\dfrac{a}{b} > \dfrac{c}{d}$

If $ad < bc$, then $\dfrac{a}{b} < \dfrac{c}{d}$

1. If $a = \dfrac{15}{16}, b = \dfrac{8}{9}$ then which is true
   (a) $a > b$
   (b) $a < b$
   (c) $a = b$
   (d) can't be determine

   Sol. (a) $15 \times 9 = 135,$ $\qquad 16 \times 8 = 128$
   Here $135 > 128$
   $\therefore \quad a > b$

If in any given sequence of fractions, the difference in consecutive numerators is equal or greater than the difference in consecutive denominators, then the fraction having larger numerator is larger and the fraction having smaller numerator is smaller.

This is not applicable for compound fractions i.e. improper fractions

2. Which of the following fractions is smallest?

   (a) $\dfrac{5}{12}$ (b) $\dfrac{7}{13}$ (c) $\dfrac{9}{14}$ (d) $\dfrac{11}{15}$

Sol. (a) $\begin{pmatrix} \text{Difference in} \\ \text{consecutive} \\ \text{numerators} \end{pmatrix} > \begin{pmatrix} \text{Difference in} \\ \text{consecutive} \\ \text{denominators} \end{pmatrix}$

or $2 > 1$

Hence the fraction having smaller numeratoer is the smallest

i.e. $\dfrac{5}{12}$.

⊕ Shortcut Approach - 3

If in any given sequence of fractions, numerator is increasing by a definite value and denominator is also increasing by a different definite value but increase in the value of numerator is less than increase in the value of denominator, then

(i) If $\dfrac{\text{increase in numerator}}{\text{increase in denominator}}$ > First fraction, the fraction with greatest numerator is greatest.

(ii) If $\dfrac{\text{increase in numerator}}{\text{increase in denominator}}$ < First fraction, the fraction with greater numerator is least.

3. **Which of the fraction is largest among $\dfrac{2}{5}, \dfrac{5}{11}, \dfrac{8}{17}, \dfrac{11}{23}$?**

(a) $\dfrac{2}{5}$ (b) $\dfrac{11}{23}$ (c) $\dfrac{5}{11}$ (d) $\dfrac{8}{17}$

Sol. (b) Here, $\dfrac{\text{Increase in numerator}}{\text{Increase in denominator}}$ first fraction

or $\dfrac{3}{6} > \dfrac{2}{5}$

Hence the fraction with greatest numerator is the greatest i.e.

$\dfrac{11}{23}$.

⊕ Shortcut Approach - 4

A fraction between any two given fractions $\dfrac{x_1}{y_1}$ and $\dfrac{x_2}{y_2}$ is $\dfrac{x_1 + x_2}{y_1 + y_2}$.

Using this you can find any number of fractions between any two given fractions.

4. **Which of the following fractions lie between $\dfrac{3}{5}$ and $\dfrac{2}{3}$?**

(a) $\dfrac{2}{5}$ (b) $\dfrac{1}{3}$ (c) $\dfrac{1}{15}$ (d) $\dfrac{5}{8}$

Sol. (d) Fraction lie between $\dfrac{3}{5}$ and $\dfrac{2}{3} = \dfrac{3+2}{5+3} = \dfrac{5}{8}$

Shortcut Approach - 5

If a man spends $\dfrac{x_1}{y_1}$ part of his salary on food, $\dfrac{x_2}{y_2}$ part of his salary on

clothing, $\dfrac{x_3}{y_3}$ part of his salary on education and so on. After these expenditures,

$$\text{Balance salary} = (\text{Salary}) \times \left[1 - \left(\dfrac{x_1}{y_1} + \dfrac{x_2}{y_2} + \dfrac{x_3}{y_3} + ... \right) \right]$$

5. **A person gave ₹ 500 to his eldest son. Then the gave $\dfrac{1}{10}$ part of his total wealth to his second son and the amount of money received by his third son equal to the total amount received by his first and second son. How much money the person had?**

(a) 1250   (b) 1750   (c) 1500   (d) 1000

Sol. (a) Let the total money be ₹ x.

$$\text{Fraction for eldest son's share} = \dfrac{500}{x}$$

$$\text{Fraction for third son's share} = \left(\dfrac{500}{x} + \dfrac{1}{10} \right)$$

Now remaining money

$$= \text{Total money} \times \left[1 - \left(\dfrac{x_1}{y_1} + \dfrac{x_2}{y_2} + ... \right) \right]$$

$$\Rightarrow\ 500 = x \times \left[1 - \left(\dfrac{1}{10} + \left(\dfrac{500}{x} + \dfrac{1}{10} \right) \right) \right]$$

$$\Rightarrow \quad 500 = x \times \left[1 - \frac{2x + 5000}{10x}\right]$$

$$\Rightarrow \quad 500 = x \times \left[\frac{10x - 2x - 5000}{10x}\right]$$

$$\Rightarrow \quad 5000 = 8x - 5000$$

$$\Rightarrow \quad 10000 = 8x \Rightarrow x = ₹1250$$

⊕ Shortcut Approach - 6

For any single activity,

(i)   Part done + Part remained = 1

(ii)   Total amount

$$\text{Total amount} = \frac{\text{Amount spent}}{\text{Balance part}} = \frac{\text{Amount remained}}{\text{Part remained}}$$

6. $\dfrac{1}{8}$ **part of a pencil is black and** $\dfrac{1}{2}$ **part of the remaining is white. If the remaining part is blue and length of this blue part is** $3\dfrac{1}{2}$ **cm, then find the length of the pencil.**

(a) 6 cm   (b) 7 cm   (c) 8 cm   (d) 9 cm

Sol. (c) Length of the pencil $= \dfrac{\text{Amount remained}}{\text{Part remained}}$

$$= \frac{3\frac{1}{2}}{1 - \left[\frac{1}{8} + \frac{1}{2}\left(1 - \frac{1}{8}\right)\right]} = \frac{3\frac{1}{2}}{1 - \left(\frac{1}{8} + \frac{7}{16}\right)}$$

$$= \frac{3\frac{1}{2}}{1 - \frac{9}{16}} = \frac{7}{2\left(\frac{7}{16}\right)} = \frac{7}{\frac{7}{8}} = 8 \text{ cm}$$

⊕ Shortcut Approach - 7

The denominator of a fraction (or rational number) is 'D' more than its numerator. If the numerator is increased by x and the denominator is decreased by y, we get P, then the fraction (or rational number) is given by

$$\frac{x - P(D - y)}{x + (yP - D)}.$$

7. The numerator of a fraction is 4 less than its denominator. If the numerator is decreased by 2 and the denominator is increased by 1, then the denominator becomes eight times the numerator, then find the fraction

(a) $\dfrac{3}{7}$ (b) $\dfrac{4}{8}$ (c) $\dfrac{2}{7}$ (d) $\dfrac{3}{8}$

Sol. (a)   Here, $D = 4$, $x = (-2)$, $y = (-1)$ and $P = \dfrac{1}{8}$

$$\therefore \quad \text{Required fraction} = \frac{x - P(D - y)}{x + (yP - D)}$$

$$= \frac{-2 - \dfrac{1}{8}[4 - (-1)]}{-2 + \left[(-1)\left(\dfrac{1}{8}\right) - 4\right]} = \frac{-2 - \dfrac{5}{8}}{-2 - \dfrac{33}{8}}$$

$$= \frac{\dfrac{-21}{8}}{\dfrac{-49}{8}} = \frac{-21}{-49} = \frac{3}{7}$$

Exercise

1. Find the value of

$$\frac{1}{2\times 3}+\frac{1}{3\times 4}+\frac{1}{4\times 5}+\frac{1}{5\times 6}+.....+\frac{1}{9\times 10}$$

(a) $\dfrac{3}{2}$ (b) $\dfrac{2}{5}$

(c) $\dfrac{2}{3}$ (d) $\dfrac{3}{5}$

2. The ascending order of $\dfrac{3}{4},\dfrac{5}{12},\dfrac{11}{18}$ and $\dfrac{17}{24}$ is

(a) $\dfrac{17}{24},\dfrac{11}{18},\dfrac{5}{12},\dfrac{3}{4}$

(b) $\dfrac{3}{4},\dfrac{17}{24},\dfrac{11}{18},\dfrac{5}{12}$

(c) $\dfrac{5}{12},\dfrac{11}{18},\dfrac{17}{24},\dfrac{3}{4}$

(d) $\dfrac{11}{18},\dfrac{17}{24},\dfrac{5}{12},\dfrac{3}{4}$

3. Which of the following fractions are in ascending order?

(a) $\dfrac{11}{52},\dfrac{7}{26},\dfrac{4}{13}$

(b) $\dfrac{7}{26},\dfrac{4}{13},\dfrac{11}{52},$

(c) $\dfrac{4}{13},\dfrac{7}{26},\dfrac{11}{52},$

(d) $\dfrac{7}{26},\dfrac{11}{52},\dfrac{4}{13},$

4. Which of the fraction is smallest among

$$\dfrac{2}{5},\dfrac{5}{11},\dfrac{8}{17},\dfrac{11}{23}?$$

(a) $\dfrac{2}{5}$ (b) $\dfrac{11}{23}$

(c) $\dfrac{5}{11}$ (d) $\dfrac{8}{17}$

5. If the numerator of a fraction is increased by 200% and the denominator of the fraction is increased by 150%, the resultant fraction is 9/35. What is the original fraction?

(a) $\dfrac{3}{10}$

(b) $\dfrac{2}{15}$

(c) $\dfrac{3}{16}$

(d) None of there

6. What is value of the expression

$$\sqrt{7\sqrt{7\sqrt{7\sqrt{7\sqrt{.............\infty}}}}} \; ?$$

(a) 49   (b) 7
(c) 1   (d) 0

7. Evaluate $\sqrt{6+\sqrt{6+\sqrt{6+}}}$ -- ----- ∞

(a) –2   (b) 3
(c) 6   (d) –6

8. The product of 2 numbers is 1575 and their quotient is 9/7. Then the sum of the numbers is–

(a) 74   (b) 78
(c) 80   (d) 90

9. $199\dfrac{1}{7}+199\dfrac{2}{7}++199\dfrac{3}{7}+199\dfrac{4}{7}$

$+199\dfrac{5}{7}+199\dfrac{6}{7}$ is equal to

(a) 603   (b) 600
(c) 598   (d) 597

10. A man reads 3/8 of a book on a day and 4/5 of the remainder on the second day. If the number of pages still unread are 40, then how many pages did the book contain?
(a) 300   (b) 500
(c) 320   (d) 350

11. For all real values of x and y if $(4x - y)$ is divisible by 3, then $(4x^2 + 7\ xy - 2y^2)$ is always divisible by
(a) 12   (b) 3
(c) −11   (d) 1

12. Find the value of

$$\dfrac{1}{\sqrt{1}+\sqrt{2}}+\dfrac{1}{\sqrt{2}+\sqrt{3}}+\dfrac{1}{\sqrt{3}+\sqrt{4}}$$

$$+\ldots+\dfrac{1}{\sqrt{99}+\sqrt{100}}\ \text{is}$$

(a) 8   (b) 6
(c) 10   (d) 9

Hints & Solution

1. **(b)** Given expression

$$= \left(\dfrac{1}{2}-\dfrac{1}{3}\right)+\left(\dfrac{1}{3}-\dfrac{1}{4}\right)+\left(\dfrac{1}{4}-\dfrac{1}{5}\right)+\left(\dfrac{1}{5}-\dfrac{1}{6}\right)+$$

$$\ldots+\left(\dfrac{1}{9}-\dfrac{1}{10}\right)=\left(\dfrac{1}{2}-\dfrac{1}{10}\right)=\dfrac{4}{10}=\dfrac{2}{5}$$

2. **(c)** Use Shortcut Approach-2

3. **(a)** Use Shortcut Approach-2

4. **(a)** Use Shortcut Approach-3

5. **(d)** Let the original fraction be $\dfrac{x}{y}$.

Numerator is increased by 200%.

∴ Numerator $= x + 200\%$ of x

$$= x + \dfrac{200x}{100} = \dfrac{100x + 200x}{100} = 300$$

$$x/100$$

And denominator of the fraction is increased by 150%.

Denominator

$$= y + \dfrac{150y}{100} = \dfrac{100y + 150y}{100}$$

$$= \dfrac{250y}{100}$$

Then, according to the question,

$$\dfrac{300x/100}{250y/100}=\dfrac{9}{35}$$

$$\Rightarrow \dfrac{300x}{250y}=\dfrac{9}{35}$$

$$\therefore\ \dfrac{x}{y}=\dfrac{9}{35}\times\dfrac{250}{300}=\dfrac{3}{14}$$

6. **(b)** Let

$$x = \sqrt{7\sqrt{7\sqrt{7\sqrt{\cdots\cdots\infty}}}}$$

$$\Rightarrow x=\sqrt{7x}$$

Squaring both sides and solving for x, we get x^2-

$7x = 0$ or $x = 0, 7$. But x can't be zero, so $x = 7$.

7. **(b)** $\therefore$ Two consecutive factor of $6 = 3 \times 2$

$\therefore \sqrt{6 + \sqrt{6 + \sqrt{6 + }}} \text{-------}\infty$

$= +3, -2$

Since, sum can not be negative here.

$\therefore$ Sum $= 3$

8. **(c)** Let two numbers are x and y then, $x.y = 1575$

and $\dfrac{x}{y} = \dfrac{9}{7} \Rightarrow y = \dfrac{7}{9}x$

$\therefore \quad x.\dfrac{7}{9}x = 1575$

$x^2 = \dfrac{1575 \times 9}{7}$

$x = 45$

then $y = \dfrac{7}{9} \times 45 = 35$

$\therefore \quad x + y = 45 + 35 = 80$

9. **(d)** Required sum

$= \left(199\dfrac{1}{7} + 199\dfrac{6}{7}\right) + \left(199\dfrac{2}{7} + 199\dfrac{5}{7}\right)$

$\quad + \left(199\dfrac{3}{7} + 199\dfrac{4}{7}\right)$

$= 199 \times 3 = 597$

10. **(c)** Let the number of pages be x.

Number of pages read in

first day $= \dfrac{3x}{8}$

Remaining pages

$= x - \dfrac{3x}{8} = \dfrac{5}{8}x$

Number of pages read on second day

$= \dfrac{4}{5} \times \dfrac{5}{8}x = \dfrac{1}{2}x$

Now, remaining pages

$= x - \left(\dfrac{3x}{8} + \dfrac{x}{2}\right)$

$= \left(x - \dfrac{7x}{8}\right)$

$= \left(\dfrac{8x - 7x}{8}\right) = \dfrac{x}{8}$

According to the question,

$\dfrac{x}{8} = 40 \Rightarrow x = 40 \times 8 \Rightarrow x = 320$

11. **(b)** $4x^2 + 7xy - 2y^2 = (4x - y)(x + 2y)$

$(4x - y)$ is divisible by 3

$4x^2 + 7xy - 2y^2$ is also divisible by 3

12. **(d)**

$\dfrac{1}{\sqrt{1} + \sqrt{2}} = \dfrac{1}{\sqrt{2} + \sqrt{1}}$

$\quad + \dfrac{\sqrt{2} - \sqrt{1}}{\sqrt{2} - \sqrt{1}} = \sqrt{2} - \sqrt{1}$

$\dfrac{1}{\sqrt{1} + \sqrt{2}} + \dfrac{1}{\sqrt{2} + \sqrt{3}} + \dfrac{1}{\sqrt{3} + \sqrt{4}}$

$\quad \dots \dfrac{1}{\sqrt{99} + \sqrt{100}}$

$= \sqrt{2} - \sqrt{1} + \sqrt{3} - \sqrt{2} +$

$\quad \dots + \sqrt{100} - \sqrt{99}$

$= \sqrt{100} - \sqrt{1} = 10 - 1 = 9$

Square and Square Roots, Cube and Cube Roots, Indices and Surds

Easier method to find the square root of 3 or 4 digits number:

Step-(i) : Square root of 3 or 4 digits number is always a 2 digits number. Ten's digit of the square root is the largest digit whose square is less than or equal to the number form from the digit(s) remains after leaving the two digits from right from the given number.

Step-(ii) :Guess the unit digit of the square root on the basis of unit digit of the given number as explained in the following examples.

(i) $\sqrt{3481} = ?$

    $(5)^2 < 34 < 36 \Rightarrow$ Ten's digit of $\sqrt{3481} = 5$

    Since unit digit of $3481 = 1$

    Therefore, unti digit of $\sqrt{3481}$ is 1 or 9.

    Thus $\sqrt{3481}$ is 51 or 59.

    Now 51 is close to 50 and 59 is close to 60.

    Now $(50)^2 = 2500$ and $(60)^2 = 3600$.

    But 3481 is closer to 3600.

    $\therefore \sqrt{3481} = 59$

(ii) $\sqrt{324} = ?$

    $(1)^2 < 3 < (2)^2 \Rightarrow$ Ten's digit of 324 is 1.

    Since unit digit of $324 = 4$.

    Therefore, unit digit of $\sqrt{324}$ is 2 or 8.

    Thus $\sqrt{324} = 12$ or 18.

    Now, 12 is close to 10 and 18 is close to 20.

    Now $(10)^2 = 100$ and $(20)^2 = 400$.

    But 324 is closer to 400.

    $\therefore \sqrt{324} = 18$

1.   **Find the square root of $\sqrt{2304}$**

    (a) 48   (b) 42

    (c) 47   (d) None of these

Sol. **(a)** $(4)^2 < 23 < (5)^2 \Rightarrow$ Ten's digit of $\sqrt{2304} = 4$

Since unit digit of $2304 = 4$

Therefore, unit digit of $\sqrt{2304}$ is 2 or 8

Thus, $\sqrt{2304}$ is 42 or 48

Now 42 is close to 40 and 48 is close to 50

Now, $(40)^2 = 1600$

$\qquad (50)^2 = 2500$

$\therefore \quad \sqrt{2304} = 48$

2. **Find the square root of $\sqrt{5184}$**

(a) 78 (b) 71

(c) 72 (d) None of these

Sol. **(c)** $(7)^2 < 51 < (8)^2 \Rightarrow$ Ten's digit of $\sqrt{5184} = 7$

Since unit digit of $5184 = 4$

Therefore, unit digit of $\sqrt{5184}$ is 2 or 8

Thus, $\sqrt{5184}$ is 72 or 78

Now, 72 is close to 70 and 78 is close to 80

Now, $(70)^2 = 4900$,

$\qquad (80)^2 = 6400$,

$\therefore \quad \sqrt{5184} = 72$

Shortcut Approach - 2

Approximate Square Root of a number :

Divide the given number by a divisor around approximate square root of the number. Find the average of the divisor and quotient. This average is the approximate square root of the given number.

(i) $\sqrt{850} = ?$

Take 30 as divisor.

$850 \div 30 = 28.33$

Average of 30 and $28.33 = 29.17$.

Hence, approximate square root of $850 = 29.17$.

(ii) $\sqrt{1171} = ?$

Take 35 as divisor.

$1171 \div 35 = 33.46$

Average of 35 and $33.46 = \dfrac{35 + 33.46}{2} = 34.23$

Hence approximate square root of $1171 = 34.23$.

Note that, we can take divisor as any other number nearby the square root of 1171. If we take 30 as divisor, then

$1171 \div 30 = 39.03$.

Average of 30 and 39.03 $= \dfrac{30 + 39.03}{2} = 34.52$

Hence approximate square root of $1171 = 34.52$.

3. **Find the approximate square root of 624.**

    (a) 23.98   (b) 24.98

    (c) 25.98   (d) None of these.

Sol. **(b)**   Consider 25 as divisor

        $624 \div 25 = 24.96$

        Average of 25 and 24.96

$$= \dfrac{25 + 24.96}{2} = \dfrac{49.96}{2} = 24.98$$

        Hence, approximate square root of 624 is $= 24.98$

4. **Find the Approximate square root of 1550.**

    (a) 37. 375   (b) 38. 375

    (c) 39. 375   (d) None of these.

Sol. **(c)**   Consider 40 as divisor

        $1550 \div 40 = 38.75$

        Average of 40 and 38.75

$$= \dfrac{40 + 38.75}{2} = \dfrac{78.75}{2} = 39.375$$

        Hence, approximate square root of 1550 is 39.375

Shortcut Approach - 3

If in a given number, number of digits is n and if n is even, then square root of that number will have $\dfrac{n}{2}$ digits and if n is odd, then number of digits will be $\dfrac{n+1}{2}$.

5. **How many digits are there in square root of 6594624.**

    (a) 7   (b) 6   (c) 5   (d) 4

Sol. **(d)** Since number of digits in 6594624 is 7 and 7 is odd number
Hence, number of digits in square root

$$= \frac{7+1}{2} = 4 \text{ digits}$$

6. **How many digits are there in square root of 20820969.**
(a) 4   (b) 5   (c) 6   (d) 8

Sol. **(a)** Since number of digits in 20820969 is 8 and 8 is even number
Hence, number of digits in square root

$$= \frac{n}{2} = \frac{8}{2} = 4 \text{ digits}$$

⊕ Shortcut Approach - 3 (a)

7. **Find the greatest 8 digit number which is a perfect square.**
(a) 99970001   (b) 99980001
(c) 99990001   (d) None of these

Sol. **(b)** Greatest 8 digits number = 99999999

		9999
	9	99 99 99 99
	9	81
	189	1899
	9	1701
	1989	19899
	9	17901
	19989	199899
	9	179901
	19998	19998

Clearly greatest 8-digits number which is a perfect square will
be 19998, less than 99999999. Therefore, required number
= 99999999 – 19998 = 99980001

8. **Find the greatest 9 digit number which is a perfect square.**
(a) 999970884   (b) 999960884
(c) 999950884   (d) None of these

Sol.　**(c)**　Greatest 9 digits number $= 999999999$

	31622
3	999999999
3	9
61	99
1	61
626	3899
6	3756
6322	14399
2	12644
63242	175599
	126484
	49115

Clearly greatest 9-digits number which is a perfect square will be 49115 less than 999999999.

Therefore, required number

$= 999999999 - 49115 = 999950884$

To calculate cube of a number the following two formulae are used

(i)　$(a + b)^3 = a^3 + 3ab\,(a - b) + b^3$

(ii)　$(a - b)^3 = a^3 - 3ab\,(a - b) - b^3$

You can easily understand it by the following illustrations.

9.　Find the cube of 19.

　　(a) 6559　　(b) 6659　　(c) 6759　　(d) 6859

Sol.　**(d)**　$(19)^3 = (10 + 9)^3$

$= (10)^3 + 3 \times 10 \times 9\,(10 + 9) + (9)^3$

$= 1000 + 270 \times (19) + 729$

$= 1729 + 5130 = 6859$

10.　Find the cube of 28.

　　(a) 23952　　　　　　(b) 22952

　　(c) 21952　　　　　　(d) None of these

Sol.　**(c)**　$(28)^3 = (30 - 2)^3$

$= (30)^3 - 3 \times 30 \times 2 \times (30 - 2) - (2)^3$

$= 27000 - 180 \times (28) - 8$

$= 27000 - 5040 - 8 = 21952$

Cube Root By Successive Subtraction:

If we subtract 1, 7, 19, 37, 61, 91 .... from a given number, till we get zero then the number of subtractions will give the cube root of the given number.

The numbers 1, 7, 19, 37 .... are obtained by putting m = 1, 2, 3, 4.......... in
$[1 + m \times (m - 1) \times 3]$

Example : $64 - 1 = 63, 63 - 7 = 56, 56 - 19 = 37,$
$37 - 37 = 0.$

Here number of subtractions till we get zero is 4. Therefore $\sqrt[3]{64} = 4$

Cube root of any number upto 3-digits is a single digit number. We can easily find the cube root of any perfect cube number upto 3 digits. Using the relation between unit digit of a perfect cube number and unit digit of its cube root. Cube root of any 4, 5 or 6 digits number is a 2-digits number. To find the cube root of any 4, 5 or 6 digits number follow the steps :

(i) Put a slash before the last three digits from right of given perfect cube number. 103823 can represent as 103 / 823, 1331 can represent as 1 / 331.

(ii) The number on right side of slash will give us the unit place digit of cube root and that on left hand side will give ten's digit of cube root.

(iii) The unit place digit of cube root can be found by looking at unit place digit of the given number and the relation between unit digit of a perfect cube number and unit digit of its cube root . For example, cube root of 287496 will have 6 at units place in its cube root because the number itself has 6 in its unit place.

(iv) To find the ten's place digit of the cube root, we take the number which lies to the left of the slash. Now we find two perfect cubes between which the left hand part i.e., number before slash, lies. For example in 287/496, left part 287 lies between 216 (cube of 6) and 343 (cube of 7).

(v) Now out of the numbers 6 and 7 obtained above we take the smaller number as ten's place digit of the cube root. Thus cube root of 287496, which is a perfect cube, is 66.

Thus by simple observation we will be able to find cube root of any given perfect cube number upto 6 digits.

11. Find the cube root of 729, by successive substraction method.

    (a) 9   (b) 11

    (c) 13   (d) None of these.

Sol.. (a) $729 - 1 = 728, 728 - 7 = 721,$
$721 - 19 = 702, 702 - 37 = 665,$
$665 - 61 = 604, 604 - 91 = 513,$
$513 - 127 = 386, 386 - 169 = 217,$
$217 - 217 = 0$

Here number of subtractions fill we get zero is 9. Therefore
$\sqrt[3]{729} = 9$

12. **Find the cube root of 343, by successive substraction method.**
    (a) 9   (b) 8
    (c) 7   (d) None of these.

Sol. **(c)** $343 - 1 = 342$, $342 - 7 = 335$,
$335 - 19 = 316$, $316 - 37 = 279$,
$279 - 61 = 218$, $218 - 91 = 127$,
$127 - 127 = 0$

Here number of subtraction fill we get zero is 7. Therefore

$$\sqrt[3]{343} = 7$$

Shortcut Approach - 6

Finding cube root by Approximation

Divide the given number by a divisor around approximate cube root of the number. Divide the quotient by the same divisor again. Take average of the two divisors and final quotient. This is approximate cube root of the number.

13. **Find the cube root of 3400.**
    (a) 15.037   (b) 14.037
    (c) 16.037   (d) 13.037

Sol. **(a)** Let, take 15 as divisor,
$3400 \div 15 = 226.666$
$226.666 \div 15 = 15.111$
So, average of 15, 15, 15.111 is 15.037

14. **Find the cube root of 1750.**
    (a) 15.05   (b) 14.05   (c) 13.05   (d) 12.05

Sol. **(d)** Let take 12 as divisor,
$1750 \div 12 = 145.833$
$145.833 \div 12 = 12.152$
So, average of 12, 12, 12.152 is 12.05

Shortcut Approach - 7

If x is a positive real number and a, b and c are real number; then

(i)
$$\left(\frac{x^b}{x^c}\right)^a \cdot \left(\frac{x^c}{x^a}\right)^b \cdot \left(\frac{x^a}{x^b}\right)^c = 1$$

(ii)
$$\left(\frac{x^a}{x^b}\right)^{a+b} \cdot \left(\frac{x^b}{x^c}\right)^{b+c} \cdot \left(\frac{x^c}{x^a}\right)^{c+a} = 1$$

(iii) $\left(\dfrac{x^a}{x^b}\right)^{(a^2+b^2+ab)} \cdot \left(\dfrac{x^b}{x^c}\right)^{(b^2+c^2+bc)}$

$\cdot \left(\dfrac{x^c}{x^a}\right)^{(c^2+a^2+ca)} = 1$

15. Find the value of the following:

$$\left(\dfrac{13^3}{13^6}\right)^2 \cdot \left(\dfrac{13^6}{13^2}\right)^3 \cdot \left(\dfrac{13^2}{13^3}\right)^6$$

(a) 11   (b) 111

(c) 1   (d) None of thses

Sol. (c) $\left(\dfrac{(13)^6}{(13)^{12}}\right)\left(\dfrac{(13)^{18}}{(13)^6}\right)\cdot\left(\dfrac{(13)^{12}}{(13)^{18}}\right) = 1$

16. Find the value of the following.

$$\left(\dfrac{(121)^7}{(121)^8}\right)^{7+8} \cdot \left(\dfrac{(121)^8}{(121)^9}\right)^{8+9} \cdot \left(\dfrac{(121)^9}{(121)^7}\right)^{9+7}$$

(a) 121   (b) 1

(c) 11   (d) None of these

Sol. (b) $\dfrac{(121)^{7\times15}}{(121)^{8\times15}} \cdot \dfrac{(121)^{8\times17}}{(121)^{9\times17}} \cdot \dfrac{(121)^{9\times16}}{(121)^{7\times16}} = 1$

17. Find the value of the following.

$$\left(\dfrac{(49)^3}{(49)^9}\right)^{(3^2+9^2+3\times9)} \cdot \left(\dfrac{(49)^9}{(49)^{27}}\right)^{(9^2+(27)^2+9\times27)}$$

$$\cdot \left(\dfrac{(49)^{27}}{(49)^3}\right)^{((27)^2+(3)^2+27\times3)}$$

(a) 1   (b) 49

(c) $(49)^2$ (d) None of these.

Sol. (a)

$$\frac{(49)^{3\cdot\left(3^2+9^2+3\times9\right)}}{(49)^{9\cdot\left(3^2+9^2+3\times9\right)}} \cdot \frac{(49)^{9\left(9^2+(27)^2+9\times27\right)}}{(49)^{27\left(9^2+(27)^2+9\times27\right)}}$$

$$\cdot \frac{(49)^{27\left((27)^2+3^2+27\times3\right)}}{(49)^{3\left((27)^2+3^2+27\times3\right)}} = 1$$

If the sum of a number and its square is x, then the number is given by

$$\left[\frac{\sqrt{1+4x}-1}{2}\right].$$

18. If the sum of a number and its square is 110, what is the number?

    (a) 10   (b) 21

    (c) 11   (d) None of these.

Sol. (a) The required number $= \dfrac{\sqrt{1+4\times110}-1}{2}$

$$= \frac{\sqrt{441}-1}{2} \Rightarrow \frac{21-1}{2} = 10$$

19. If the sum of a number and its square is 240, what is the number?

    (a) 13   (b) 14

    (c) 15   (d) None of these

Sol. (c) The required number

$$= \frac{\sqrt{1+4\times240}-1}{2} = \frac{\sqrt{961}-1}{2}$$

$$= \frac{31-1}{2} = 15$$

⊕ Shortcut Approach - 9

The difference between the squares of two consecutive numbers is the sum of the two consecutive numbers and it is always an odd number.

20. Find the value of

$$(47)^2 + (31)^2 + (21)^2 - (46)^2 - (30)^2 - (20)^2$$

(a) 190   (b) 195   (c) 205   (d) 215

Sol. (b) $(47)^2 + (31)^2 + (21)^2 - (46)^2 - (30)^2 - (20)^2$

$$= ((47)^2 - (46)^2) + ((31)^2 - (30)^2) + ((21)^2 - (20)^2)$$

$$= (47 + 46) + (31 + 30) + (21 + 20)$$

$$\Rightarrow \quad 93 + 61 + 41 = 195$$

21. Find the value of

$$(91)^2 + (81)^2 + (71)^2 - (90)^2 - (80)^2 - (70)^2$$

(a) 480   (b) 485   (c) 481   (d) 483

Sol. (d) $(91)^2 + (81)^2 + (71)^2 - (90)^2 - (80)^2 - (70)^2$

$$= ((91)^2 - (90)^2) + ((81)^2 - (80)^2) + ((71)^2 - (70)^2)$$

$$= (91 + 90) + (81 + 80) + (71 + 70)$$

$$= 181 + 161 + 141 = 483$$

⊕ Shortcut Approach - 10

A number is divided by a certain number N_1 and gives a remainder R. If the same number is divided by another number N_2, where $N_1 > N_2$ and N_1 is divisible by N_2, then the new remainder is obtained by dividing R by N_2.

22. A number when divided by 357, gives a remainder 39. What remainder would be obtained by dividing the same number by 17.

(a) 6   (b) 3   (c) 5   (d) 8

Sol. (c)

$$
\begin{array}{r}
17)\overline{\,39\,}(2 \\
\underline{34} \\
5
\end{array}
$$

Required number $= 5$

23. A number when divided by 899, gives a remainder 63. What remainder would be obtained by dividing the same number by 29.

(a) 0   (b) 3   (c) 5   (d) 8

Sol. (c)

$$29) \overline{63} (2$$

$$\underline{58}$$

$$5$$

Required number $= 5$

If the sum of two numbers be x and difference is y, then the difference of their squares is xy.

24. The sum of two number be 100 and their difference is 37. The difference of their square is:

(a) 2700   (b) 3700   (c) 3900   (d) 2900

Sol. (b) The required number

$$= xy = 100 \times 37 = 3700$$

25. The sum of two number is 291 and their difference is 89, the difference of their square is

(a) 25799   (b) 25699   (c) 25599   (d) 25899

Sol. (d) The required number

$$= xy = 291 \times 89 = 25899$$

If the difference between the squares of two consecutive numbers is x,

then the numbers are $\left(\dfrac{x-1}{2}\right)$ and $\left(\dfrac{x+1}{2}\right)$.

26. The difference between the squares of two consecutive number is 31, find the numbers.

(a) 15, 16   (b) 14, 15

(c) 13, 14   (d) None of these

Sol. (a) The required number

$$= \left(\dfrac{x-1}{2}\right) \text{ and } \left(\dfrac{x+1}{2}\right)$$

$$= \frac{31-1}{2} \text{ and } \frac{31+1}{2}$$

$$= 15 \text{ and } 16$$

27. The difference between the squares of two consecutive number 201, find the numbers.

    (a) 101, 102   (b) 102, 103

    (c) 100, 101   (d) None of these

Sol. **(c)**   The required number

$$= \left(\frac{201-1}{2}\right) \text{ and } \left(\frac{201+1}{2}\right) = 100 \text{ and } 101$$

⊕ Shortcut Approach - 13

If the two consecutive numbers are x and y, then the difference of their squares is given by $(x + y)$.

28. Two consecutive numbers are 171 and 172, then the difference of their squares.

    (a) 345   (b) 343

    (c) 353   (d) None of these

Sol. **(b)**   The required number $= x + y$

$$= 171 + 172 = 343$$

29. Two consecutive numbers are 1178 and 1179 then the difference of their squares.

    (a) 2357   (b) 2457

    (c) 2557   (d) None of these

Sol. **(a)**   The required number $= x + y$

$$= 1178 + 1179 = 2357$$

⊕ Shortcut Approach - 14

If the product of the two numbers is x and the sum of their squares is y, then

(i)   the sum of the two numbers is given by $\sqrt{y + 2x}$ and

(ii)   the difference of the two numbers is given by $\sqrt{y - 2x}$.

30. The product of two numbers is 3976. The sum of their squares is 8177. Find the difference of the two numbers.

(a) 17   (b) 18   (c) 16   (d) 15

Sol. **(d)**   As given that x = 3976, y = 8177

$$\text{The required difference} = \sqrt{y - 2x}$$

$$= \sqrt{8177 - 2 \times 3976}$$

$$= \sqrt{225} = 15$$

31. The product of two numbers is 5429. The sum of their squares is 11642. Find the sum of the two numbers.

(a) 151   (b) 152   (c) 150   (d) 153

Sol. **(c)**   As given that x = 5429, y = 11642

$$\text{The required sum} = \sqrt{y + 2x}$$

$$= \sqrt{11642 + 2 \times 5429}$$

$$= \sqrt{22500} = 150$$

Exercise

1. Find the value of x if

$$\sqrt{x}^{\sqrt{x}^{\sqrt{x}^{\sqrt{x}^{.\cdot^{.\infty}}}}} = 9$$

   (a) $\sqrt{3}$ (b) $3^{\frac{1}{4}}$

   (c) $3^{\frac{1}{6}}$ (d) $3^{\frac{4}{9}}$

2. What number must be added to the expression $16a^2 - 12a$ to make it a perfect square?
   (a) 9/4   (b) 11/2
   (c) 13/2   (d) 16

3. Which one among $2^{1/2}$, $3^{1/3}$, $4^{1/4}$, $6^{1/6}$ and $12^{1/12}$ is the largest?
   (a) $2^{1/2}$ (b) $3^{1/3}$
   (c) $4^{1/4}$ (d) $6^{1/6}$

4. Arrange the following in descending order.

   $$\sqrt[3]{3},\ \sqrt[4]{4},\ \sqrt[6]{6},\ \sqrt[12]{12}$$

   (a) $\sqrt[4]{4} > \sqrt[12]{12} > \sqrt[6]{6} > \sqrt[3]{3}$

   (b) $\sqrt[12]{12} > \sqrt[6]{6} > \sqrt[4]{4} > \sqrt[3]{3}$

   (c) $\sqrt[3]{3} > \sqrt[4]{4} > \sqrt[6]{6} > \sqrt[12]{12}$

   (d) $\sqrt[4]{4} > \sqrt[6]{6} > \sqrt[3]{3} > \sqrt[12]{12}$

5. The largest number among
   $\sqrt{7}-\sqrt{5}, \sqrt{5}-\sqrt{3}, \sqrt{9}-\sqrt{7}, \sqrt{11}-\sqrt{9}$ is
   (a) $\sqrt{7}-\sqrt{5}$

   (b) $\sqrt{5}-\sqrt{3}$

   (c) $\sqrt{9}-\sqrt{7}$

   (d) $\sqrt{11}-\sqrt{9}$

6. The value of $\left[x^{(b-c)}\right]^{b+c}$
   $\left[x^{(c-a)}\right]^{(c+a)}\left[x^{(a-b)}\right]^{(a+b)}$ is
   (a) 0   (b) 1
   (c) x
   (d) $x^{a^2+b^2+c^2}$

7. If $x^{\frac{1}{3}} + y^{\frac{1}{3}} = z^{\frac{1}{3}}$, then $\{(x + y - z)^3 + 27\,xyz\}$ will be equal to
   (a) -1 (b) 1
   (c) 0   (d) 27

8. If $P = 124$, then
   $$\sqrt[3]{P\left(P^2 + 3P + 3\right) + 1} = ?$$
   (a) 5   (b) 7
   (c) 123   (d) 125

9. If $a = 2 + \sqrt{3}$, then what is the value of $(a^2 + a^{-2})$?
   (a) 12   (b) 14
   (c) 16   (d) 18

10. If p, q, r be integers such that $p^2 = q^2 \cdot r$ then :
    (a) p is an even number
    (b) q is an even number
    (c) r is an even number
    (d) r is a perfect square

11. What is the least number which must be subtracted from 369 to make it a perfect cube?
    (a) 8   (b) 26
    (c) 2   (d) 25

12. Simplify:

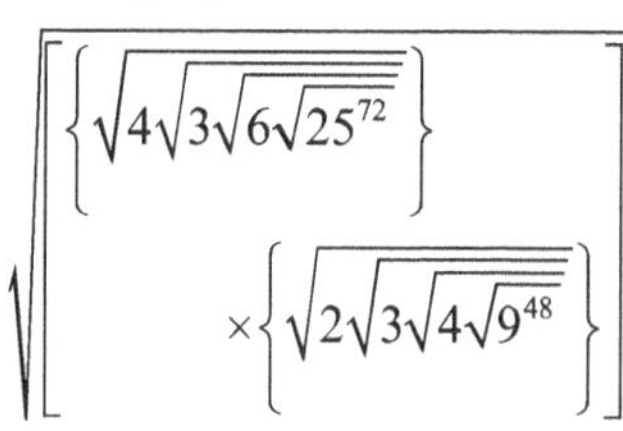

$$\sqrt{\left[\left\{\sqrt{4\sqrt{3\sqrt{6\sqrt{25^{72}}}}}\right\} \times \left\{\sqrt{2\sqrt{3\sqrt{4\sqrt{9^{48}}}}}\right\}\right]}$$

   (a) 75   (b) 45
   (c) 1/5   (d) 15

Hints & Solution

1. **(d)** From the given information we can say that

$$\left(\sqrt{x}\right)^9 = 9 = 3^2 \text{ hence } \sqrt{x} = 3^{\frac{2}{9}} \text{ or } x = 3^{\frac{4}{9}}$$

2. **(a)** $16a^2 - 12a = (4a)^2 - 2(4a)(3/2)$

∴ The number is $(3/2)^2 = (9/4)$.

3. **(b)** In this question it is adv[isable to raise all the numbers to the power of 12, so the numbers become,

$$(2^{1/2})^{12}, (3^{1/3})^{12}, (4^{1/4})^{12}, (6^{1/6})^{12}, (12^{1/12})^{12}$$

or $2^6, 3^4, 4^3, 6^2, 12$

or $64, 81, 64, 36, 12$

So, $3^{1/3}$ is the largest.

4. **(c)** $\sqrt[3]{3} \quad \sqrt[4]{4} \quad \sqrt[6]{6} \quad \sqrt[12]{12}$

$$\downarrow \quad \downarrow \quad \downarrow \quad \downarrow$$

$$3^{\frac{1}{3}} \quad 4^{\frac{1}{4}} \quad 6^{\frac{1}{6}} \quad 12^{\frac{1}{12}}$$

LCM of $(3, 4, 6, 12) = 12$.

$$3^{\frac{1}{3} \times 12} = 3^4 = 81$$

$$4^{\frac{1}{4} \times 12} = 4^3 = 64$$

$$6^{\frac{1}{6} \times 12} = 6^2 = 36$$

$$12^{\frac{1}{12} \times 12} = 12^1 = 12$$

$81 > 64 > 36 > 12$

$3^{1/3} > 4^{1/4} > 6^{1/6} > 12^{1/12}$.

5. **(b)** If $b - a = d - c = f - e$ ....then putting smaller value in

$$\sqrt{b} - \sqrt{a}, \sqrt{d} - \sqrt{c}, \sqrt{f} - \sqrt{e}$$

we get the largest difference.

So, $\sqrt{5} - \sqrt{3}$ here will be the largest

Trick : $\sqrt{7} - \sqrt{5} = \dfrac{2}{\sqrt{7} + \sqrt{5}}$

$$\sqrt{11} - \sqrt{9} = \dfrac{2}{\sqrt{11} + \sqrt{9}} \text{ etc}.$$

∵ Numerator is same, so that number will be largest whose denominator is the smallest.

6. **(b)** Use Short Approach -7

7. **(c)** If $a + b + c = 0$, then $a^3 + b^3 + c^3 = 3abc$

After putting

$$a = x^{\frac{1}{3}}, b = y^{\frac{1}{3}}, c = -z^{\frac{1}{3}}$$

$$x + y - z = -3x^{\frac{1}{3}} y^{\frac{1}{3}} z^{\frac{1}{3}}$$

or, $(x + y - z)^3 = -27 \, xyz$

or, $(x + y - z)^3 + 27 \, xyz = 0$

8. **(d)** $\sqrt[3]{P\left(P^2 + 3P + 3\right) + 1}$

$$= \sqrt[3]{P^3 + 3P^2 + 3P + 1}$$

$$= \sqrt[3]{(P+1)^3} = P + 1$$

∵ $P = 124 \Rightarrow P + 1 = 125$

9.   **(b)**   Given that, $a = 2 + \sqrt{3}$

Then $\dfrac{1}{a} = 2 - \sqrt{3}$ [b y conjugate property]

Now, we have,

$$a^2 + a^{-2} = \left(a + \dfrac{1}{a}\right)^2 - 2$$

$$= \left(2 + \sqrt{3} + 2 - \sqrt{3}\right)^2 - 2$$

$$= (4)^2 - 2 = 16 - 2 = 14$$

10.   **(d)**   Options (a), (b) and (c) are irrelevent.

as $(25)^2 = (5)^2 \times 25$

or $(27)^2 = (9)^2 \times 9$

or $(6)^2 = (4)^2 \times 9$

or $(6)^2 = (3)^2 \times 4$ etc.

11.   **(b)**   **Go through option.** If you subtract 2, 8 or 25 from 369, then you will not obtain a perfect cube number. So (b) is the correct answer.

Alternatively : If you write down the nearest perfect cube such that $k \le 369$, where k is a perfect cube, then $7^3 = 343$, which is just below 369.

So $369 - 343 = 26$

12. (b)

$$\sqrt{4\sqrt{3\sqrt{6\sqrt{25^{72}}}}} = 5^{\frac{2\times72}{4\times3\times6}} = 5^2 = 25$$

and

$$\sqrt{2\sqrt{3\sqrt{4\sqrt{9^{48}}}}} = 3^{\frac{2\times48}{4\times3\times2}} = 3^4 = 81$$

Hence required value is

$$\sqrt{81 \times 25} = \sqrt{2025} = 45$$

Fundamental Operations, Vbodmas Rule, Algebraic Identities, Approximation and Simplification (Including Basic Calculations)

Shortcut Approach - 1

Application of the formula :

$(a + b)^2 = a^2 + 2ab + b^2$

(or)

$(a + b)^2 = a^2 + b^2 + 2ab$

1. $16 \times 16 + 128 + 4 \times 4 = ?$

(a) 20   (b) 100   (c) 400   (d) 500

Sol. (c) Put $a = 16$ and $b = 4$, then the given expression *becomes*

$16 \times 16 + 128 + 4 \times 4 = (a)^2 + 2 \times a \times b + (b)^2$

$= (a + b)^2 = (16 + 4)^2 = 400$

2. **If the sum of two numbers is 3 and the sum of their squares is 12, then their product is equal to:**

(a) $\dfrac{3}{2}$

(b) $\dfrac{2}{3}$

(c) $-\dfrac{3}{2}$

(d) $-\dfrac{2}{3}$

Sol. (c) Here, $x + y = 3$ and $x^2 + y^2 = 12$

Now $(x + y)^2 = (3)^2 \Rightarrow x^2 + y^2 + 2xy = 9$

$\Rightarrow 12 + 2xy = 9 \Rightarrow xy = \dfrac{-3}{2}$

Shortcut Approach - 2

Application of the fomrula :

$(a - b)^2 = a^2 - 2ab + b^2$

(or)

$(a - b)^2 = a^2 + b^2 - 2ab$

3. **The sum of two numbers is 42 and their product is 437. Then the absolute difference between the numbers is:**

(a) 3   (b) 4   (c) 5   (d) 7

Sol. (b) $x + y = 42$ and $xy = 437$

Now, $(x - y)^2 = x^2 + y^2 - 2xy = x^2 + y^2 + 2xy - 4xy$

$= (x + y)^2 - 4xy = (42)^2 - 4(437) = 16$

$\Rightarrow \quad x - y = 4$

4. The product of two numbers is 120. The sum of their squares is 289. The difference of these two numbers is

(a) 9   (b) 7   (c) 8   (d) 6

Sol. (b) $xy = 120$ and $x^2 + y^2 = 289$

$\therefore \quad (x - y)^2 = x^2 + y^2 - 2xy = 289 - 2(120) = 49$

$\Rightarrow \quad x - y = 7$

5. Find the value of

$$\frac{0.5 \times 0.5 + 0.1 \times 0.1 - 0.2 \times 0.5}{0.4}$$

(a) 0.2   (b) 0.3   (c) 0.4   (d) 0.6

Sol. (c) $\dfrac{0.5 \times 0.5 + 0.1 \times 0.1 - 2 \times 0.1 \times 0.5}{0.5 - 0.1}$

Substitute $a = 0.5$ and $b = 0.1$

$$\Rightarrow \quad \frac{a^2 + b^2 - 2ab}{a - b} = \frac{(a - b)^2}{a - b} = a - b = 0.4$$

⊕ Shortcut Approach - 3

Application of the formula :

$a^2 - b^2 = (a + b)(a - b)$

6. $\left[\dfrac{(0.1)^2 - (0.01)^2}{0.0001}\right] + 1$ **is equal to**

(a) 1010   (b) 110   (c) 101   (d) 100

Sol. (d) $\left[\dfrac{(0.1)^2 - (0.01)^2}{0.0001} + 1\right]$

$$\Rightarrow \left[\frac{(0.1 + 0.01)(0.1 - 0.01)}{0.0001} + 1\right] = \left[\frac{0.11 \times 0.09}{0.0001} + 1\right]$$

$= [99 + 1] = 100$

7. The product of two consecutive odd numbers is 4899. What is the smaller number?

 (a) 67 (b) 69 (c) 71   (d) 73

Sol. (b) Let the numbers be $(x-1)$ and $(x+1)$

$$\therefore \quad (x-1)(x+1) = 4899$$

$$\Rightarrow \quad x^2 - 1 = 4899$$

$$\Rightarrow \quad x = \sqrt{4900} = 70$$

$$\therefore \quad \text{The smaller number} = x - 1 = 69$$

8. $\dfrac{998^2 - 997^2 - 45}{98^2 - 97^2} = ?$

 (a) 1995 (b) 195 (c) 95 (d) 10

Sol. (d) $\dfrac{(998+997)(998-997) - 45}{(98+97)(98-97)}$

$$= \frac{1995 - 45}{195} = \frac{1950}{195} = 10$$

Shortcut Approach - 4

Application of the formula :

$$(a+b)^2 + (a-b)^2 = 2(a^2 + b^2)$$

9. Solve: $\dfrac{(835+378)^2 + (835-378)^2}{835 \times 835 + 378 \times 378}$

 (a) 1 (b) 2 (c) 3   (d) 4

Sol. (b) $\Rightarrow \dfrac{(835+378)^2 + (835-378)^2}{(835 \times 835 + 378 \times 378)}$

$$= \frac{2\left((835)^2 + (378)^2\right)}{\left((835)^2 + (378)^2\right)} = 2$$

Shortcut Approach - 5

Application of the formula:

$$(a+b)^2 - (a-b)^2 = 4ab$$

10. Solve: $\dfrac{(999+588)^2 - (999-588)^2}{999 \times 588}$

     (a) 4   (b) 3   (c) 2   (d) 1

Sol. (a) $\Rightarrow \dfrac{(999+588)^2 - (999-588)^2}{999 \times 588}$

$$= \dfrac{4 \times 999 \times 588}{999 \times 588} = 4$$

11. $\left(\dfrac{4}{3}+\dfrac{3}{4}\right)^2 - \left(\dfrac{4}{3}-\dfrac{3}{4}\right)^2 = ?$

     (a) 1   (b) 2   (c) 3   (d) 4

Sol. (d) The given expression is

$$(a+b)^2 - (a-b)^2 = 4ab = 4\left(\dfrac{4}{3}\right)\left(\dfrac{3}{4}\right) = 4$$

⊕ Shortcut Approach - 6

Application of the formula :
$$(a+b)^3 = a^3 + 3a^2b + 3ab^2 + b^3$$
$$(a+b)^3 = a^3 + b^3 + 3ab\,(a+b)$$

12. **If $xy\,(x+y)=1$, then the value of $\dfrac{1}{x^3 y^3} - x^3 - y^3$.**

     (a) 3   (b) -3 (c) 1   (d) -1

Sol. (a) $xy\,(x+y)=1 \Rightarrow x+y = \dfrac{1}{xy}$

$$\Rightarrow (x+y)^3 = \dfrac{1}{x^3 y^3} \Rightarrow x^3 + y^3 + 3xy\,(x+y) = \dfrac{1}{x^3 y^3}$$

$$\Rightarrow \; = \dfrac{1}{x^3 y^3} - x^3 - y^3 = 3xy\,(x+y) = 3$$

⊕ Shortcut Approach - 7

Application of the formula :
$$(a-b)^3 = a^3 - 3a^2b + 3ab^2 - b^3$$

       or

$$(a-b)^3 = a^3 - b^3 - 3ab\,(a-b)$$

13. **If $x-y=1$, then $x^3 - y^3 - 3(xy-2)$ is equal to**

     (a) 7   (b) 6   (c) 10   (d) 4

Sol. (a) As given expression is

$$\Rightarrow \quad x-y=1$$
$$\Rightarrow \quad (x-y)^3 = 1^3$$
$$\Rightarrow \quad x^3 - y^3 - 3(xy)(x-y) = 1$$
$$\Rightarrow \quad x^3 - y^3 - 3xy = 1$$
$$\Rightarrow \quad x^3 - y^3 - 3xy + 6 = 1 + 6 = 7$$

14. If $p - 2q = 4$, then the value of $p^3 - 8q^3 - 24pq - 64$ is

    (a) 0   (b) 3   (c) -1 (d) 2

Sol. (a) As given expression is

$$\Rightarrow \quad p - 2q = 4$$
$$\Rightarrow \quad (p - 2q)^3 = (4)^3$$
$$\Rightarrow \quad p^3 - (2q)^3 - 3p(2q)(p - 2q) = (4)^3$$
$$\Rightarrow \quad p^3 - 8q^3 - 24pq = 64 \quad (\because p - 2q = 4)$$

Then the value of

$$p^3 - 8q^3 - 24pq - 64 = 0$$

⊕ Shortcut Approach - 8

Application of the formula :
$$a^3 + b^3 = (a + b)(a^2 - ab + b^2)$$

15. If $\dfrac{a}{b} + \dfrac{b}{a} = 1$, then the value of $a^3 + b^3$ is

    (a) 0   (b) 1   (c) 2   (d) 3

Sol. (a) $\dfrac{a}{b} + \dfrac{b}{a} = 1$

$$\Rightarrow \quad a^2 + b^2 = ab$$
$$\Rightarrow \quad (a^2 + b^2 - ab) = 0 \qquad \qquad \text{...(i)}$$
$$\therefore \quad a^3 + b^3 = (a + b)(a^2 + b^2 - ab) = 0 \quad (\because \text{From eq (i)})$$

16. The value of

$$\left(\sqrt[3]{3.5} + \sqrt[3]{2.5}\right)\left\{\left(\sqrt[3]{3.5}\right)^2 - \sqrt[3]{8.75} + \left(\sqrt[3]{2.5}\right)^2\right\} \text{ is:}$$

    (a) 5.375   (b) 1
    (c) 6   (d) 5

Sol. (c) As given expression

$$\Rightarrow \left(\sqrt[3]{3.5} + \sqrt[3]{2.5}\right)\left\{\left(\sqrt[3]{3.5}\right)^2 - \sqrt[3]{8.75} + \left(\sqrt[3]{2.5}\right)^2\right\}$$

Let $a = \sqrt[3]{3.5}, b = \sqrt[3]{2.5}$

$$\Rightarrow \quad (a+b)(a^2 - ab + b^2)$$

$$\Rightarrow \quad (a^3 + b^3) = \left(\left(\sqrt[3]{3.5}\right)^3 + \left(\sqrt[3]{2.5}\right)^3\right) = 6$$

Shortcut Approach - 9

Application of the formula :

$$a^3 - b^3 = (a-b)(a^2 + ab + b^2)$$

17. The value of $\dfrac{(0.96)^3 - (0.1)^3}{(0.96)^2 + (0.096) + (0.01)}$ is

(a) 0.86   (b) 1.06   (c) 0.95   (d) 0.97

Sol. (a) $\dfrac{(0.96)^3 - (0.1)^3}{(0.96)^2 + (0.096) + (0.01)}$

$$= \dfrac{(0.96 - 0.1)\left((0.96)^2 + (0.96)\times(0.1) + (0.1)^2\right)}{(0.96)^2 + (0.096) + (0.01)}$$

$$= \dfrac{(0.96 - 0.1)(10.96)^2 + 0.096 + 0.01)}{\left((0.96)^2 + (0.096) + 0.01\right)}$$

$$= 0.86$$

Shortcut Approach - 10

Application of the formula :

$$a^3 + b^3 + c^3 = 3abc, \text{ if } a + b + c = 0$$

18. $\dfrac{(m-n)^3 + (n-r)^3 + (r-m)^3}{6(m-n)(n-r)(r-m)} = \,?$

(a) $\dfrac{1}{2}$ (b) $\dfrac{1}{10}$ (c) $\dfrac{1}{5}$ (d) $\dfrac{1}{6}$

Sol. (a) $\dfrac{(m-n)^3 + (n-r)^3 + (r-m)^3}{6(m-n)(n-r)(r-m)}$

$$\Rightarrow \dfrac{3\times(m-n)(n-r)(r-m)}{6(m-n)(n-r)(r-m)} = \dfrac{1}{2}$$

19. Find the value of

$$\frac{(a-b)^2}{(b-c)(c-a)}+\frac{(b-c)^2}{(a-b)(c-a)}+\frac{(a-c)^2}{(a-b)(b-c)}.$$

   (a) 0   (b) 1   (c) 2   (d) 3

Sol. (d)
$$\frac{(a-b)^2}{(b-c)(c-a)}+\frac{(b-c)^2}{(a-b)(c-a)}+\frac{(a-c)^2}{(a-b)(b-c)}$$

$$=\frac{(a-b)^3+(b-c)^3+(c-a)^3}{(a-b)(b-c)(c-a)}$$

$$=\frac{3.(a-b)(b-c)(c-a)}{(a-b)(b-c)(c-a)}=3$$

⊕ Shortcut Approach - 11

Application of the formula:

$$a^3+b^3+c^3-3abc=(a+b+c)(a^2+b^2+c^2-ab-bc-ca)$$

or $a^3+b^3+c^3-3abc$

$$=\frac{1}{2}(a+b+c)\{(a-b)^2+(b-c)^2+(c-a)^2\}$$

20. If $a+b+c=6$ and $a^2+b^2+c^2=20$, then the value of $a^3+b^3+c^3-3abc$ is

   (a) 64   (b) 70   (c) 72   (d) 76

Sol. (c) $(a+b+c)^2=(6)^2$

        $\Rightarrow\quad a^2+b^2+c^2+2(ab+bc+ca)=36$

        $\Rightarrow\quad (ab+bc+ca)=8$ $(\because a^2+b^2+c^2=20)$

        Now, $a^3+b^3+c^3-3abc$

        $=(a+b+c)(a^2+b^2+c^2-ab-bc-ca)$

        $=6(20-8)=72$

21. If $(a-b)=3$, $(b-c)=5$ and $(c-a)=1$, then the value of

$$\frac{a^3+b^3+c^3-3abc}{a+b+c}\text{ is}$$

   (a) 17.5   (b) 20.5 (c) 10.5   (d) 35

Sol. (a) $$\frac{a^3+b^3+c^3-3abc}{a+b+c}$$

$$= \frac{\frac{1}{2}(a+b+c)\left[(a-b)^2+(b-c)^2+(c-a)^2\right]}{a+b+c}$$

$$= \frac{1}{2}\left[(3)^2+(5)^2+(1)^2\right]$$

$$= \frac{1}{2}\times(9+25+1)=17.5$$

⊕ Shortcut Approach - 12

Application of the formula:

$(a+b+c)^2 = a^2+b^2+c^2+2ab+2bc+2ca$

22. If $\dfrac{x^2+y^2+z^2-64}{xy-yz-zx} = -2$ and $x+y=3z$, then the value of z is

    (a) 2   (b) 3

    (c) 4   (d) None of these

Sol. (c) As given that,

$$\frac{x^2+y^2+z^2-64}{xy-yz-zx} = -2$$

$$\Rightarrow \quad x^2+y^2+z^2-64 = -2(xy-yz-zx)$$
$$\Rightarrow \quad [x+y+(-z)]^2 = 64$$

$$\Rightarrow \quad (3z-z)^2 = 64 \left[\because x+y=3z\right]$$
$$\Rightarrow \quad 2z=8 \Rightarrow z=4$$

23. If $a+b+c=3$, $a^2+b^2+c^2=6$ and $\dfrac{1}{a}+\dfrac{1}{b}+\dfrac{1}{c}=1$, where a, b, c are all non-zero, then 'abc' is equal to

    (a) $\dfrac{2}{3}$ (b) $\dfrac{3}{2}$ (c) $\dfrac{1}{2}$ (d) $\dfrac{1}{3}$

Sol. (b) As given that

$$a+b+c=3$$
$$(a+b+c)^2=9$$
$$\Rightarrow \quad (a^2+b^2+c^2+2ab+2bc+2ca)=9$$
$$\Rightarrow \quad (6+2(ab+bc+ca)=9\,[\,\because (a^2+b^2+c^2=6)]$$
$$\Rightarrow \quad 2(ab+bc+ca)=3$$
$$\Rightarrow \quad ab+bc+ca=3/2$$

dividing both side *by* (*abc*)

$$\Rightarrow \quad \left[\frac{1}{a}+\frac{1}{b}+\frac{1}{c}\right]=\frac{3}{2}\left[\frac{1}{abc}\right]$$

$$\Rightarrow \quad 1=\frac{3}{2}\left[\frac{1}{abc}\right]\left(\because \frac{1}{a}+\frac{1}{b}+\frac{1}{c}=1\right)$$

$$\Rightarrow \quad abc=3/2$$

⊕ Shortcut Approach - 13

To simplify a continued Fraction :
You can easily understand this through the following example,

$$5+\cfrac{1}{6+\cfrac{1}{6+\cfrac{1}{10}}}$$

To simplify a continued fraction, begin at the bottom and work upwards as follow :

$$5+\cfrac{1}{6+\cfrac{1}{6+\cfrac{1}{10}}}$$

First take up the lowest complex fraction $\cfrac{1}{6+\cfrac{1}{10}}$

Multiply the numerator and denominator by 10 and thus we get $\dfrac{10}{61}$.

Next multiply the numerator and denominator of the fraction $\cfrac{1}{6+\cfrac{10}{61}}$ by

61 and thus we get $\dfrac{61}{376}$.

Hence, the given fraction $=5+\dfrac{61}{376}$ or $5\dfrac{61}{376}$

24. Find the value of $1+\cfrac{2}{3+\cfrac{4}{5+\cfrac{6}{7}}}$

(a) $1\dfrac{82}{151}$ (b) $2\dfrac{31}{151}$ (c) $2\dfrac{49}{159}$ (d) $1\dfrac{49}{150}$

Sol. (a) $1 + \dfrac{2}{3 + \dfrac{4}{5 + \dfrac{6}{7}}} = 1 + \dfrac{2}{3 + \dfrac{28}{41}}$

$$= 1 + \dfrac{82}{151} = 1\dfrac{82}{151}$$

Shortcut Approach - 14

To find the value of $\sqrt{x + \sqrt{x + \sqrt{x + ...}}}$, find the factors of x, such that the difference between the factors is 1, then the larger factor will be the result.

25. $\sqrt{6 + \sqrt{6 + \sqrt{6 + ...}}}$ **is equal to**

(a) 3   (b) 4   (c) 5   (d) 6

Sol. (a) $\sqrt{6 + \sqrt{6 + \sqrt{6 + ...}}}$

The factors of 6 with *difference* one *are* 2 *and* 3
Here 3 is the larger factors.

Hence $\sqrt{6 + \sqrt{6 + \sqrt{6 + ...}}} = 3$

26. $\sqrt{12 + \sqrt{12 + \sqrt{12 + \sqrt{12.....}}}} = ?$

(a) 3   (b) 4   (c) 6   (d) 12

Sol. (b) $\sqrt{12 + \sqrt{12 + \sqrt{12 + \sqrt{12 + ...}}}}$

The two factors of 12 with difference one are 4 and 3.
Here, 4 is the bigger factor.

Hence, $\sqrt{12 + \sqrt{12 + \sqrt{12 + \sqrt{12......}}}} = 4$

27. The value of $\sqrt{20 + \sqrt{20 + \sqrt{20 + ...}}}$ **is**

(a) 4   (b) 5
(c) 6   (d) greater than 6

Sol. (b) As given expression is

$$\Rightarrow \quad \sqrt{20+\sqrt{20+\sqrt{20+......}}}$$

The factors of 20 with difference 1 are 4 and 5.
Here 5 is the larger factor.

Hence $\sqrt{20+\sqrt{20+\sqrt{20+......}}} = 5$

28. $\left(\sqrt{56+\sqrt{56+\sqrt{56+.....}}}\right) \div 2^2 = ?$

    (a)   0   (b)   1   (c)   2   (d) 8

Sol. (c) As given expression

$$\Rightarrow \quad \left(\sqrt{56+\sqrt{56+\sqrt{56+....}}}\right) \div 2^2$$

The factor of 56 with difference one are 7 and 8.
Here 8 is the larger factor

Hence, $\left(\sqrt{56+\sqrt{56+\sqrt{56+....}}}\right) = 8$

$$\Rightarrow \quad 8 \div 2^2 = 2$$

Shortcut Approach - 15

To find the value of $\sqrt{x-\sqrt{x-\sqrt{x-.....}}}$ find the factors of x, such that the difference between the factors is 1, then the smaller factor will be the result.

29. $\sqrt{2-\sqrt{2-\sqrt{2-\sqrt{2.....}}}} = ?$

    (a)   0   (b)   1   (c)   2   (d) 3

Sol. (b) As given expression is

$$\sqrt{2-\sqrt{2-\sqrt{2-\sqrt{2}}}}$$

The factors of 2 with difference one are 1 and 2.
Here 1 is the smaller factor

Hence, $\sqrt{2-\sqrt{2-\sqrt{2-\sqrt{2}}}} = 1$

Shortcut Approach - 16

$$\sqrt{x\sqrt{x\sqrt{x.......... \; n \text{ times}}}} = (x)^{\frac{2^n-1}{2^n}}$$

30. The value of $\sqrt{2\sqrt{2\sqrt{2\sqrt{2\sqrt{2}}}}}$ will be

    (a) 2   (b) $2^{15/32}$ (c) $2^{31/32}$ (d) 4

Sol. (c) $\sqrt{2\sqrt{2\sqrt{2\sqrt{2\sqrt{2}}}}} = (2)^{\left[\frac{2^5-1}{2^5}\right]} = 2^{(31/32)}$

⊕ Shortcut Approach - 17

$$\sqrt{x\sqrt{x\sqrt{x\sqrt{x.......\infty}}}} = x$$

31. $\sqrt{3\sqrt{3\sqrt{3...}}}$ is equal to

    (a) $\sqrt{3}$ (b) 3   (c) $2\sqrt{3}$ (d) $3\sqrt{3}$

Sol. (b) $\sqrt{3\sqrt{3\sqrt{3.....}}} = 3$

      Alternate Method

      Let $\sqrt{3\sqrt{3\sqrt{3.....}}} = x$

      or, $\sqrt{3x} = x$

      Squaring *both* side

      $3x = x^2$

      $0 = x^2 - 3x$

      $0 = x(x-3)$

      $x = 3$

32. If $\sqrt{7\sqrt{7\sqrt{7\sqrt{7...}}}} = (343)^{y-1}$, then y will be equal to

    (a) 2/3   (b) 1   (c) 4/3   (d) 3/4

Sol. (c) $\sqrt{7\sqrt{7\sqrt{7\sqrt{7.....}}}} = (343)^{y-1}$

      $\sqrt{7\sqrt{7\sqrt{7\sqrt{7.....}}}} = 7$

      $7 = (343)^{y-1}$ $\Rightarrow (7)^1 = (7)^{3(y-1)}$

      $\Rightarrow 3(y-1) = 1$ $\Rightarrow 3y - 3 = 1$

      $\Rightarrow 3y = 4$ $\Rightarrow y = 4/3$

Exercise

1. If $(X + (1/X)) = 4$, then the value of $X^4 + 1/X^4$ is
(a) 124
(b) 64
(c) 194
(d) Can't be determined

2. If $x^4 + \dfrac{1}{x^4} = 119$ and $x > 1$,

then the value of

$x^3 - \dfrac{1}{x^3}$ is

(a) 54   (b) 18
(c) 72   (d) 39

3. If 'a' be a positive number,

then the least value of $a + \dfrac{1}{a}$ is

(a) 1   (b) 0

(c) 2   (d) $\dfrac{1}{2}$

4. If

$$x = \sqrt{a} + \dfrac{1}{\sqrt{a}}, y = \sqrt{a} - \dfrac{1}{\sqrt{a}},$$

then the value of $x^4 + y^4 - 2x^2y^2$ is
(a) 16   (b) 20   (c) 10   (d) 5

5. The value of

$$\left(2 - \dfrac{1}{3}\right) \times \left(2 - \dfrac{3}{5}\right) \times \left(2 - \dfrac{5}{7}\right)$$

$$\times ... \times \left(2 - \dfrac{999}{1001}\right)$$

(a) $\dfrac{1001}{5}$ (b) 999

(c) 1003   (d) $\dfrac{1003}{3}$

6. The value of

$$\dfrac{\begin{array}{l}0.051 \times 0.051 \times 0.051 \\ + 0.041 \times 0.041 \times 0.041\end{array}}{\begin{array}{l}0.051 \times 0.051 - 0.051 \times 0.041 \\ + 0.041 \times 0.041\end{array}} \text{ is}$$

(a) 0.092   (b) 1.002
(c) 0.0092   (d) 1.0002

7. Calculate the number of digits in the product of $4^{11111} \times 5^{22222}$
(a) 22222   (b) 22220
(c) 22221   (d) 22223

8. If $(x + y + z) = 6$ and $(xy + yz + zx) = 11$, then the value of $(x^3 + y^3 + z^3 - 3xyz)$ is :
(a) 81
(b) 54
(c) 18
(d) none of these

9. If $\left(x + \dfrac{1}{x}\right) = 2\sqrt{3}$, then the

value of $\left(x^3 + \dfrac{1}{x^3}\right)$ is :

(a) $12\sqrt{3}$
(b) 18
(c) $18\sqrt{3}$
(d) None of these

10. If $x = 997, y = 998, z = 999$, then the value of $x^2 + y^2 + z^2 - xy - yz - zx$ will be
(a) 3   (b) 9
(c) 16   (d) 4

11. If $x^2 + y^2 + 2x + 1 = 0$, then the value of $x^{31} + y^{35}$ is
(a) -1 (b) 0
(c) 1   (d) 2

12.

$$\dfrac{\dfrac{1}{3}\cdot\dfrac{1}{3}\cdot\dfrac{1}{3}+\dfrac{1}{4}\cdot\dfrac{1}{4}\cdot\dfrac{1}{4}-3.\dfrac{1}{3}\cdot\dfrac{1}{4}\cdot\dfrac{1}{5}+\dfrac{1}{5}\cdot\dfrac{1}{5}\cdot\dfrac{1}{5}}{\dfrac{1}{3}\cdot\dfrac{1}{3}+\dfrac{1}{4}\cdot\dfrac{1}{4}+\dfrac{1}{5}\cdot\dfrac{1}{5}-\left(\dfrac{1}{3}\cdot\dfrac{1}{4}+\dfrac{1}{4}\cdot\dfrac{1}{5}+\dfrac{1}{5}\cdot\dfrac{1}{3}\right)}$$

is equal to

(a) $\dfrac{2}{3}$　　(b) $\dfrac{3}{4}$

(c) $\dfrac{47}{60}$　　(d) $\dfrac{49}{60}$

Hints & Solution

1. (c)

$$\left[X+\dfrac{1}{X}\right]^2 = X^2 + \dfrac{1}{X^2} + 2 = 16$$

$$\text{or } X^2 + \dfrac{1}{X^2} = 14$$

Now,

$$X^4 + \dfrac{1}{X^4} + 2 = 196 \text{ or } X^4 + \dfrac{1}{X^4} = 194.$$

2. (d) Use Short Approach -9

3. (c) The least value of $a + \dfrac{1}{a}$ is 2 where $a = 1$.

4. (a) Use Short Approach -3

5. (d)

$$\left(2-\dfrac{1}{3}\right)\times\left(2-\dfrac{3}{5}\right)\times\left(2-\dfrac{5}{7}\right)$$

$$\times ..... \times\left(2-\dfrac{999}{1001}\right)$$

$$=\dfrac{5}{3}\times\dfrac{7}{5}\times\dfrac{9}{7}\times .... \times\dfrac{1003}{1001}=\dfrac{1003}{3}$$

6. (a) Use Short Approach -8

7. (d) $4^{11111} \times 5^{22222}$

$$=\left(2^2\right)^{11111} \times 5^{22222}$$

$$=2^{22222} \times 5^{22222} \quad \left[\left(a^m\right)^n = a^{mn}\right]$$

$$= 10^{22222} \;[a^m \times b^m = (ab)^m]$$

Hence, number of digits
$$= 22222 + 1 = 22223.$$

8. (c) Use Short Approach -11

9. (c) Use Short Approach -8

10. (a) $x^2+y^2+z^2-xy-yz-zx$

$$=\dfrac{2}{2}(x^2+y^2+z^2-xy-yz-zx)$$

$$=\dfrac{1}{2}(2x^2+2y^2+2z^2-2xy-2yz-2zx)$$

$$=\dfrac{1}{2}(x^2+y^2-2xy+y^2+z^2-2yz+x^2+z^2-2xy)$$

$$=\dfrac{1}{2}[(x-y)^2+(y-z)^2+(z-x)^2]$$

$$=\dfrac{1}{2}[(997-998)^2+(998-999)^2+(999-997)^2]$$

$$=\dfrac{1}{2}[1^2+1^2+2^2]=\dfrac{1}{2}\times 6=3$$

11. (a) $x^2+y^2+2x+1=0$
$$\Rightarrow (x+1)^2+y^2=0$$
$$\Rightarrow x+1=0 \Rightarrow x=-1 \text{ and } y=0$$
$$\therefore x^{31}+y^{35}=-1$$

12. (c) $\because a^3+b^3+c^3-3abc = (a+b+c)(a^2+b^2+c^2-ab-bc-ca)$

Here

$$a=\dfrac{1}{3}, b=\dfrac{1}{4}, c=\dfrac{1}{5}$$

So,

$$a+b+c = \dfrac{1}{3}+\dfrac{1}{4}+\dfrac{1}{5}=\dfrac{47}{60}$$

06 Chapter

Polynomials and Rational Expressions (Inducing Factorization of Polynomials, Factor Theorem & Remainder Theorem)

Let $f(x)$ be a Polynimial of degree greater than or equal to 1. Then if $f(x)$ is divided by $(x–a)$ where 'a' be any real number then the nemainder $= f(a)$.

1. Find the remainder when $x^3 + 2x^2 - 5x + 3$ is divided by $x - 2$.

    (a) 7   (b) 9   (c) 1   (d) 0

Sol. (b) Let $p(x) = x^3 + 2x^2 - 5x + 3$

Remainder $= p(2) = 2^3 + 2 \times 2^2 - 5 \times 2 + 3 = 8 + 8 - 10 + 3 = 9$

2. Find the remainder when $x^4 + x^2 + 1$ is divided by $x + 1$.

    (a) 0   (b) 5   (c) 2   (d) 3

Sol. (d) Let $p(x) = x^4 + x^2 + 1$

Now $x + 1 = x - (-1)$

Hence, remainder $= p(-1) = (-1)^4 + (-1)^2 + 1 = 3$

Let $p(x)$ be a polynimial of degree greater than or equal to 1 and 'a' be any real number such that $p(a) = 0$ then $(x - a)$ is a factor of $p(x)$

3. Is $(x - 2)$ is a factor of $x^3 + 3x^2 - 12x + 4$?

Sol. Let $p(x) = x^3 + 3x^2 - 12x + 4$

Now $p(2) - (2)^3 + 3(2)^2 - 12 \times 2 + 4 = 8 + 12 - 24 + 4 = 0$

Hence $x - 2$ is a factor of $x^3 + 3x^2 - 12x + 4$

If a number α is zero of a linear polynomial $f(x)$, if $f(\alpha) = 0$

4. If α is the zero of $2x + 5$ then what is velue of α?

    (a) $\dfrac{5}{2}$ (b) $\dfrac{-5}{2}$ (c) $\dfrac{-2}{5}$ (d) 0

Sol. (b) Let $f(x) = 2x + 5$

Since α is the zero of the given polynomial,

Therefore $f(\alpha) = 0$

$$\Rightarrow 2\alpha + 5 = 0 \quad \Rightarrow \alpha = \frac{-5}{2}$$

Shortcut Approach - 4

If α and β are zeros of a Quarditic Polynomial $ax^2 + bx + c$ with $a \neq 0$ then

$$\alpha + \beta = \frac{-b}{a} \text{ and } \alpha.\ \beta = \frac{c}{a}$$

5.   **Find is sum of zeros of $5x^2 + 34x + 24$?**

     (a) $\dfrac{-34}{5}$ (b) $\dfrac{-24}{5}$ (c) -5 (d) $\dfrac{34}{5}$

Sol.   (a)   sum of zero of Quarditic Polynomial $= \dfrac{-b}{a} = \dfrac{-34}{5}$

Shortcut Approach - 5

If α, β and γ are zeros of a cubic Polynomial $ax^3 + bx^2 + cx + d$, $a \neq 0$, then

(i) $\alpha + \beta + \gamma = \dfrac{-b}{a}$ (ii) $\alpha\ \beta + \gamma\ \beta + \gamma\ \alpha = \dfrac{c}{a}$

(iii) $\alpha\ \beta\ \gamma = \dfrac{-d}{a}$

6.   **Find the Product of zeros of the polynomial $5x^3 + 17x^2 + 19x + 25$**

     (a) $\dfrac{-19}{5}$ (b) -5 (c) 5 (d) None of these

Sol.   (b)   Product of zeros of a cubic polynomial $= \dfrac{-d}{a} = \dfrac{-25}{5} = -5$

Shortcut Approach - 6

If $p(x)$ and $q(x)$ are two different polynomials then
$$L.C.M \times H.C.F = P(x) \times q(x)$$

7.   If L.C.M and H.C.F of two polynomials are $(x-1)^2 (x+2)^3(x+3)$ and $(x-1)(x+3)$ and one of the two polynomials is $(x-1)(x+2)^3(x+3)$ then second polynomial is

     (a) $(x+3)(x-1)^2$ (b) $(x+3)^2(x-1)$

     (c) $(x+3)^2(x-1)^2$ (d) None of these

Sol.   (a)   Second Polynomial $= \dfrac{L.C.M \times H.C.F}{First\ Polynomial}$

$$= \frac{(x-1)^2(x+2)^3(x+3)(x-1)(x+3)}{(x-1)(x+2)^3(x+3)} = (x+3)(x-1)^2$$

Exercise

1. Factorize : $(a-b)^3 + (b-c)^3 + (c-a)^3$
   (a) $3(a+b)(a-b)(a+c)$
   (b) $3(abc)$
   (c) $3(a-b)(b-c)(c-a)$
   (d) $3(a+b)(b+c)(c+a)$

2. If $(x^3 - 5x^2 + 4p)$ is divisible by $(x+2)$, then the value of p is
   (a) 7   (b) -2
   (c) 3   (d) -7

3. If $(x+2)$ and $(x-1)$ are the factors of $(x^3 + 10x^2 + mx + n)$, the values of m and n are :
   (a) $m=5, n=-3$
   (b) $m=17, n=-8$
   (c) $m=7, n=-18$
   (d) $m=23, n=-19$

4. Find the remainder when $5p^3 - 13p^2 + 21p - 14$ is divided by $(3 - 2p + p^2)$.
   (a) -5 (b) -15
   (c) -10 (d) 5

5. If $p(y) = 3y^4 - 5y^3 + y^2 + 8$, then $p(-1)$ will be
   (a) 2   (b) 15
   (c) 17   (d) -17

6. For what value of k is the polynomial $2x^4 + 3x^3 + 2kx^2 + 3x + 6$ exactly divisible by $(x+2)$?
   (a) 1   (b) -1
   (c) 2   (d) -2

7. If $4x^4 - 3x^3 - 3x^2 + x - 7$ is divided by $1 - 2x$ then remainder will be –
   (a) $\dfrac{57}{8}$ (b) $-\dfrac{59}{8}$
   (c) $\dfrac{55}{8}$ (d) $-\dfrac{55}{8}$

8. If the polynomials $(2x^3 + ax^2 + 3x - 5)$ and $(x^3 + x^2 - 2x + a)$ leave the same remainder when divided by $(x-2)$, find the value of a.
   (a) -8 (b) 4
   (c) -3 (d) $\dfrac{6}{3}$

9. If $(x-a)$ and $(x-2)$ are two factors of $x^3 - ax^2 + 14x + b$, the values of a and b are
   (a) $a=6, b=7$
   (b) $a=-8, b=-7$
   (c) $a=7, b=-8$
   (d) $a=7, b=8$

10. Let r_1 and r_2 be the remainders when the polynomials
    $p(x) = x^3 + x^2 - 5kx - 7$
    and $q(x) = x^3 + kx^2 - 12x + 6$
    are divided by $x+1$ and $x-2$ respectively.
    If $2r_1 - r_2 = 10$, the value of k is.
    (a) $\dfrac{7}{3}$ (b) $\dfrac{3}{7}$
    (c) $\dfrac{5}{7}$ (d) $\dfrac{7}{5}$

11. If $x = \dfrac{4}{3}$ is a root of the polynomial $f(x) = 6x^3 - 11x^2 + kx - 20$, then find the value of k.
    (a) 10   (b) 19
    (c) -5 (d) 3

12. If two zeroes of the polynomial $x^4 - 6x^3 - 26x^2 + 138x - 35$ are $2 \pm \sqrt{3}$, then the other zeroes are
    (a) 5, 7   (b) $-5, 7$
    (c) $-5, -7$ (d) $5, -7$

Hints & Solution

1. **(c)** $\because \ (a-b)+(b-c)+(c-a)=0$

$\therefore \ (a-b)^3+(b-c)^3+(c-a)^3$
$=3(a-b)(b-c)(c-a)$

2. **(a)** Since $(x+2)$ divides the polynomial (x^3-5x^2+4p) Hence,

$f(-2)=0.$
$f(x)=x^3-5x^2+4p$
$\Rightarrow \ f(-2)=(-2)^3-5.(-2)^2+4p=0$
$\Rightarrow \ f(-2)=-8-20+4p=0$
$\Rightarrow p=7$

3. **(c)** Use Shortcut Approach -2

4. **(a)**

$$
\begin{array}{r}
5p-3 \\
p^2-2p+3 \overline{)\ 5p^3-13p^2+21p-14} \\
5p^3-10p^2+15p \\
\hline
-3p^2+6p-14 \\
-3p^2+6p-9 \\
\hline
-5 \\
\hline
\end{array}
$$

Hence, the remainder is -5.

5. **(c)** $p(-1)=3(-1)^4-5(-1)^3+(-1)^2+8$
$=3+5+1+8=17$

6. **(b)** $f(-2)=2\times(-2)^4+3(-2)^3+2k\times(-2)^2+3\times(-2)+6$
$=32-24+8k-6+6=8k+8$
$\therefore \ f(-2)=0 \Rightarrow 8k+8=0 \Rightarrow k=-1$

7. **(b)** Use Shortcut Approach -1

8. **(c)** Let $f(x)=2x^3+ax^2+3x-5$ and $g(x)=x^3+x^2-2x+a.$
When $f(x)$ is divided by $(x-2)$, remainder $=f(2)$.
When $g(x)$ is divided by $(x-2)$, remainder $=g(2)$.

Now, $f(2)=(2\times2^3+a\times2^2+3\times2-5)=(17+4a).$
And, $g(2)=(2^3+2^2-2\times2+a)=(8+a)$
$\therefore \ 17+4a=8+a \Rightarrow 3a=-9 \Rightarrow a=-3.$

9. **(c)** Use Shortcut Approach -1

10. **(a)** Here, we will use remainder theorem to find r_1 and r_2. Remainder theorem states that if a polynomial $f(x)$ is divided by $(x-a)$, then the remainder is given by $f(a)$.
Let us perform synthetic division of $p(x)$ and $q(x)$ by $(x+1)$ and $(x-2)$ respectively.

$$
\begin{array}{r|rrrr}
-1 & 1 & 1 & -5k & -7 \\
   &   & -1 & 0 & 5k \\
\hline
   & 1 & 0 & -5k & 5k-7=r_1 \\
\end{array}
$$

and

$$
\begin{array}{r|rrrr}
2 & 1 & k & -12 & 6 \\
  &   & 2 & 2k+4 & 4k-16 \\
\hline
  & 1 & k+2 & 2k-8 & 4k-10=r_2 \\
\end{array}
$$

Given that $2r_1-r_2=10$
$\Rightarrow \ 2(5k-7)-(4k-10)=10$
$\Rightarrow \ 10k-14-4k+10=10$
$\Rightarrow \ 6k=14$
$\therefore \ k=\dfrac{7}{3}$

11. **(b)** Let $f(x)=6x^3-11x^2+kx-20$

$f\left(\dfrac{4}{3}\right)=6\left(\dfrac{4}{3}\right)^3-11\left(\dfrac{4}{3}\right)^2+k\left(\dfrac{4}{3}\right)-20=0$

$\Rightarrow \ 6.\dfrac{64}{27}-11.\dfrac{16}{9}+\dfrac{4k}{3}-20=0$

$\Rightarrow \ 128-176+12k-180=0$

$\Rightarrow \ 12k+128-356=0 \Rightarrow k=19$

12. **(b)** Use Shortcut Approach −5

◈ Shortcut Approach - 1

Shortcut Approach to solve quadratic equation
$ax^2 + bx + c = 0$, if $b^2 - 4ac \geq 0$,

then roots are real sum of the roots $= -\dfrac{b}{a}$

Product of the roots $= \dfrac{c}{a}$

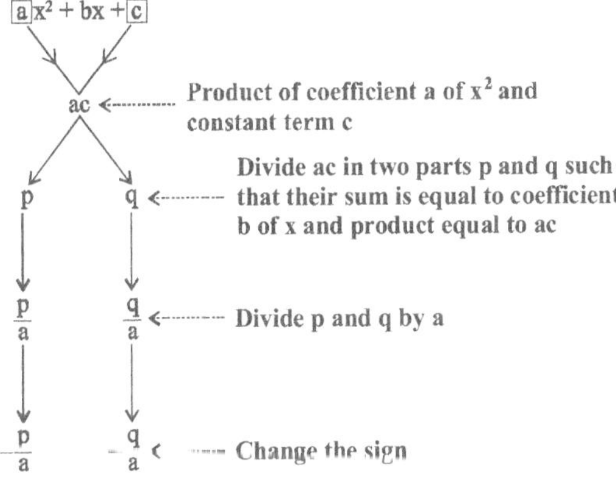

Here $\dfrac{-p}{a}$ and $\dfrac{-q}{a}$ are two roots or solutions of quadratic equation ax^2

$+ bx + c = 0$ i.e. $x = -\dfrac{p}{a}$ or $-\dfrac{q}{a}$.

1. Solve : $2x^2 + 6 = 7x$

   (a) $\dfrac{3}{2}, 2$ (b) $\dfrac{1}{2}, 2$

   (c) $\dfrac{5}{2}, 2$ (d)   None of these

Sol. (a) $2x^2 + 6 = 7x$

      $\Rightarrow 2x^2 - 7x + 6 = 0$

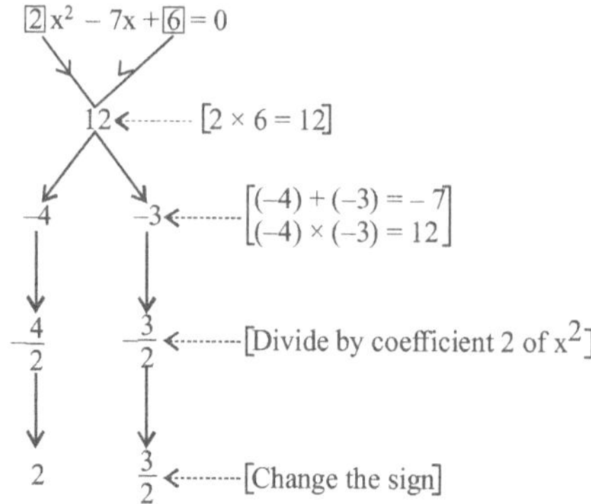

$\therefore$ Solutions or roots of given quadratic equation

$$2x^2 + 6 = 7x \text{ are } \frac{3}{2} \text{ and } 2.$$

2. *Solve* $x - \dfrac{1}{x} = 1\dfrac{1}{2}$

  (a) $\dfrac{1}{2}, 2$ (b) $\dfrac{-1}{2}, 2$

  (c) $\dfrac{3}{2}, 2$ (d) $\dfrac{-3}{2}, 2$

Sol. (b) $\quad x - \dfrac{1}{x} = 1\dfrac{1}{2}$

$\Rightarrow \quad \dfrac{x^2 - 1}{x} = \dfrac{3}{2} \qquad\qquad \Rightarrow \quad 2(x^2 - 1) = 3x$

$\Rightarrow \quad 2x^2 - 2 = 3x \qquad\qquad \Rightarrow \quad 2x^2 - 3x - 2 = 0$

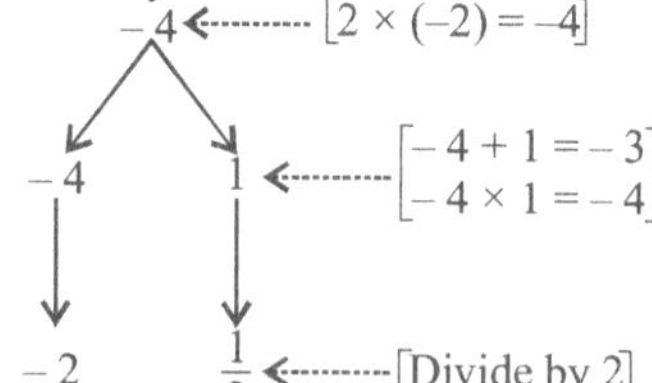

Either $2x + 1 = 0$ or $x - 2 = 0$

$\Rightarrow \quad 2x = -1$ or $x = 2$

$\Rightarrow \quad x = \dfrac{-1}{2}$ or $x = 2$

$\therefore \quad x = \dfrac{-1}{2}$, 2 are solutions.

⊕ Shortcut Approach - 2

If present age of the father is F times the age of his son. T years hence, the father's age become Z times the age of son then present age of his

son is given by $\dfrac{(Z-1)T}{(F-Z)}$

3. Present age of the father is 9 times the age of his son. One year later, father's age become 7 times the age of his son. What are the present ages of the father and his son.

(a) 27 years   (b)   30 years
(c) 36 years   (d)   45 years

Sol. (a) By the formula

$$\text{Son's age} = \frac{(7-1)}{(9-7)} \times 1 = \frac{6}{2} \times 1 = 3 \text{ years.}$$

So, father's age $= 9 \times$ son's age $= 9 \times 3 = 27$ years.

⊕ Shortcut Approach - 3

If T_1 years earlier the age of the father was n times the age of his son, T_2 years hence, the age of the father becomes m times the age of his son then his son's age is given by

$$\text{Son's age} = \frac{T_1(n-1) + T_2(m-1)}{n-m}$$

4. 10 years ago, Shakti's mother was 4 times older than her. After 10 years, the mother will be twice older than the daughter. What is the present age of Shakti?

(a) 15 years   (b)   20 years
(c) 24 years   (d)   30 years

Sol. (b) By using formula,

$$\text{Shakti's age} = \frac{10(4-1) + 10(2-1)}{4-2} = 20 \text{ years.}$$

⊕ Shortcut Approach - 4

Present age of Father : Son = a : b
After / Before T years = m : n

Then son's age $= b \times \dfrac{T(m-n)}{an-bm}$

and father's age $= a \times \dfrac{T(m-n)}{an-bm}$

5.   The ratio of the ages of the father and the son at present is 3 : 1. Four years earlier, the ratio was 4 : 1. What are the present ages of the son and the father?

(a)   10 years, 30 years

(b)   20 years, 50 years

(c)   12 years, 36 years

(d)   None of these

Sol. (c)   Ratio of present age of father and son = 3 : 1

4 years before = 4 : 1

$$\text{Son's age} = 1 \times \frac{4(4-1)}{4 \times 1 - 3 \times 1} = 12 \text{ years.}$$

$$\text{Father's age} = 3 \times \frac{4(4-1)}{4 \times 1 - 3 \times 1} = 36 \text{ years.}$$

Exercise

1. If $ax^2 + bx + c = 0$ has real and different roots, then
   (a) $b^2 - 4ac = 0$
   (b) $b^2 - 4ac > 0$
   (c) $b^2 - 4ac < 0$
   (d) $b^2 - 4ac \leq 0$

2. When 24 is subtracted from a number, it reduces to its four-seventh. What is the sum of the digits of that number ?
   (a) 1
   (b) 9
   (c) 11
   (d) Data inadequate

3. The roots of the equation
   $$2\sqrt{x} + 2x^{-\frac{1}{2}} = 5 \text{ can be found}$$
   by solving
   (a) $4x^2 - 25x + 4 = 0$
   (b) $4x^2 + 25x + 4 = 0$
   (c) $4x^2 - 17x + 4 = 0$
   (d) None of these

4. The roots of the equation $ax^2 + bx + c = 0$ will be reciprocal if
   (a) $a = b$
   (b) $a = bc$
   (c) $c = a$
   (d) $b = c$

5. Determine the value of k for which the quadratic equation $4x^2 - 3kx + 1 = 0$ has equal roots :

   (a) $\pm \left(\dfrac{2}{3} \right)$ (b) $\pm \left(\dfrac{4}{3} \right)$

   (c) ± 4 (d) ± 6

6. Find the value of k so that the sum of the roots of the quadratic equation is equal to the product of the roots : $(k + 1)x^2 + 2kx + 4 = 0$
   (a) -2 (b) -4
   (c) 6 (d) 8

7. If r and s are roots of $x^2 + px + q = 0$, then what is the value of $\dfrac{1}{r^2} + \dfrac{1}{s^2}$?

   (a) $p^2 - 4q$

   (b) $\dfrac{p^2 - 4q}{2}$

   (c) $\dfrac{p^2 - 4q}{q^2}$

   (d) $\dfrac{p^2 - 2q}{q^2}$

8. If -4 is a root of the quadratic equation $x^2 - px - 4 = 0$ and the quadratic equation $x^2 - px + k = 0$ has equal roots, find the value of k :
   (a) 9/4   (b) 1
   (c) 2.5   (d) 3

9. Find the quadratic equation whose roots are $\sqrt{3}$ and $2\sqrt{3}$:

(a) $x^2 + 3\sqrt{3}x - 6 = 0$

(b) $x^2 - 3\sqrt{3}x + 6 = 0$

(c) $x^2 + 3\sqrt{3}x + 5 = 0$

(d) None of these

10. For what value of c the quadratic equation
$x^2 - (c + 6)x + 2(2c - 1) = 0$
has sum of the roots as half of their product?

(a) 5   (b) -4

(c) 7   (d) 3

11. If p and q are the roots of $x^2 + px + q = 0$, then

(a) $p = 1$ (b) $p = 1$ or 0

(c) $p = -2$ (d) $p = -2$ or 0

12. A two digit number is such that the product of its digits is 12. When 9 is added to the number, the digits interchange their places, find the number :

(a) 62   (b) 34

(c) 26   (d) 43

Hints & Solution

1. **(b)** Use Short Approach -1

2. **(c)** Let the number be x, then

$$ATQ, x - 24 = \frac{4}{7}x$$

$$7x - 168 = 4x$$
$$3x = 168 \implies x = 56$$

$\therefore$ Sum of its digits $= 5 + 6 = 11$

3. **(c)** $2\sqrt{x} + \dfrac{2}{\sqrt{x}} = 5$

Equaring both sides,

$$\left(2\sqrt{x} + \frac{2}{\sqrt{x}}\right)^2 = (5)^2$$

$$4x + \frac{4}{x} + 8 = 25$$

$$4x^2 - 17x + 4 = 0$$

4. **(c)** Since roots are reciprocal, product of the roots $= 1$

$$\Rightarrow \frac{c}{a} = 1 \implies c = a.$$

5. **(b)** $4x^2 - 3kx + 1 = 0$
$$D = b^2 - 4ac = 0$$
$$\therefore 9k^2 - 4 \times 1 \times 4 = 0$$

$$\Rightarrow k^2 = \frac{16}{9} \Rightarrow k = \pm\frac{4}{3}$$

6. **(a)** $\alpha + \beta = \alpha\beta$

$$\Rightarrow \frac{-b}{a} = \frac{c}{a} \Rightarrow -b = c$$

$$\therefore -2k = 4 \Rightarrow k = -2$$

7. **(d)** Use Short Approach -1

8. **(a)** Since -4 is a root of $x^2 - px - 4 = 0$

$\therefore$ $(-4)^2 - p(-4) - 4 = 0 \Rightarrow$ $p = -3$

$\therefore$ The equation becomes $x^2 + 3x + k = 0$
Since both the roots of this equation are equal.

$\therefore$ Sum of the roots $(\alpha + \alpha)$

$$= 2\alpha = -3 \implies \alpha = -\frac{3}{2}$$

$\therefore$ Product of the roots

$$(\alpha.\alpha) = \alpha^2 = (-3/2)^2 = \frac{9}{4} = k$$

$$\therefore \quad k = \frac{9}{4}$$

9. **(b)** **Method – I.**
If α and β be the roots of a quadratic equation, then the equation will be $(x - \alpha)(x - \beta) = 0$

$$\therefore \quad \left(x - \sqrt{3}\right)\left(x - 2\sqrt{3}\right) - 0$$

$$\Rightarrow \quad x^2 - 3\sqrt{3}x + 6 = 0$$

Method – II.
The required equation
$$x^2 - (\alpha + \beta)x + (\alpha.\beta) = 0$$

$$\Rightarrow x^2 - \left(\sqrt{3} + 2\sqrt{3}\right)x + \left(\sqrt{3}.2\sqrt{3}\right) = 0$$

$$\Rightarrow \quad x^2 - 3\sqrt{3}x + 6 = 0$$

10. **(c)** Use Short Approach -1

11. **(b)** Since p and q are the roots of given equation $x^2 + px + q = 0$, then $p + q = -p \Rightarrow q = -2p$ and $pq = q \Rightarrow p = 1$

So, when $p = 1$, then $q =$

Again, when $q = 0$, then $p = 0$ hence,

$p = 1, 0$ and $q = -2, 0$

Thus, option (b) is most appropriate.

12. **(b)** Let the tens digit be x and unit digit be y. Then the two digit number $= 10x + y$ but

$$x \times y = 12 \Rightarrow y = \frac{12}{x}$$

$\therefore$ the number is $\left(10x + \dfrac{12}{x}\right)$

Again

$$10x + \frac{12}{x} + 9 = 10 \times \left(\frac{12}{x}\right) + x$$

$\Rightarrow \quad 10x^2 + 12 + 9x = 120 + x^2$

$\Rightarrow \quad 9x^2 + 9x - 108 = 0$

$\Rightarrow \quad x^2 + x - 12 = 0$

$\Rightarrow \quad (x + 4)(x - 3) = 0$

$\Rightarrow \quad x = -4, 3$

but x cannot be negative

$\therefore \quad x = 3$ only

$$\therefore \quad y = \frac{12}{x} = \frac{12}{3} = 4$$

$\therefore$ the number $= 10x + y$
$= 10 \times 3 + 4 = 34$

Ratio, Proportion, Variation and Partnership

To divide a given quantity into a given ratio
Suppose any given quantity a is to be divided in the ratio $m : n$, then

$$\text{First part} = \frac{ma}{m+n}; \quad \text{Second part} = \frac{na}{m+n}$$

1. **Divide 1458 into two parts such that one may be to the other as 2 : 7**
   (a) 324, 1134   **(b) 358, 1100**
   (c) 462, 996   **(d) 458, 1000**

Sol. (a) First part $= \dfrac{2 \times 1458}{2+7} = \dfrac{2 \times 1458}{9} = 324$

Second part $= \dfrac{7 \times 1458}{2+7} = 1134$

(i)   If $a : b = N_1 : D_1$, $b : c = N_2 : D_2$
      Then $a : b : c = N_1N_2 : D_1N_2 : D_1D_2$.

(ii) If $a : b = N_1 : D_1$, $b : c = N_2 : D_2$, $c : d = N_3 : D_3$
      Then $a : b : c : d = N_1N_2N_3 : D_1N_2N_3 : D_1D_2N_3 : D_1D_2D_3$

(iii) If $a : b = N_1 : D_1$, $b : c = N_2 : D_2$, $c : d = N_3 : D_3$, $d : e = N_4 : D_4$
      Then $a : b : c : d : e = N_1N_2N_3N_4 : D_1N_2N_3N_4 : D_1D_2N_3N_4 : D_1D_2D_3N_4 : D_1D_2D_3D_4$.

2. **The ratio of A : B = 1 : 3, B : C = 2 : 5 and C : D = 2 : 3. Find the value of A : B : C : D.**
   (a) 3 : 9 : 12 : 15   **(b) 4 : 12 : 30 : 45**
   (c) 5 : 10 : 15 : 20   **(d) 4 : 8 : 12 : 20**

Sol. (b) As given that,
   A : B = 1 : 3, B : C = 2 : 5 and C : D = 2 : 3
   We know that
   $A : B : C : D = N_1N_2N_3 : D_1N_2N_3 : D_1D_2N_3 : D_1D_2D_3$
   $= (1 \times 2 \times 2) : (3 \times 2 \times 2) : (3 \times 5 \times 2) : (3 \times 5 \times 3)$
   $A : B : C : D = 4 : 12 : 30 : 45$

3.   If ratio $A : B = 1 : 2$, $B : C = 3 : 4$ and $C : D = 5 : 6$ find $D : C : B : A$ = ?

     (a) $6 : 5 : 4 : 2$ (b) $6 : 4 : 2 : 1$

     (c) $6 : 3 : 2 : 1$ (d) $48 : 40 : 30 : 15$

Sol. (d) $A : B = 1 : 2$, $B : C = 3 : 4$ and $C : D = 5 : 6$

     $A : B : C : D$

     $= (1 \times 3 \times 5) : (2 \times 3 \times 5) : (2 \times 4 \times 5) : (2 \times 4 \times 6)$

     $= 15 : 30 : 40 : 48$

     $D : C : B : A = 48 : 40 : 30 : 15$

⊕ Shortcut Approach - 3

If the ratio between two numbers is $a : b$ and if each number is increased by x, the ratio becomes $c : d$. Then two numbers are given by $\dfrac{xa(c-d)}{ad-bc}$ and

$$\dfrac{xb(c-d)}{ad-bc}$$

4.   Two numbers are in the ratio of $2 : 3$. If 15 is added to both the numbers, then the ratio between two numbers becomes $\dfrac{11}{14}$. Find the greater number.

     (a) 18   (b) 30   (c) 27   (d) 9

Sol. (c)   Numbers are

$$\dfrac{15 \times 2(11-14)}{2 \times 14 - 3 \times 11} \text{ and } \dfrac{15 \times 3(11-14)}{2 \times 14 - 3 \times 11}$$

$$\Rightarrow \dfrac{-30 \times 3}{-5} \text{ and } \dfrac{-45 \times 3}{-5} \Rightarrow 18 \text{ and } 27$$

     Hence gretest number is 27

⊕ Shortcut Approach - 4

If two numbers are in the ratio of $a : b$ and the sum of these numbers is x, then these numbers will be $\dfrac{ax}{a+b}$ and $\dfrac{bx}{a+b}$.

5.   Two glasses **A** and **B** with their capacities in the ratio $2 : 3$. If the total capacities of the glasses is 45 litres. Find the capacity of glass A.

     (a) 5   (b) 6   (c) 7   (d) 18

Sol. (d)   Capacity of glass

$$(A) = \frac{ax}{(a+b)} = \frac{2 \times 45}{(2+3)} = 18$$

6.   Amit and Sudesh have invested in the ratio of 4 : 7. If both invested an amount of ₹ 49500, then find the investment of sudesh.

(a) ₹31500   (b) ₹1800

(c) ₹31000   (d) ₹18500

Sol. (a)   Investment of Sudesh $= \left(\dfrac{bx}{a+b} \right)$

$$= \frac{7 \times 49500}{(7+4)} = 31500$$

⊕ Shortcut Approach - 5

If two numbers are in the ratio $a : b$ and the difference between these numbers is x, then these numbers will be

(i) $\dfrac{ax}{a-b}$ and $\dfrac{bx}{a-b}$ respectively (if $a > b$)

(ii) $\dfrac{ax}{b-a}$ and $\dfrac{bx}{b-a}$ respectively (if $a < b$)

7.   The ratio of two numbers is 10:7 and their difference is 105. The sum of the numbers is:

(a) 595   (b) 805

(c) 1190   (d) 1610

Sol. (a) $\dfrac{ax}{a-b} + \dfrac{bx}{a-b}$ $\qquad$ ($\because a > b$)

$$= \frac{10 \times 105}{(10-7)} + \frac{7 \times 105}{(10-7)} = 10 \times 35 + 7 \times 35 = 595$$

8.   A certain sum of money is divided between A and B in the ratio 3:7. If B gets ₹ 800 more than A, find the total sum.

(a) ₹ 2400   (b) ₹ 3200   (c) ₹ 3000   (d) ₹ 2000

Sol. (d) $\left(\dfrac{ax}{b-a} \right) + \left(\dfrac{bx}{b-a} \right)$ $\qquad$ ($\because b > a$)

$$= \frac{(3 \times 800)}{(7-3)} + \frac{(7 \times 800)}{(7-3)} = \frac{800}{4}(3+7) = 2000$$

Shortcut Approach - 6

If three numbers are in the ratio $a : b : c$ and the sum of these numbers is x, then these numbers will be

$$\frac{ax}{a+b+c}, \frac{bx}{a+b+c} \text{ and } \frac{cx}{a+b+c} \text{ respectively.}$$

9.　　If ₹ 126.50 is divided among A, B and C in the ratio of 2 : 5: 4, the share of B exceeds that of A by
　　(a) ₹ 36.50　　　　　　(b) ₹ 35.50
　　(c) ₹ 34.50　　　　　　(d) ₹ 33.50

Sol. (c)　Share of

$$B = \frac{bx}{a+b+c} = \frac{5 \times 126.50}{2+5+4} = 57.5$$

Share of

$$A = \frac{ax}{a+b+c} = \frac{2 \times 126.50}{2+5+4} = 23.0$$

then, the share of B exceeds that of A = B – A
= 57.5 – 23 = ₹34.50

10.　If ₹ 900 is divided among A, B, C; the division is such that $\frac{1}{2}$ of

A's money $= \frac{1}{3}$rd of B's money

$= \frac{1}{4}$th of C's money. Find the amount (in ₹) received by A, B, C.

　　(a) 300, 400, 200　　　(b) 350, 450, 100
　　(c) 200, 300, 400　　　(d) 400, 150, 130

Sol. (c)　As given that,

$$\frac{A}{2} = \frac{B}{3} = \frac{C}{4} \Rightarrow A : B : C = 2 : 3 : 4$$

∵　Amount received by

$$A = \left(\frac{ax}{a+b+c}\right) = \frac{2 \times 900}{(2+3+4)} = 200$$

∵　Amount received by

$$B = \left(\frac{bx}{a+b+c}\right) = \frac{3 \times 900}{(2+3+4)} = 300$$

∵　Amount received by

$$C = \frac{cx}{(a+b+c)} = \frac{4 \times 900}{(2+3+4)} = 400$$

Shortcut Approach - 7

If two numbers X and Y are in the ratio $x : y$. Then

(i) $\dfrac{X+Y}{X-Y} = \dfrac{x+y}{x-y}$, if $x > y$. (ii) $\dfrac{Y+X}{Y-X} = \dfrac{y+x}{y-x}$, if $x < y$.

11. The prices of a scooter and a moped are in the ratio of $9 : 5$. If a scooter costs ₹ 4200 more than a moped, find the total price of both vehicles.

(a) ₹14000   (b) ₹14700

(c) ₹ 15000   (d) ₹15200

Sol. (b) Here, $\dfrac{X+Y}{X-Y} = \dfrac{x+y}{x-y}$

$$\Rightarrow \quad \frac{X+Y}{4200} = \frac{9+5}{9-5} \Rightarrow X+Y = 4200 \times \frac{14}{4}$$

$$\Rightarrow \quad X+Y = ₹\,14700$$

Shortcut Approach - 8

If the sum of two numbers is A and their difference is a, then the ratio of numbers is given by $(A + a) : (A - a)$.

12. The sum of two numbers is 40 and their difference is 4. The ratio of the numbers is :

(a) $21 : 19$ (b) $11 : 9$

(c) $22 : 9$ (d) $11 : 18$

Sol. (b) Ratio of two numbers $= \dfrac{A+a}{A-a} = \left[\dfrac{40+4}{40-4}\right] = \dfrac{44}{36} = \dfrac{11}{9}$

13. The ratio between sum and difference of two numbers is $5 : 1$. Find the ratio between the numbers.

(a) $5 : 2$ (b) $3 : 2$

(c) $2 : 3$ (d) $2 : 5$

Sol. (b) As given, ratio of sum and difference of two numbers $= 5 : 1$

So, the sum of two numbers $= 5$ and their difference is 1, the ratio of two numbers

$$= \frac{5+1}{5-1} = \frac{6}{4} = \frac{3}{2}$$

⊕ Shortcut Approach - 9

A number which, when added to the terms of the ratio $a : b$ makes it equal to the ratio $c : d$ is $\dfrac{ad - bc}{c - d}$.

14. **What must be added to each term of the ratio 7 : 11 so as to make it equal to 3:4 ?**
(a) 1 (b) 2
(c) 3 (d) 5

Sol. **(d)**   Required number $= \dfrac{ad - bc}{c - d} = \dfrac{(7)(4) - (11)(3)}{3 - 4} = \dfrac{-5}{-1} = 5$

⊕ Shortcut Approach - 10

A number which when subtracted from the terms of the ratio $a : b$ makes it equal to the ratio $c : d$ is $\dfrac{bc - ad}{c - d}$.

15. **What number should be subtracted from both terms of the ratio 15 : 19 in order to make it 3 :4 ?**
(a) 9 (b) 2
(c) 5 (d) 3

Sol. **(d)**   Required number $= \dfrac{bc - ad}{c - d}$

$$= \dfrac{(19)(3) - (15)(4)}{3 - 4} = \dfrac{57 - 60}{-1} = 3$$

⊕ Shortcut Approach - 11

The ratio between two numbers is $a : b$, if each number is increased by x, the ratio becomes $c : d$. Then sum of two numbers $= \dfrac{x(a + b)(c - d)}{ad - bc}$.

16. **Two numbers are in the ratio 2 : 3. If 3 be added to both of them, then their ratio becomes 3 : 4. Find the sum of the numbers.**
(a) 10 (b) 15
(c) 20 (d) 25

Sol. **(b)**   Sum of two numbers $= \dfrac{x(a + b)(c - d)}{ad - bc}$

$$= \dfrac{3(2 + 3)(3 - 4)}{2(4) - (3)(3)} = \dfrac{3 \times 5 \times (-1)}{(-1)} = 15$$

Shortcut Approach - 12

Income of two persons are in the ratio of $a : b$ and their expenditures are in the ratio $c : d$. If each of them saves ₹ x then their incomes are given by

$$\frac{xa(d-c)}{ad-bc} \text{ and } \frac{xb(d-c)}{ad-bc}.$$

17. **The ratio of monthly incomes of A, B is 6 : 5 and their monthly expenditures are in the ratio 4 : 3. If each of them saves ₹ 400 per month, find the sum of their monthly incomes.**
    (a) ₹ 2300   (b) ₹ 2400
    (c) ₹ 2200   (d) ₹ 2500

Sol. (c) Sum of incomes $= \dfrac{xa(d-c)}{ad-bc} + \dfrac{xb(d-c)}{ad-bc}$

$$= \frac{400(6)(3-4)}{(6)(3) - \xi \mathcal{H}( )(6)(3) -(5)(4)} + \frac{400(5)(3-4)}{} = \frac{-2400}{-2} + \frac{-2000}{-2}$$

$$= 1200 + 1000 = ₹ 2200$$

Shortcut Approach - 13

Income of two persons are in the ratio $a : b$ and their expenditure are in the ratio $c : d$. If each of them saves ₹ x, then their expenditures are given by

$$\frac{xc(b-a)}{ad-bc} \text{ and } \frac{xd(b-a)}{ad-bc}.$$

18. **The incomes of Ram and Shyam are in the ratio 8 : 11 and their expenditure are in the ratio 7 : 10. If each of them saves ₹ 500, what are their incomes and expenditures?**
    (a) 4000, 5500, 3500, 5000
    (b) 5000, 5000, 4000, 3500
    (c) 4000, 5000, 3500, 4500
    (d) None of these

Sol. (a) Expenditure of Ram $= \dfrac{(11-8)\times 500 \times 7}{8\times 10 - 11\times 7} = \dfrac{3\times 500 \times 7}{3} = 3500$

Expenditure of Shyam $= \dfrac{500\times 10(11-8)}{3} = 5000$

Income of Ram $= \dfrac{500\times 8(10-7)}{8\times 13 - 7\times 11} = 4000$

Income of Shyam $= \dfrac{500\times 11(10-7)}{3} = 5500$

Shortcut Approach - 14

Two candles of the same height are lighted at the same time. The first is consumed in T_1 hours and the second in T_2 hours. Assuming that each candle burns at a constant rate, the time after which the ratio of first candle to second candle becomes $x : y$ is given by $\dfrac{T_1 T_2 \left(\dfrac{x}{y} - 1\right)}{\left(\dfrac{x}{y}\right) T_1 - T_2}$ hours.

19. **Two candles of the same height are lighted at the same time. The first is consumed in 7 hours and the second is consumed in 4 hours. Assuming that each candle burns at a constant rate, in how many hours, after being lighted, was the first candle four times the height of the second ?**

    (a) **3.5 hrs**   (b) **2.5 hrs**

    (c) **2 hrs**   (d) **3 hrs**

Sol. (a) If out of two candles of the same height, the first burns in T_1 hour and the second burns in T_2 hour, then after $\dfrac{T_1 T_2 \left(\dfrac{x}{y} - 1\right)}{\left(\dfrac{x}{y}\right)(T_1) - T_2}$

hours, the ratio of the height of remaining parts will be $4 : 1$

Here, $T_1 = 7\text{hrs}$, $T_2 = 4\text{hrs}$

$\therefore$ Required time $= \dfrac{(7)(4)(4-1)}{(4)(7)-4} = \dfrac{84}{24} = 3.5\text{ hrs}$

Shortcut Approach - 15

If on adding x to four numbers a, b, c and d; the resulting numbers become proportional, then $x = \dfrac{bc - ad}{(a+d)-(b+c)}$.

20. **What must be deducted from each of the numbers 7, 10, 12 and 18 so that the resultant numbers are in proportion ?**

    (a) **1**   (b) **2**

    (c) **3**   (d) **4**

Sol. (b) Required number $= \dfrac{bc - ad}{(a+d)-(b+c)} = \dfrac{(10)(12)-(7)(18)}{(7+18)-(10+12)} = \dfrac{-6}{3} = (-2)$

Thus, 2 must be subtracted from each of the numbers.

Shortcut Approach - 16

Two numbers are in the ratio $a : b$. If p is added to the first number and q is added to the second number respectively, then ratio of the resulting numbers become $m : n$. Then,

The original first number $= \dfrac{a(mq - np)}{an - bm}$ and the original second number

$$= \dfrac{b(mq - np)}{an - bm}$$

21. **In a class, the number of boys and girls is in the ratio of 4: 5. If 10 more boys join the class, the ratio of numbers of boys and girls becomes 6 : 5. How many girls are there in the class?**

   (a) **20**
   (b) **30**
   (c) **25**
   (d) **Couldn't be determined**

Sol. (c)   Number of girls $= \dfrac{b\left(mq - np\right)}{an - bm}$

$$= \dfrac{5\left[(6)(0) - (5)(10)\right]}{(4)(5) - (5)(6)} = \dfrac{5 \times (-50)}{(-10)} = 25$$

Exercise

1. Two numbers are in the ratio of $3:4$. If 5 is subtracted from each, the resulting numbers are in the ratio $2:3$. Find the numbers
   (a) 12, 16   (b) 24, 32
   (c) 60, 80   (d) 15, 20

2. Find the fourth proportional to $12X^3, 9aX^2, 8a^3X$.
   (a) $4a^3$ (b) $6a^4$
   (c) $5a$ (d) $7a^5$

3. In a partnership, A invests $\dfrac{1}{6}$ of the capital for $\dfrac{1}{6}$ of the time, B invests $\dfrac{1}{3}$ of the capital for $\dfrac{1}{3}$ of the time and C, the rest of the capital for whole time. Find A's share of the total profit of ₹ 2,300.
   (a) ₹ 100   (b) ₹ 200
   (c) ₹ 300   (d) ₹ 400

4. If 12 men can build a wall 100 m long, 3 m high, and 0.5 m thick in 25 days, in how many days will 20 men build a wall $60\,m \times 4\,m \times 0.25\,m$?
   (a) 6 days   (b) 8 days
   (c) 12 days   (d) 15 days

5. In a camp, there is a meal for 120 men or 200 children. If 150 children have taken the meal, how many men will be catered to with the remaining meal ?
   (a) 20   (b) 30
   (c) 40   (d) 50

6. The ratio of males and females in a city is $7:8$ and the percentage of children among males and females is 25% and 20% respectively. If the number of adult females in the city is 156800 what is the total population?
   (a) 245000   (b) 367500
   (c) 196000   (d) 171500

7. A and B invested ₹ 12,000 and ₹ 18,000 respectively in a business for the whole year. At the year-end, there was a total profit of ₹ 2,000. What is the share of A in the profit?
   (a) ₹ 800
   (b) ₹ 1, 200
   (c) ₹ 1,600
   (d) None of these

8. A bag contains an equal number of one rupee, 50 paise and 25 paise coins respectively. If the total value is ₹ 35, how many coins of each type are there?
   (a) 20 coins
   (b) 30 coins
   (c) 28 coins
   (d) 25 coins

9. Three friends A, B and C started a business by investing a sum of money in the ratio of $5:7:6$. After 6 months C withdraws half of his capital. If the sum invested by 'A' is ₹ 40,000, out of a

total annual profit of ₹ 33,000, *C*'s share will be

(a) ₹9,000   (b) ₹12,000
(c) ₹11,000 (d) ₹10,000

10. In a journey of 45 km performed by tonga, rickshaw and cycle in that order, the distance covered by the three ways in that order are in the ratio of 8 : 1 : 3 and charges per kilometre in that order are in the ratio of 8 : 1 : 4. If the tonga charges being 24 paise per kilometre, the total cost of the journey is

(a) ₹ 9.24
(b) ₹ 10
(c) ₹ 12
(d) None of these

11. King Dashrath decided to distribute gold coins to his three queens in the following way : 2nd queen would get 5/7th of what the 1st queen would get and the 3rd queen would get 3/5th of what the 2nd queen would get. 1st queen got 60 gold coins more than the 3rd queen. How many gold coins were distributed to the three queens?

(a) 120   (b) 175
(c) 225   (d) 250

12. Anil started a manufacturing unit with a certain amount of money. After a few months, Dheeraj became his partner, contributing three times of what Anil had contributed. At the end of the year, each was entitled to half the total profit. If Anil started the unit in January, then when did Dheeraj join as a patner?

(a) August
(b) September
(c) July
(d) October

Hints & Solution

1. **(d)** Use Short Approach -3

2. **(b)** Let r be the 4th proportional.

    Then

    $$\frac{12X^3}{9aX^2} = \frac{8a^3X}{r} \Rightarrow r = 6a^4$$

3. **(a)** Use Short Approach -6

4. **(a)** Let the required days be x.
    More men, less days (Indirect proportion)
    More size, more days (Direct proportion)

    Men 20   12
    size 100×3×0.5   60×4×0.25 } :: 25 : x

    $\therefore 20 \times 100 \times 3 \times 0.5 \times x = 12 \times 60 \times 4 \times 0.25 \times 25$

    $\Rightarrow x = 6$ days

5. **(b)** There is a meal for 200 children. 150 children have taken the meal. Remaining meal is to be catered to 50 children.

    Now, 200 children $\equiv$ 120 men

    $\therefore$ 50 children

    $$\equiv \left(\frac{120}{200} \times 50\right) \text{ men} = 30 \text{ men}.$$

6. **(b)** Number of females

    $$= 156800 \times \frac{100}{80} = 196000$$

    $\therefore$ Number of males $= \frac{7}{8} \times 196000 = 171500$

    $\therefore$ Total population $= 196000 + 171500 = 367500$

7. **(a)** Use Short Approach -4

8. **(a)** Let number of each type of coin $= x$. Then,

    $1 \times x + .50 \times x + .25x = 35$

    $\Rightarrow 1.75x = 35 \Rightarrow x = 20$ coins

9. **(a)** Use Short Approach -6

10. **(a)** Total distances covered under each mode $= 32, 4$ and 12 km respectively.

    Total charges $= 32 \times 24 + 4 \times 3 + 12 \times 12$

    $= 924$ paise $= ₹9.24$.

11. **(c)** Let x gold coins were given to 1st queen. Then no. of gold coins given

    to 2nd queen $= \frac{5}{7}x$

    And no. of gold coins given to 3rd queen

    $$= \frac{3}{7}x$$

    then,

    $$x - \frac{3}{7}x = 60 \Rightarrow \frac{4x}{7} = 60$$

    $x = 105$

    Required no.

    $$= 105 + \frac{5}{7} \times 105 + \frac{3}{7} \times 105 = 225$$

12. **(b)** Use Short Approach -6

Average

If average of n consecutive odd numbers x, then the difference between the smallest and the largest numbers is given by $2(n-1)$.

Note that the above formula is independent of x. Therefore, this formula always holds good irrespective of the value of x.

1. **If A, B, C and D are four consecutive odd numbers and their average is 52, what is the difference between A and D?**
   (a) 6 (b) 7 (c) 8 (d) 9

Sol. (a) Difference $= 2(n-1) = 2(4-1) = 6$

If the average of n numbers is A and on rechecking, it is noticed that some of the numbers n (i.e. $x_1, x_2, x_3, ..., x_n$) are wrongly taken as ($x'_1, x'_2, x'_3,$ ....., x'_n), then their correct average

$$= A + \frac{(x_1 + x_2 + x_3 + ... + x_n) - (x'_1 + x'_2 + x'_3 + ... + x'_n)}{n}$$

2. **The mean of 50 observations was 36. It was found later that an observation 48 was wrongly taken as 23. The corrected (new) mean is:**
   (a) 35. 2 (b) 36.1 (c) 36. 5 (d) 39.1

Sol. (c) Correct average

$$= 36 + \frac{48 - 23}{50}$$

$$= 36 + \frac{25}{50} = 36.5$$

3. **The arithmetic mean of 100 numbers was computed as 89.05. It was later found that two numbers 92 and 83 have been misread as 192 and 33 respectively, what is the correct arithmetic mean of the numbers?**
   (a) 88.55 (b) 87.55
   (c) 89.55 (d) Data Insufficient

Sol. (a) Correct average

$$= 89.05 + \frac{(92+83)-(192+33)}{100}$$

$$= 89.05 + \frac{175-225}{100} = 89.05 - \frac{50}{100} = 89.05 - 0.5 = 88.55$$

Shortcut Approach - 3

Let the average weight of n balls is a units. If the weight of a bag is included, the average weight increases by b units, then weight of the bag $= a + b\,(n + 1)$.

4. **The average run scored by a batsman in 20 innings is 32. After 21st innings, the runs average becomes 34. How much runs does the batsman score in his 21st innings?**

    (a) 70   **(b)** 72   **(c)** 74   **(d)** 76

Sol. (c) After 21st innings, the runs average increases by 2.

    $\therefore$ Runs scored in 21st innings $= a + b\,(n+1)$

    $= 32 + 2\,(20+1) = 32 + 42 = 74$

5. **The average weight of 21 boys was recorded as 64 kg. If the weight of the teacher was added, the average increased by one kg. what was the teacher's weight?**

    (a) 86 kg   **(b)** 64 kg   **(c)** 72 kg   **(d)** 98 kg

Sol. (a) Teacher's weight $= a + b\,(n + 1)$

    $= 64 + 1\,(21 + 1) = 64 + 22$

    $= 86\,\text{kg}$

Shortcut Approach - 4

Let there were n students in a hostel. If the number of students increases by a, the expenses of mess increase by ₹ b per day while the average expenditure per head diminishes by ₹ c, then the original expenditure of

the mess $= n\left[\dfrac{c(n+a)+b}{a}\right]$

6. **There were 52 students in a hostel. If the number of students increases by 13, the daily expenses of the mess increases by ₹65, while average expenses per student decreases by ₹1. Find the original expenditure of the mess.**

    (a) ₹480   **(b)** ₹500   **(c)** ₹520   **(d)** ₹545

Sol. (c) Original expenditure $= n\left[\dfrac{c(n+a)+b}{a}\right]$

$$= 52\left[\dfrac{1(52+13)+65}{13}\right]$$

$$= 52 \times \dfrac{130}{13} = ₹\,520$$

7. **There were 35 students in a hostel. If the number of students increases by 7, the daily expenses of the mess increases by ₹42, while average expenses per student decreases by ₹1. Find the original expenditure of the mess.**
   (a) ₹420 (b) ₹500
   (c) ₹520 (d) ₹545

Sol. (a) Original expenditure $= 35\left[\dfrac{1(7+35)+42}{7}\right]$

$$= 35 \times \dfrac{84}{7} = ₹\,420$$

Shortcut Approach - 5

If the average of $(a + b + 1)$ result is x, that of the first a is y and that of the last b is z, then value of the $(n + 1)$th result $=$ Total of $(a + b + 1)$ results $-$ (Total of first a results $+$ Total of last b results)
$= (a + b + 1)x - (ay + bz)$

8. **The average of 9 numbers is 30. The average of first 5 numbers is 25 and that of the last 3 numbers is 35. What is the 6th number?**
   (a) 20 (b) 30
   (c) 40 (d) 50

Sol. (c) The value of 6th number
$$= (a + b + 1)x - (ay + bz)$$
$$= (5 + 3 + 1)30 - (5 \times 25 + 3 \times 35)$$
$$= 270 - (125 + 105) = 40$$

Shortcut Approach - 6

If the average age of m boys is x and the average age of n boys out of m boys is y, then the average age of the rest of the boys $= \dfrac{mx - ny}{m - n}$

9. The average age of 30 girls is 13 years. The average of first 18 girls is 15 years. Find out the average age of remaining 12 girls.
   (a) 12 yrs   (b) 10 yrs   (c) 16 yrs   (d) 10.5 yrs

Sol. (b) Average age

$$= \left[\frac{mx - ny}{m - n} \right]$$

$$= \left[\frac{30 \times 13 - 18 \times 15}{30 - 18} \right]$$

$$= \frac{(390 - 270)}{12} = 10 \text{ years}$$

10. The sum of five numbers is 555. The average of first two numbers is 75 and the third number is 115. What is the average of last two numbers?
    (a) 145   (b) 290
    (c) 265   (d) 150

Sol. (a) Average of last two number

$$= \left[\frac{555 - (75 \times 2) - (115 \times 1)}{5 - 2 - 1} \right] = 145$$

⊕ Shortcut Approach - 7

If the average of n quantities is equal to x. When a quantity is removed, the average becomes y. Then the value of the removed quantity $= n (x - y) + y$.

11. The average age of a family of 6 members is 25 years. The average age of the family after the demise of a 40 years old member will be
    (a) 20 yrs   (b) 21 yrs   (c) 22 yrs   (d) 23 yrs

Sol. (c) $40 = n (x - y) + y$
$40 = 6 (25 - y) + y$
$40 = 150 - 5y$
$5y = 110$
$y = 22$ years

12. The average monthly income of a family of 4 earning members was ₹7350. One of the earning members died. Thereby the average came down to ₹6500. The monthly income of the deceased was:
    (a) ₹8500   (b) ₹8200
    (c) ₹9900   (d) ₹10750

Sol. (c) Monthly income of the deceased person $= 4 (7350 - 6500) + 6500$
$= 3400 + 6500 = ₹9900$

If the average of the first and the second of three numbers is x more or less than the average of the second and the third of these numbers, then the difference between the first and the third of these three numbers is given by $2x$.

Note that, here only 2 numbers (i.e. first and second or second and third) are involved in calculating average, therefore, we multiply x by 2. If n numbers are involved, for getting answer, we multiply x by n.

13. **Average rainfall on Monday, Tuesday, Wednesday and Thursday is 420.5 cm and average on Tuesday, Wednesday, Thursday and Friday is 440.5 cm. If the ratio of rainfall for monday and Friday is 20:21, find the rainfall in cm on Monday and Friday.**

   (a) 1700, 1470
   (b) 1682, 1762
   (c) 1800, 1890   (d)   1600, 1680

Sol. (d) The difference between the rainfall on Monday
   and Friday $= 4 \times (440.5 - 420.5) = 80$
   So, $21x - 20x = 80$ $\therefore$ $x = 80$
   Hence, rainfall on Monday and Friday
   $= 20 \times 80$ and 21×80
   $= 1600$ cm and 1680 cm

14. **The mean temperature from Monday to Wednesday was 37°C and from Tuesday to Thursday was 34°C. If the temperature on Thursday was 4/5th that of Monday, the temperature on Thursday was:**

   (a) 34°C   (b) 35°C

   (c) 36°C   (d) 37°C

Sol. (c) Difference between the temperature on Monday
   and Thursday $= 3 \times (37°C - 34°C) = 9°C$

   So, $x - \dfrac{4x}{5} = 9 \Rightarrow x = 45°C$

   Hence, temperature on Thursday

   $= \dfrac{4}{5} \times 45° = 36°C$

If a batsman in his nth innings makes a score of x and thereby increases his average by y, then the average after n innings $= x - y(n-1)$.

15. **Sachin Tendulkar has a certain average for 11 innings. In the 12th innings, he score 120 runs and there by increases his average by 5 runs. His new average is**
    (a) 60   (b) 62
    (c) 65   (d) 66

Sol. (c) Average $= x - y\,(n-1)$
    $= 120 - 5\,(12 - 1)$
    $= 120 - 5 \times 11$
    $\Rightarrow 120 - 55 = 65$

16. **A cricketer had a certain average of runs for his 64 innings. In his 65th innings, he is bowled out for no score on his part, This brings down his average by 2 runs his new average of runs is:**

    (a) 130   (b) 128
    (c) 70   (d) 68

Sol. (b) Average $= x - y\,(n-1)$
    $= 0 - (-2)(65 - 1)$
    $= 0 + 2 \times 64 = 128$

⊕ Shortcut Approach - 10

If a cricketer has completed n innings and his average is x runs. The number of runs, he must make in his next innings so as to raise his average to $y = n\,(y - x) + y$.

17. **A cricketer has completed 10 innings and his average is 21.5 runs. How many runs must be made in his next innings so as to raise his average to 24?**
    (a) 47   (b) 48
    (c) 49   (d) 50

Sol. (c) Required runs
    $= n\,(y - x) + y$
    $= 10\,(24 - 21.5) + 24 = 49$ runs

⊕ Shortcut Approach - 11

The average of marks obtained by n candidates in a certain examination is T. If the average marks of passed candidates is P and that of the failed candidates is F. Then the number of candidates who passed the examination

$$= \text{Total candidates} \times \frac{(\text{Total Average} - \text{Failed Average})}{\text{Passed Average} - \text{Failed Average}} = \frac{n(T - F)}{P - F}$$

18. The average of marks obtained by 120 candidates in a certain examination is 35. If the average mark of passed candidates is 39 and that of the failed candidates is 15, what is the number of candidates who passed the examination?

   (a) 90   (b) 85

   (c) 100   (d) 120

Sol. (c) No. of passed students

$$= \frac{n(T-F)}{P-F} = \frac{120(35-15)}{(39-15)} = 100$$

Shortcut Approach - 12

The average weight of n persons is increased by x kg. when some of them whose weight $[y_1 + y_2 + ...$ where, $y_1 + y_2 + ... = y$ kg] are replaced by the same number of persons. Then the weight of the new persons

= Weight of removed person (s) + (No. of persons) ×

(Increase in average)

$= y + nx.$

19. The average age of 8 persons is increased by 2 years, when one of them, whose age is 24 years, is replaced by a new person. The age of the new person is:

   (a) 42 yrs   (b) 40 yrs

   (c) 38 yrs   (d) 45 yrs

Sol. (b) The age of the new man $= y + nx$

   $= 24 + 8 \times 2 - 40$ years

20. The average age of 8 men is increased by 2 years when two of them whose ages are 21 and 23 years are replaced by two new men. The average age of the two new men is:

   (a) 22 yrs   (b) 24 yrs

   (c) 28 yrs   (d) 30 yrs

Sol. (d) The average of the two new men is

$$= \frac{\text{Total age of new persons}}{\text{No. of new persons}} = \frac{(y+nx)}{2}$$

$$= \frac{(21+23)+8(2)}{2} = \frac{60}{2} = 30 \text{ years}$$

Shortcut Approach - 13

The average age of n persons is decreased by x years. When some of them aged $[y_1 + y_2 + \ldots$ where, $y_1 + y_2 + \ldots = y$ years$]$ are replaced by the same number of persons. Then the total age of the new persons

= Total age of removed persons – (No. of persons) × (Decrease in average)

$= y - nx$.

21. **Out of 10 teachers of a school, one teacher retires and in his place, a new teacher of age 25 years joins. As a result, average age of teachers is reduced by 3 years. The age (in years of the retired teacher is:**

    (a) 50 (b) 58 (c) 60 (d) 55

Sol. **(d)** Let, the age of the retired teacher $= x$

$$25 = x - (10 \times 3)$$
$$x = 25 + 30 = 55 \text{ years}$$

Shortcut Approach - 14

If the average of n results (where n is an odd number) is a and the average

of first $\dfrac{n+1}{2}$ results is b and that of last $\dfrac{n+1}{2}$ is c.

Then $\left(\dfrac{n+1}{2}\right)$ th result

$$= \frac{n+1}{2}(b+c) - na.$$

or (the middle value)

22. **The average of 11 numbers is 10.8. If the average of the first six numbers be 10.4 and that of the last six is 11.5, the middle (6th) number is:**

    (a) 10.3 (b) 12.6 (c) 13.5 (d) 15.5

Sol. **(b)** Middle number (6th) $= \dfrac{n+1}{2}(b+c) - na$

$$= \frac{11+1}{2}(10.4 + 11.5) - 11 \times 10.8$$

$$= 131.4 - 118.8 = 12.6$$

If the average value of all the members of group is x, the average value of the first part of member is y, the average value of the remaining part of members is z and the number of the first part of members is n, then the number of the other part of members is $\dfrac{n(x-y)}{z-x}$.

or

$$= \dfrac{\text{No. of 1st part members} \times (\text{Total average of whole group} - \text{Average of 1st part})}{\text{Average of other part} - \text{Total average of whole group}}$$

23. **The average salary of the entire staff in a office is ₹ 120 per month. The average salary of officers is ₹ 460 and that of non-officers is ₹ 110. If the number of officers is 15, then find the number of non-officers in the office.**

    (a) 510   (b) 520   (c) 530   (d) 540

Sol. (a) No. of non-officers

$$= \dfrac{15(120-460)}{110-120} = \dfrac{15\times(-340)}{(-10)} = 15 \times 34 = 510$$

Exercise

1. The average age of 24 students and the class teacher is 16 years. If the class teacher's age is excluded, the average reduces by one year. What is the age of the class teacher?
   (a) 50 years (b) 45 years
   (c) 40 years
   (d) Data inadequate

2. A person covers half his journey by train at 60 kmph, the remaining half by bus at 30 kmph and the rest by cycle at 10 kmph. Find his average speed during the entire journey.
   (a) 36 kmph
   (b) 24 kmph
   (c) 48 kmph
   (d) None of these

3. The average of 10 numbers is 40.2. Later it is found that two numbers have been wrongly copied. The first is 18 greater than the actual number and the second number added is 13 instead of 31. Find the correct average.
   (a) 40.2   (b) 40.4
   (c) 40.6   (d) 40.8

4. Rahul Ghosh walks from A to B at 8 km/h and comes back from B to A at 12 km/h. What is his average speed for the entire journey?

   (a) 8.8 km/h
   (b) 9.6 km/h
   (c) 10.2 km/h
   (d) 11.4 km/h

5. The average marks of 40 students in an English exam is 72. Later it is found that three marks 64, 62 and 84 were wrongly entered as 68, 65 and 73. The average after mistakes are rectified as–
   (a) 70   (b) 72
   (c) 71.9   (d) 72.1

6. The average of 7, 14, 21, 28..........77 is :
   (a) 7   (b) 11
   (c) 42   (d) 66

7. Three years ago, the average age of a family of 8 members was 30 years. If one child is also included in the family, the present average age of the family remained the same as three years ago. The present age of the child is
   (a) 6 yrs   (b) 1 year
   (c) 3 yrs   (d) 4 yrs

8. The average salary of all the workers in a workshop is ₹8,000. The average salary of 7 technicians is ₹12,000 and the average salary of the rest is ₹6,000. The total number of workers in the workshop is :

(a) 21   (b) 20
(c) 23   (d) 22

9. A car covers 1/5 of the distance from A to B at the speed of 8 km/hour, 1/10 of the distance at 25 km per hour and the remaining at the speed of 20km per hour. Find the average speed of the whole journey-
(a) 12.625 km/hr
(b) 13.625 km/hr
(c) 14.625 km/hr
(d) 15.625 km/hr

10. The average weight of 47 balls is 4 gm. If the weight of the bag (in which the balls are kept) be included, the calculated average weight increases by 0.3 gm. What is the weight of the bag?
(a) 14.8 gm   (b) 15.0 gm
(c) 18.6 gm
(d) None of these

11. Brian Lara, the famous batsman, scored 6,000 runs in certain number of innings. In the next five innings he was out of form and hence, could make only a total of 90 runs, as a result of which his average fell by 2 runs. How many innings did he play in all, if he gets out in all the innings?
(a) 105   (b) 95
(c) 115   (d) 104

12. The batting average for 40 innings of a cricketer is 50 runs. His highest score exceeds his lowest score by 172 runs. If these two innings are excluded, the average of the remaining 38 innings is 48 runs. The highest score of the player is-
(a) 165   (b) 170
(c) 172   (d) 174

Hints & Solution

1. **(c)** Use short approach -7

2. **(b)** Recognise that the journey by bus and that by cycle are of equal distance. Hence, we can use the short cut illustrated earlier to solve this part of the problem.

   Using the process explained above, we get average speed of the second half of the journey as

   $10 + 1 \times 5 = 15$ kmph

   Then we employ the same technique for the first part and get $15 + 1 \times 9 = 24$ kmph

3. **(a)** Use short approach -2

4. **(b)** Average speed

$$= \frac{2 \times 8 \times 12}{8 + 12} = \frac{192}{20}$$
$$= 9.6 \text{ km/h}$$

5. **(d)** Use short approach -2

6. **(c)** $\dfrac{7 + 14 + 21 + \dots 77}{11}$

$$= \frac{7(1 + 2 + \dots 11)}{11}$$

$$= \frac{7 \times 11 \times 12}{11 \times 2} = 42$$

$$\left[\because 1 + 2 + 3 \dots n = \frac{n(n+1)}{2} \right]$$

Alternatively : Since all the numbers are in A.P Further there are odd number of numbers (i.e., 11) in the sequence. Thus the middle most term is the average of the sequence, which is 42.

7. **(a)** The present average age of 8 members will be 33 years.

   Let the present age of child be 'x'. So,

$$\frac{8 \times 33 + x}{8 + 1} = 30 \Rightarrow x$$
$$= 6 \text{ years.}$$

8. **(a)** Use short approach -6

9. **(d)** If the whole journey be x km. The total time taken

$$= \left(\frac{\dfrac{x}{5}}{8} + \frac{\dfrac{x}{10}}{25} + \frac{\dfrac{7x}{10}}{20} \right) \text{hrs}$$

$$= (x/40 + x/250 + 7x/200) \text{ hrs}$$
$$= (25x + 4x + 35x)/1000$$
$$= 64x/1000 \text{ hrs}$$

$$\therefore \quad \text{Average speed} = \frac{x}{\dfrac{64x}{1000}}$$

$$= 15.625 \text{ km/hr}$$

10. **(d)** Use short approach -3

11. **(a)** Use short approach -10

12. **(d)** Use short approach -2

Percentage

If a is $x\%$ of b, then $x = \dfrac{a}{b} \times 100\%$

1. **50 kg is what percent of 250 kg?**
   (a) 26% (b) 15%
   (c) 20% (d) 18%

Sol. (c) Required percent $= \left(\dfrac{50}{250} \times 100\right)\% = 20\%$

If the price of a commodity increases by r%, then the reduction in consumption so as not to increase the expenditure, is $\left(\dfrac{r}{100 + r} \times 100\right)\%$

2. **The price of sugar is increased by 25%. If a family wants to keep its expenses on sugar unaltered, then the family will have to reduce the consumption of sugar by**
   (a) 20% (b) 21%
   (c) 22% (d) 25%

Sol. (a) Required percentage

$$= \left(\dfrac{r}{100 + r} \times 100\right)\%$$

$$= \left(\dfrac{25}{100 + 25} \times 100\right)\% = 20\%$$

3. **The price of cooking oil is increased by 25%. By what percent a family should reduce the consumption of cooking oil so as not to increase the expenditure on this account?**
   (a) 20% (b) 25%
   (c) 50% (d) 40%

Sol. (a) Required percentage

$$= \left(\frac{25}{100+25} \times 100 \right)\% = \left(\frac{25}{125} \times 100 \right)\% = 20\%$$

4. The price of commodity rises from ₹6 per kg to ₹7.50 per kg. If the expenditure cannot increase, then percentage of reduction in consumption is :

    (a) 15   (b) 20   (c) 25   (d) 30

Sol. (b) % increase in price

$$= \left(\frac{(7.50-6)}{6} \times 100 \right)\% = \left(\frac{1.50}{6} \times 100 \right)\% = 25\%$$

$\therefore$ Required percentage

$$= \left(\frac{25}{100+25} \times 100 \right)\% = 20\%$$

⊕ Shortcut Approach - 3

If the price of a commodity decreases by r%, then, increase in consumption, so as not to decrease expenditure on this item is $\left[\dfrac{r}{(100-r)} \times 100 \right]\%$,

5. If the price of tea falls down by 6% by how much percent must a householder increase its consumption, so as not to decrease expenditure?

    (a) $5\dfrac{16}{47}\%$ (b) $4\dfrac{18}{67}\%$ (c) $6\dfrac{18}{47}\%$ (d) $6\dfrac{17}{47}\%$

Sol. (c) Required percentage

$$= \left(\frac{r}{100-r} \times 100 \right)\% = \left(\frac{6}{100-6} \times 100 \right)\% = 6\frac{18}{47}\%$$

⊕ Shortcut Approach - 4

If the price of a commodity is changed by $x\%$ and its consumption changed by $y\%$, then

$$\frac{\textbf{New expenditure}}{\textbf{Initial expenditure}} = \frac{(100-x)(100+y)}{(100)^2}$$

Put x as $(+x)$ and y as $(+y)$ in the case of 'increase' and x as $(-x)$ and y as $(-y)$ in the case of 'decrease'.

6. The price of consumer goods increased by 50% and its consumption decreased by 25%. Find the ratio of new expenditure to initial expenditure.

(a) $8:9$ (b) $9:8$ (c) $7:8$ (d) $11:8$

Sol. (b) Required ratio

$$= \frac{\text{New expenditure}}{\text{Initial expenditure}} = \frac{(100+50)(100-25)}{(100)^2}$$

$$= \frac{150 \times 75}{(100)^2} = \frac{9}{8} = 9:8$$

Shortcut Approach - 5

If three successive discounts of $x\%$, $y\%$ and $z\%$ are allowed on an amount then a single discount that equivalent to the three successive discounts will be $\left[x+y+z - \dfrac{xy+yz+zx}{100} + \dfrac{xyz}{100^2} \right]\%.$

or

Finding single discount rate equivalent to the series of two discounts
= 1st discount + 2nd discount

$$- \frac{\text{1st discount} \times \text{2nd discount}}{100}$$

7. Successive discount of 50% and 50% is equivalent to

(a) 100% (b) 75% (c) 50% (d) 25%

Sol. (b) Required equivalent single discount

$$= \left[(50+50) - \frac{(50 \times 50)}{100} \right]\%$$

$$= (100-25)\% = 75\%$$

Shortcut Approach - 6

If the value is increased successively by $x\%$ and $y\%$ then the final increase is given by $\left[x+y+\dfrac{xy}{100} \right]\%,$

8. A number is increased by 20% and then again by 20%. By what per cent should the increased number be reduced so as to get back the original number?

(a) $30\dfrac{5}{9}\%$ (b) $19\dfrac{11}{13}\%$ (c) 40% (d) 44%

Sol. (d) % Increase in number

$$= \left(20 + 20 + \frac{20 \times 20}{100}\right)\%$$

$$= (40 + 4)\% = 44\%$$

Hence, the increased number should be reduced by 44% so as to get back the original number.

Shortcut Approach -7

If the value is decreased successively by $x\%$ and $y\%$ then the final decrease is given by $\left[x + y - \dfrac{xy}{100}\right]\%$,

9. The population of a city is decreased by 20% in a year. In the next year, the population is again decreased by 30%. Find per cent decrease in population of the city from the original population.

(a) 44% (b) 50% (c) 55% (d) 56%

Sol. (a) Population is decreased by

$$= \left[20 + 30 - \frac{20 \times 30}{100}\right]\% = \left(50 - \frac{600}{100}\right)\% = 44\%$$

Shortcut Approach - 8

If the value is first increased by $x\%$ and then decreased by $y\%$, then there is $\left(x - y - \dfrac{xy}{100}\right)\%$ increase or decrease, according to the +ve or –ve sign respectively.

10. A number is increased by 20% and then it is decreased by 10%. Find the net increase or decrease per cent.

(a) 10 % increase

(b) 10% decrease

(c) 8% increase

(d) 8% decrease

Sol. (c) Change in the number

$$= \left(x - y - \frac{xy}{100}\right)\% = \left(20 - 10 - \frac{20 \times 10}{100}\right)\%$$

$= 8\%$ increase

11. If price of a book is first decreased by 25% and then increased by 20%, the net change in the price of the book will be :

 (a)   10 % decrease   (b)   5% decrease

 (c)   No change   (d)   5% increase

Sol. (a) Change in the price

$$= \left(20 - 25 - \frac{20 \times 25}{100}\right)\%$$

$= (-5 - 5)\% = (-10)\%$

$= 10\%$ decrease

⊕ Shortcut Approach - 9

A man spends x% of his income. His income is increased by y% and his expenditure also increases by z%, then the percentage increase or decrease in his savings is given by

$$\left[\frac{100y - xz}{100 - x}\right]\%,$$

according to the +ve or –ve sign.

12. A man spends 75% of his income. His income is increased by 20% and he increases his expenditure by 10%. His savings are increased by :

 (a)   10%   (b)   25%   (c)   37%   (d)   50%

Sol. (d) % increase in savings

$$-\left[\frac{(100 \times 20) - (75 \times 10)}{100 - 75}\right]\% - \left(\frac{2000 - 750}{25}\right)\% = 50\%$$

13. The monthly income of a person was ₹13500 and his monthly expenditure is ₹9000. Next year his income increased by 14% and his expenditure increased by 7%. The percentage of increase in his savings is :

 (a)   7%   (b)   21%   (c)   28%   (d)   35%

Sol. (c) Percentage expenditure

$$= \left(\frac{9000}{13500} \times 100\right)\% = \frac{200}{3}\%$$

$\therefore$ % increase in saving

$$= \left[\frac{(100 \times 14) - \left(\dfrac{200}{3} \times 7 \right)}{100 - \dfrac{200}{3}} \right] \% = \left[\frac{\dfrac{2800}{3}}{\dfrac{100}{3}} \right] \% = 28\%$$

⊕ Shortcut Approach - 10

The pass marks in an examination is $x\%$. If a candidate who secures y marks fails by z marks, then the maximum marks, is given by

$$\left[\frac{100(y+z)}{x} \right].$$

14. In an examination a candidate must secure 40% marks to pass. A candidate who gets 220 marks, fails by 20 marks. What are the maximum marks for the examination?

(a) 1200   (b) 800   (c)   600   (d)   450

Sol. (c)   Maximum marks

$$= \frac{100(220 + 20)}{40} = 600$$

⊕ Shortcut Approach - 11

Theorem : If one factor is increased by x% and the other increases by

y% then the effect on the product is given by $\left[x + y + \dfrac{xy}{100} \right]\%$ **increase.**

15. The number of seats in a cinema hall is increased by 25%. The cost of a ticket is also increased by 10%. The overall percentage increase in the revenue is :

(a) 10.5%   (b) 27.5%   (c)   37.5%   (d)   40.5%

Sol. (c)   Overall percentage increase in revenue

$$= \left[x + y + \frac{xy}{100} \right] \%$$

$$= \left[25 + 10 + \frac{250}{100} \right] \%$$

$$= 37.5\%$$

⊕ Shortcut Approach - 12

If one of the sides of a rectangle is increased by $x\%$ and the other is decreased by $y\%$, then the increase or decrease per cent in area is given by $\left(x - y - \dfrac{xy}{100}\right)\%$, according to the +ve or –ve sign.

16. If the length is increased by 20% and the breadth is decreased by 25%, then what will be the effect on the area?

    (a) 10% decrease

    (b) 10% increase

    (c) 20% increase

    (d) 20% decrease

Sol. (a) Effect on area

$$= \left(x - y - \frac{xy}{100}\right)\% = \left(20 - 25 - \frac{20 \times 25}{100}\right)\%$$

$$= (-10)\% = 10\% \text{ decrease}$$

⊕ Shortcut Approach - 13

If one of the sides of a rectangle is increased by $x\%$ and the other is increased by $y\%$ then the per cent value by which area changes is given by $\left[x + y + \dfrac{xy}{100}\right]\%$ increase.

17. If the sides of a square are increased by 30%, find the per cent increase in its area.

    (a) 70%   (b) 68%   (c)   69%   (d)   71%

Sol. (c) % increase in area

$$= \left[30 + 30 + \frac{30 \times 30}{100}\right]\% = (60 + 9)\% = 69\%$$

Exercise

1. If the price of sugar is increased by 7%, then by how much per cent should a housewife reduce her consumption of sugar, to have no extra expenditure?
   (a) 7 over 107%
   (b) 107 over 100%
   (c) 100 over 107%
   (d) 7%

2. A positive number is by mistake divided by 6 instead of being multiplied by 6. What is the % error on the basis of correct answer?
   (a) 3%   (b) 97%
   (c) 17%   (d) 83%

3. When the price of a radio was reduced by 20%, its sale increased by 80%. What was the net effect on the sale?
   (a) 44% increase
   (b) 44% decrease
   (c) 66% increase
   (d) 75% increase

4. A store raised the price of an item by exactly 10 per cent. Which of the following could not be the resulting price of the item ?
   (a) ₹5.50   (b) ₹7.60
   (c) ₹11.00   (d) ₹12.10

5. The price of consumer goods increased by 50% and its consumption decreased by 25%. Find the ratio of new expenditure to initial expenditure.
   (a) 8 : 9   (b) 9 : 8
   (c) 7 : 8   (d) 11 : 8

6. 10 litres of water is added to 50 litres of a solution containing 20% of alcohol in water. What is the concentration of alcohol in the solution now?

   (a) 20%   (b) $16\dfrac{2}{3}\%$

   (c) $12\dfrac{1}{2}\%$ (d) $33\dfrac{1}{3}\%$

7. p is six times as large as q. The percent that q is less than p, is :

   (a) $16\dfrac{2}{3}$ (b) 60

   (c) $83\dfrac{1}{3}$ (d) 90

8. In a class, the no. of boys is more than the no. of girls by 12% of the total strength. The ratio of boys to girls is :
   (a) 15 : 11   (b) 11 : 14
   (c) 14 : 11   (d) 8 : 11

9. In some quantity of ghee, 60% is pure ghee and 40% is vanaspati. If 10 kg of pure ghee is added, then the

strength of vanaspati ghee becomes 20%. The original quantity was :

(a) 10 kg   (b) 15 kg

(c) 20 kg   (d) 25 kg

10. The ratio of salary of a worker in July to that in June was $2\dfrac{1}{2} : 2\dfrac{1}{4}$, by what % the salary of July more than salary of June. Also find by what %, salary of June was less than that of July.

(a) $11\dfrac{1}{9}\%$ and 10%

(b) 10% and $11\dfrac{1}{9}\%$

(c) Both 10%

(d) Both $11\dfrac{1}{9}\%$

11. In an examination 80% of student passed in English 85% in mathematics and 75% in both English and mathematics. If 40 student failed in both the subject find total number of students.

(a) 350   (b) 400

(c) 450   (d) 600

12. The monthly salary of Shahid and Kareena together is $ 28, 000. The salary of Shahid and Kareena is increased by 25% and 12.5% respectively then the new salary of Kareena becomes 120% of the new salary of Shahid. The new (or increased) salary of Shahid is :

(a) $ 15,000

(b) $ 18,000

(c) $ 14,000

(d) $ 16,000

Hints & Solution

1. **(a)** Use Short Approach -2

2. **(b)** Let the number be x. Then,
% error
$$= \dfrac{6x - x/6}{6x} \times 100$$
$$= \dfrac{35}{36} \times 100 = 97.2\%$$

3. **(a)** Use Short Approach -11

4. **(b)** $5 + 10\% = 5.50$
$10 + 10\% = 11$
$11 + 10\% = 12.10$

5. **(b)** Use Shortcut Approach - 4

6. **(b)** Alcohol in solution
$= 20\%$ of $50l = 10l$
Concentration of alcohol in new solution
$$= \dfrac{10}{60} \times 100 = 16\dfrac{2}{3}\%$$

7. **(c)** Use Shortcut Approach - 1

8. **(c)**

Boys	Girls	Total
14	11	25
56	44	100

⤶⑫⤷

Since out of 100 students number of boys are greater than the numbers of girls by 12 i.e., 12%.

Alternatively:

Let the number of boy and girls be x and y respectively then $(x-y)$

$$= \frac{12\times(x+y)}{100} \Rightarrow \frac{x}{y} = \frac{14}{11}$$

9. (a) Let the original quantity be x kg. Vanaspati ghee in x kg

$$= \left(\frac{40}{100}x\right) \text{kg}$$

$$= \left(\frac{2x}{5}\right) \text{kg}.$$

Now, $\dfrac{\dfrac{2x}{5}}{x+10} = \dfrac{20}{100}$

$$\Leftrightarrow \frac{2x}{5x+50} = \frac{1}{5}$$

$$\Leftrightarrow 5x = 50 \Leftrightarrow x = 10 \,\text{kg}.$$

10. (a) Let the salary of July be

$$₹ \frac{5}{2}x$$

and the salary of June be

$$₹ \frac{9}{4}x.$$

Required percentages

$$= \frac{\dfrac{5}{2}x - \dfrac{9}{4}x}{\dfrac{9}{4}x} \times 100 \quad \text{and}$$

$$\frac{\dfrac{5}{2}x - \dfrac{9}{4}x}{\dfrac{5}{2}x} \times 100$$

$$= \frac{100}{9}\% \text{ and } \frac{100}{10}\%$$

$$= 11\frac{1}{9}\% \text{ and } 10\%$$

11. (b) $n(E) = 80\%, n(m) = 85\%$

$n(\varepsilon \cap m) = 75\%$

$n(\varepsilon \cup m) = 80 + 85 - 75$
$= 90.$

Now, $x \times \dfrac{(100-75)}{100} = 90$

$\Rightarrow \quad x = 360.$

$\therefore \quad$ Total student $= 360 + 40$
$= 400$

12. (a)
$$\begin{array}{cc} \text{S} & \text{K} \\ \begin{pmatrix} 15,000 & 18,000 \\ 12,000 & 16,000 \end{pmatrix} \end{array}$$

going in the reverse direction.

Please option (a) is correct

Alternatively :

$$\begin{array}{cc} \text{Shahid} & \text{Kareena} \end{array}$$

$$25\% \begin{pmatrix} 4x & \dfrac{48x}{9} \\ 5x & 6x \end{pmatrix}$$

$$\xrightarrow{+120\%}$$

$\Rightarrow$ Initially

$$S:K = 4x : \frac{48x}{9} = 3:4$$

$\Rightarrow$ Shahid's initial salary
$= \$\, 12,000$

Shahid's changed salary $= \$\, 15000$

Profit, Loss and Discount

If an item is bought at the rate of X items for a rupee, then the number of items sold for a rupee in order to gain x% is $\left[X \left(\dfrac{100}{100+x} \right) \right]$.

1. A man bought toffees at the rate of 15 for a rupee and sold them at the rate of 12 for a rupee. His gain percent is
   (a) 20%
   (b) 25%
   (c) 33.33%
   (d) None of these

Sol. (b) Item rate sold price $= X \left[\dfrac{100}{100+x} \right]$

$$12 = 15 \left[\dfrac{100}{100+x} \right]$$

$$12\,[100+x] = 1500$$

$$[100+x] = \dfrac{1500}{12}$$

$$x = \dfrac{1500-1200}{12}$$

$$x = \dfrac{300}{12} = 25\%$$

2. A fruit seller buys lemons at 2 for a rupee and sells them at 5 for three rupees. What is his gain percent?
   (a) 10%   (b) 15%   (c) 20%   (d) 25%

Sol. (c) Item rate sold price $= x \left[\dfrac{100}{100+x} \right]$

$$\dfrac{5}{3} = 2 \left[\dfrac{100}{100+x} \right]$$

$$(100 + x) = \left[\frac{200}{5/3}\right]$$

$$x = \frac{600 - 500}{5} = \frac{100}{5} = 20\%$$

⊕ Shortcut Approach - 2

If a man purchases 'a' items for ₹ 'b' and sells 'c' items for ₹ 'd', then the gain or loss [depending upon the respective (+ve) or (–ve) sign in the final result] made by him is $\left[\dfrac{ad - bc}{bc} \times 100\right]\%$

3. A person purchased 11 articles for ₹ 10 and at 10 articles for ₹11. Find the gain percentage.
    (a) 22% (b) 20%
    (c) 1% (d) 21%

Sol. **(d)** Profit or loss

$$= \left[\frac{ad - bc}{bc} \times 100\%\right] = \left[\frac{11 \times 11 - 10 \times 10}{10 \times 10} \times 100\right] \Rightarrow 21\%$$

⊕ Shortcut Approach - 3

When there are two successive profits of x% and y %, then the resultant profit per cent is given by $\left(x + y + \dfrac{xy}{100}\right)$.

4. A sells a cycle to B at 20% profit. Then B sells it to C at 25% profit. If C pays ₹ 225, then what is the cost price of cycle for A?
    (a) ₹100 (b) ₹125 (c) ₹150 (d) ₹175

Sol. **(c)** Resultant profit

$$= \left[x + y + \frac{x.y}{100}\right] = \left[20 + 25 + \frac{20 \times 25}{100}\right]$$

$$= 50\%$$

$$\therefore \quad C.P. = \left(\frac{100}{100 + P}\right) \times S \cdot P = \left(\frac{100}{100 + 50}\right) \times 225 = \frac{100}{150} \times 225$$

$$C.P. = ₹150$$

⊕ Shortcut Approach - 4

If a dishonest trader professes to sell his items at CP but uses false measurement, then

$$\% \text{ gain } = \frac{\text{True measurement} - \text{False measurement}}{\text{False measurement}} \times 100$$

5. A retailer profess to sell his goods at cost price. If using a false weight, he still gains 25%, find the weight he uses in place of 1 kg.

   (a) 200 g   (b) 600 g   (c) 700 g   (d) 800 g

Sol. (d) $\quad \text{Profit } \% = \left[\dfrac{\text{True weight} - \text{False weight}}{\text{False weight}}\right] \times 100$

$$25 = \left[\frac{1000 - \text{False weight}}{\text{False weight}}\right] \times 100$$

25 false weight = 100000 − 100 false weight
125 false weight = 100000
false weight = 800 gram.

⊕ Shortcut Approach - 5

If a shopkeeper sells his goods at x% profit and uses a measurement which is y% less, then

Total percentage profit

$$= \frac{\% \text{ profit} + \% \text{ less in wt}}{100 - \% \text{ less in wt}} \times 100$$

6. A trader sells wheat at 20% profit and uses weight 20% less than the actual measure. His gain percent is

   (a) 50%   (b) 25%
   (c) 10%   (d) 15%

Sol. (a) Total percentage profit

$$= \left[\frac{\text{Profit}\% - \text{loss in wt}\%}{100 - \text{loss in wt}\%}\right] \times 100$$

$$= \left(\frac{20 + 20}{100 - 20}\right) \times 100 \ = \frac{40}{80} \times 100 = 50\% \left(\text{Profit}\right)$$

⊕ Shortcut Approach - 6

If the shopkeeper sells his goods at x% loss on cost price but uses y gm

instead of z gm, then his % profit or loss is $\left[100 - x\ \dfrac{z}{y} - \right]100$ (according as

the sign is +ve or –ve.)

7. A merchant professes to sell goods at the loss of 5% but uses weight of 900 grams in place of one kilogram, what is his profit percent?

    (a)   5%   (b) $5\dfrac{5}{19}\%$

    (c)   6%   (d)   10%

Sol. (b)   Profit % $= \left[100 - x\ \dfrac{z}{y}\right] - 100$

$$= \left[[100 - 5\ \dfrac{1000}{900} - 100\right] = 95 \times \dfrac{10}{9} - 100$$

$$\Rightarrow \quad \dfrac{950 - 900}{9} = \dfrac{50}{9} = 5\dfrac{5}{9}\%$$

⊕ Shortcut Approach - 7

A dishonest dealer sells the goods at x% loss on cost price but uses y%

less weight, then his percentage profit or loss is $\left[\dfrac{y - x}{100 - y} \times 100\right]$

(according as the sign is +ve or –ve.)

8. A dishonest dealer sells his goods at 10% loss on cost price and uses 30% less weight. What is his profit or loss percent?

    (a) $28\dfrac{4}{7}\%\,\text{loss}$ (b) $28\dfrac{4}{7}\%\,\text{profit}$

    (c) $26\dfrac{4}{7}\%\,\text{profit}$ (d) $26\dfrac{4}{7}\%\,\text{loss}$

Sol. (b) $\left(\text{Profit or loss} = \dfrac{y - x}{100 - y} \times 100\right)$

$$= \left(\dfrac{30 - 10}{100 - 30}\right) \times 100 = \dfrac{2000}{70} = 28\dfrac{4}{7}\%\,(\text{profit})$$

Shortcut Approach - 8

If a seller uses 'X' gm in place of one kg (1000 gm) to sell his goods and gains a profit of x% on cost price, then his actual gain or loss percentage

is $\left[(100+x)\left[\dfrac{1000}{X}\right]-100\right]$ (according as the sign is +ve or –ve.)

9. A merchant professes to sell goods at 20% profit but uses weight of 800 grams in place of a kilogram. What is his actual profit percent?
   (a) 20%   (b) 25%   (c) 50%   (d) 33.3%

Sol. **(c)** Profit or loss $= (100+x)\left[\dfrac{1000}{X}\right]-100$

$$= (100+20)\left[\dfrac{1000}{800}\right]-100 \quad = \dfrac{120\times5-400}{4} = \dfrac{200}{4}$$

$$= 50\% \ (\text{Profit})$$

Shortcut Approach - 9

A man purchases a certain number of articles at x a rupee and the same number at y a rupee. He mixes them together and sells them at z a rupee.

then his gain or loss % $= \left[\dfrac{2xy}{z(x+y)}-1\right]\times100$ (according as the sign is

+ve or –ve .)

10. A man purchases a certain number of oranges at 4 a rupee and the same number of oranges at 5 a rupee. He mixes them together and sells them at 4 a rupee. What is his gain or loss percent?

   (a) $10\dfrac{1}{9}\%$ loss   (b) $10\dfrac{1}{9}\%$ gain

   (c) $11\dfrac{1}{9}\%$ gain   (d) $11\dfrac{1}{9}\%$ loss

Sol. **(c)** Profit or loss $= \left[\dfrac{2xy}{z(x+y)}-1\right]\times100$

$$= \left[\dfrac{2\times4\times5}{4(4+5)}-1\right]\times100$$

$$= \left[\dfrac{40-36}{36}\right]\times100 = \dfrac{4}{36}\times100 = \dfrac{100}{9} = 11\dfrac{1}{9}\% \ (\text{Profit})$$

Shortcut Approach - 10

If a tradesman marks his goods at x% above his cost price and allows

purchasers a discount of y% for cash, then there is $\left(x - y - \dfrac{xy}{100}\right)\%$

profit or loss according to +ve or –ve sign respectively.

Note : When x = y, then formula becomes $-\dfrac{x^2}{100}$

– ve sign indicates that there will be always loss.

11. What is the percentage discount (approximately) that a merchant can offer on his marked price so that he ends up selling at no profit or loss, if he initially marked his goods up by 40%?
     (a)   33.5 %   (b) 28.5%
     (c)   60%   (d) No discount

Sol. **(b)**   Let the discount % = y %

$$\text{Profit or loss} = \left(x - y - \frac{xy}{100}\right)$$

$$0 = \left(40 - y - \frac{40y}{100}\right)$$

$$y + \frac{40y}{100} = 40$$

$$y = \frac{4000}{140} = 28.5\%$$

Shortcut Approach - 11

If a man buys two items A and B for ₹ P, and sells one item A so as to loss $x\%$ and the other item B so as to gain $y\%$, and on the whole he neither gains nor loses, then

(i) the cost of the item A is $\left(\dfrac{Py}{x+y}\right)$ and

(ii) the cost of the item B is $\left(\dfrac{Px}{x+y}\right)$.

12. A man purchased two cows for ₹500. He sells the first at 12% loss and the second at 8% gain. In this bargain he neither gains nor loses. Find the selling price of each cow.

(a) ₹176, ₹324　　　　　(b) ₹324, ₹350
(c) ₹150, ₹300　　　　　(d) ₹184, ₹276

Sol. (a) The cost of first cow is $= \left(\dfrac{Py}{x+y} \right)$

$$= \left(\dfrac{500 \times 8}{8+12} \right) = \dfrac{4000}{20} = 200$$

The cost of second cow is $= \left(\dfrac{Px}{x+y} \right)$

$$= \left(\dfrac{500 \times 12}{12+8} \right) = \dfrac{6000}{20} = 300$$

So, selling price of first cow

$$\text{S.P.} = \dfrac{200(100-12)}{100} = ₹\,176$$

$$\text{Selling price of second cow} = \dfrac{300 \times (100+8)}{100} = ₹\,324$$

Shortcut Approach - 12

By selling a certain item at the rate of 'X' items a rupee, a man loses x%. If he wants to gain y%, then the number of items should be sold for a rupee is $\left[\left(\dfrac{100-x}{100+y} \right) X \right]$

13. By selling 9 articles for a rupee, a man incurred a loss of 4%. To make a gain of 44%, the number of articles to be sold for a rupee is

(a) 5　　　　(b) 3　　　　(c) 4　　　　(d) 6

Sol. (d) Number of items

$$= \left[\left(\dfrac{100-x}{100+y} \right) X \right] = \left[\dfrac{100-4}{100+44} \right] \times 9 = 6$$

⊕ Shortcut Approach - 13

When each of the two commodities is sold at the same price ₹ A, and a profit of P % is made on the first and a loss of L% is made on the second, then the percentage gain or loss is $\dfrac{100(P-L)-2PL}{(100+P)+(100-L)}$ according to the +ve or –ve sign.

14. A dealer sold two T.V. sets for ₹7400 each.

    On one he gained 10% and on the other he lost 10%. The dealers loss or gain in the transaction is

    (a) no profit, no loss   (b) 1% gain

    (c) 0.1% loss   (d) 1% loss

Sol. (d) % Profit $= \dfrac{100(P-L)-2PL}{(100+P)+(100-L)}$

$$= \dfrac{100(10-10)-2\times10\times10}{(100+10)+(100-10)} = \dfrac{-200}{200} = -1$$

So, negative sign shows the 1% loss in the transaction.

⊕ Shortcut Approach - 14

If a dealer sells an item for ₹ A, making a profit of x%, and he sells another item at a loss of y%, and on the whole he makes neither profit nor loss, then the cost of the second table is ₹ $\left[A\left(\dfrac{100}{100+x}\right)\dfrac{x}{y}\right]$.

15. A dealer sells a table for ₹400, making a profit of 25%. He sells another table at a loss of 10%, and on the whole he makes neither profit nor loss. What did the second table cost him?

    (a) ₹600   (b) ₹800

    (c) ₹700   (d) ₹900

Sol. (b) The cost of second table $= A\left[\dfrac{100}{100+x}\right]\dfrac{x}{y}$

$$= 400\left[\dfrac{100}{100+25}\right]\dfrac{25}{10} = ₹\,800$$

Shortcut Approach - 15

If a person buys an article with x per cent discount on the marked price and sells the article with y per cent profit on the marked price, then his profit per cent on the price he buys the article is given by

$$\left(\frac{x+y}{100-x}\right) \times 100 \text{ per cent.}$$

16. Sweta bought an article with 20% discount on the labelled price. She sold the article with 8% profit on the labelled price. What was her percent profit of the price she bought?
  (a) 35% (b) 25% (c) 20% (d) 15%

Sol. (a) $\text{Profit} = \left[\dfrac{x+y}{100-x}\right] \times 100$

$$= \left[\frac{20+8}{100-20}\right] \times 100 = \frac{2800}{80} = 35\%$$

Shortcut Approach - 16

A certain company declares x per cent discount for wholesale buyers. If a person buys articles from the company for ₹ A after getting discount. He fixed up the selling price of the article in such a way that he earned a profit y% on original company price. Then the total selling price is given

by $₹\, A\left(\dfrac{100+y}{100-x}\right).$

17. Surdeep bought a machinery for ₹800 after getting a discount of 20% from the company. He fixed up the selling price of garments in such a way that he earned a profit of 10% on the original company price. Find the selling price of machinery for Surdeep?
  (a) ₹900   (b) ₹1000
  (c) ₹1100   (d) ₹1200

Sol. (c) $\text{Total selling price} = A\left[\dfrac{100+y}{100-x}\right]$

$$= 800\left[\frac{100+10}{100-20}\right] = \frac{800 \times 110}{80} = ₹\,1100$$

⊕ Shortcut Approach - 17

A businessman marks an article at ₹ A and allows x % discount (on the marked price). He gains y %. If the cost price of the article is ₹ B, then the selling price of the article can be calculated from the equation given below

$$\text{Selling price} = \frac{A(100-x)}{100} = \frac{B(100+y)}{100}$$

i.e. $$\frac{\text{M.P}(100-\text{Dis}\%)}{100} = \frac{\text{CP}(100+\text{Profit}\%)}{100}$$

Note : Remember discount is given on marked price, and gain is calculated on the cost price.

18. Raman expects 20% profit by selling a fan. If the allows 40% discount on marked price then his cost price is what percent of marked price?

   (a)   40%   (b)   60%

   (c)   50%   (d)   100%

Sol. **(c)**   Selling price $= \dfrac{A(100-x)}{100} = \dfrac{B(100+y)}{100}$

$$\frac{A(100-40)}{100} = \frac{B(100+20)}{100}$$

$$A\,60 = B\,120$$

So, $\quad \dfrac{B}{A} = \dfrac{60}{120} = \dfrac{1}{2}$

$$\frac{B}{A} \times 100\% = \frac{1}{2} \times 100 = 50\%$$

Hence, cost price is 50% of marked price.

⊕ Shortcut Approach - 18

A person sells articles at ₹ A each after giving x% discount on marked price. Had he not given the discount, he would have earned a profit of y% on the cost price. Then the cost price of each article is given by ₹

$$\left[\frac{100^2\, A}{(100-x)(100+y)} \right].$$

19. A person sells a T.V at 9600 after giving a discount of 20%. If he sells the T.V at marked price then his profit is 50%. What is the cost price of T.V?

(a) ₹10000   (b) ₹12000 (c) ₹8000   (d) ₹9000

Sol. (c) Cost price of T.V. $= \left[\dfrac{(100)^2\, A}{(100-x)(100+y)} \right]$

$$= \left[\dfrac{(100)^2 \times 9600}{(100-20)(100+50)} \right]$$

$$= \dfrac{96000000}{12000} = ₹\, 8000$$

⊕ Shortcut Approach - 19

A shopkeeper sold an article for ₹ A after giving x% discount on the labelled price and made y% profit on the cost price. Had he not given the discount, the percentage profit would have been $\left[\dfrac{x+y}{100-x} \times 100 \right]$ **per cent.**

20. A person allows 30% discount on his goods and still gains 40%. If he sells a fan on marked price then what is percentage of profit?

(a) 100%   (b) 50%   (c) 60%   (d) 70%

Sol. (a) $\text{Profit} = \left[\dfrac{x+y}{100-x} \times 100 \right]\%$

$$= \left[\left(\dfrac{30+40}{100-30} \right) \times 100 \right]\%$$

$$= \left[\dfrac{70}{70} \times 100 \right]\% = 100\,\%$$

Exercise

1. Two motor cars were sold for ₹ 9,900 each, gaining 10% on one and losing 10% on the other. The gain or loss per cent in the whole transaction is :
   (a) Neither loss no gain
   (b) $\dfrac{1}{99}$ % gain
   (c) $\dfrac{100}{99}$ % profit
   (d) 1% loss

2. A dishonest dealer sells his goods at the cost price but still earns a profit of 25% by underweighing. What weight does he use for a kg?
   (a) 750 g   (b) 800 g
   (c) 825 g   (d) 850 g

3. Three successive discounts of 10%, 12% and 15% amount to a single discount of:
   (a) 36.28 %   (b) 34.68%
   (c) 37 %   (d) 32.68%

4. A man sold two steel chairs for ₹ 500 each. On one he gains 20% and on other, he loses 12%. How much does he gain or lose in the whole transaction?
   (a) 1.5% gain
   (b) 2% gain
   (c) 1.5% loss
   (d) 2% loss

5. $\dfrac{2}{3}$ of a consignment was sold at 6 % profit and the rest at a loss of 3 %. If there was an overall profit of ₹ 540, find the value of the consignment.
   (a) ₹15,000   (b) ₹18000
   (c) ₹35000   (d) ₹45000

6. A person sells 36 oranges per rupee and suffers a loss of 4%. Find how many oranges per rupee to be sold to have a gain of 8%?
   (a) 30   (b) 31
   (c) 32   (d) 33

7. Two electronic musical instruments were purchased for ₹ 8000. The first was sold at a profit of 40% and the second at loss of 40%. If the sale price was the same in both the cases, what was the cost price of two electronic musical instruments?
   (a) ₹ 2000, ₹ 5000
   (b) ₹ 2200, ₹ 5500
   (c) ₹ 2400, ₹ 5000
   (d) ₹ 2400, ₹ 5600

8. Arun bought toffees at 6 for a rupee. How many for a rupee he should sell to gain 20%?
   (a) 3   (b) 4
   (c) 5
   (d) can't be determined

9. A firm of readymade garments makes both men's and women's shirts. Its average profit is 6% of the sales. Its profit in men's shirts average 8% of the sales and women's shirts comprise 60% of the output. The average profit per sale rupee in women shirts is
   (a) 0.0466   (b) 0.0666
   (c) 0.0166
   (d) None of these

10. For a certain article, if discount is 25%, the profit is 25%. If the discount is 10%, then the profit is

(a) 10% (b) 20%
(c) 35% (d) 50%

11. By selling 66 metres of cloth a person gains the cost price of 22 metres. Find the gain per cent.

(a) 22% (b) $22\dfrac{1}{2}\%$

(c) 33% (d) $33\dfrac{1}{3}\%$

12. A fruit seller declares that he sells fruits at the cost price. However, he uses a weight of 450 g instead of 500 g. His percentage profit is :

(a) 10% (b) $11\dfrac{1}{9}\%$

(c) 12% (d) $12\dfrac{2}{9}\%$

Hints & Solution

1. **(d)** If any two transactions of SP is the same and also gain % and loss % are same then there is always a loss

$\therefore$ loss % =

$$\left(\dfrac{\text{Common gain or loss\%}}{10}\right)^2$$

$$=\left(\dfrac{10}{10}\right)^2=1\%$$

2. **(b)** Use Short Approach - 4

3. **(d)** Applying successive discounts of 10%, 12% and 15% on 100, we get

$100 \times 0.9 \times 0.88 \times 0.85$
$= 67.32$

$\Rightarrow$ Single discount
$= 100 - 67.32 = 32.68\%$

4. **(a)** Use Short Approach -13

5. **(b)** Value of consignment

$$=\dfrac{540 \times 100}{\dfrac{2}{3}\times 6 + \dfrac{1}{3}(-3)}$$

$$=\dfrac{540 \times 100}{4-1}=₹\,18{,}000$$

6. **(c)** Use Short Approach - 12

7. **(d)** Here, $SP_1 = SP_2$
$\Rightarrow 140\,CP_1 = 60\,CP_2$

$$\Rightarrow \dfrac{CP_1}{CP_2}=\dfrac{6}{14}=\dfrac{3}{7}$$

$$\therefore\ CP_1 = \dfrac{3}{(3+7)} \times 8000$$

$$=₹\,2400$$

and $CP_2 = 8000 - 2400 = ₹\,5600$

8. **(c)** Use Short Approach - 12

9. **(a)** Women's shirt comprise 60% of the output.

$\therefore$ Men's shirts comprise $(100 - 60) = 40\%$ of the out put.

$\therefore$ Average profit from men's shirt
$= 8\%$ of 40
$= 3.2$

Overall average profit

$= 6$ out of 100

$\therefore$ Average profit from women's shirts $= 2.8$ out of 60 i.e. 0.0466 out of each shirt.

10. (d) For same article,

$$\frac{100 - d_1}{100 - d_2} = \frac{100 + g_1}{100 + g_2}$$

$$\Rightarrow \quad \frac{100 - 25}{100 - 10} = \frac{100 + 25}{100 + g_2}$$

$$\Rightarrow \quad \frac{75}{90} = \frac{125}{100 + g_2}$$

$$\Rightarrow \quad 100 + g_2 = \frac{90 \times 125}{75}$$

$$= 150$$

$$\Rightarrow \quad g_2 = 50\%$$

11. (d) Let C.P. of one metre of cloth $= ₹\ 1$

then C.P. of 66 metres of cloth $= ₹\ 66$

Gain $=$ C.P. of 22 metres $= ₹\ 22$

% gain

$$= \frac{22}{66} \times 100 = 33\frac{1}{3}\%$$

Shortcut method :

If on selling 'x' articles, a man gains equal to the C.P. of 'y' articles, then % gain

$$= \frac{y}{x} \times 100$$

$$\therefore \% \text{ gain} = \frac{22}{66} \times 100$$

$$= 33\frac{1}{3}\%$$

12. (b) Use Short Approach - 8

Simple Interest & Compound Interest and Instalments

If a sum is put at SI at a certain rate r_1 % for t_1 year, again at rate r_2% at t_2 years and then so on, then

$$\text{Principal} = \frac{\text{Interest} \times 100}{t_1 r_1 + t_2 r_2 + t_3 r_3 + \dots}$$

1. The rate of interest for the first 2 years is 3% per annum, for the next 3 years is 8% per annum and for the period beyond 5 years 10% per annum. If a man gets ₹ 1520 as a simple interest for 6 years, how much money did he deposit?
   (a) 4000   (b) 3800   (c) 3900   (d) 4100

Sol. (b) Detail Method: Let his deposit = ₹ 100

Interest for first 2 years = ₹ 6

Interest for next 3 years = ₹ 24

Interest for the last year = ₹ 10

Total interest = ₹ 40

When interest is ₹ 40, deposited amount is ₹ 100

∴ when interest is ₹ 1520, deposited amount

$$= \frac{100}{40} \times 1520 = ₹\ 3800$$

Direct formula : $\text{Principal} = \dfrac{\text{Interest} \times 100}{t_1 r_1 + t_2 r_2 + t_3 r_3 + \dots}$

$$= \frac{1520 \times 100}{2 \times 3 + 3 \times 8 + 1 \times 10} = \frac{1520 \times 100}{40} = ₹\ 3800$$

Note: Here $t_3 = 6 - 5 = 1$ year

2. Manish borrowed some money at the rate of 7 per cent per annum for the first three years, 9 per cent per annum for the next six years and 10 per cent per annum for the period beyond nine years. If the total interest paid by him at the end of fifteen years is ₹ 4050, how much money did he borrow?
   (a) ₹ 2800   (b) ₹ 3600   (c) ₹ 3000   (d) ₹ 3500

Sol. (c)

$$\text{Principal} = \frac{\text{Interest} \times 100}{t_1 r_1 + t_2 r_2 + t_3 r_3 + \dots}$$

$$= \frac{4050 \times 100}{7 \times 3 + 9 \times 6 + 6 \times 10} = \frac{4050 \times 100}{135} = ₹\, 3000.$$

A sum was put at SI at a certain rate for t years. Had it been put at x% higher rate, it would have fetched ₹ 'A' more, then the sum is

$$₹ \left[\frac{A \times 100}{t \times x} \right] \text{ or } \frac{\text{More interest} \times 100}{\text{Time} \times \text{More rate}}.$$

3.   A sum was put at SI at a certain rate for 5 years. Had it been put at 5% higher rate, it would have fetched ₹ 500 more. Find the sum.
   (a)   ₹ 2500   (b) ₹ 2000   (c)   ₹ 1500   (d) ₹ 1800

Sol. (b)

$$\text{Sum} = \left[\frac{A \times 100}{t \times x} \right] = \left[\frac{500 \times 100}{5 \times 5} \right] = ₹\, 2000.$$

A sum was put at SI at a certain rate for t years. Had it been put at x% lower rate, it would have fetched ₹ A less, then the sum is

$$₹ \left[\frac{A \times 100}{t \times x} \right] \text{ or } \frac{\text{Less interest} \times 100}{\text{Time} \times \text{Less rate}}.$$

4.   A sum was put at SI at a certain rate for 5 years. Had it been put at 2% lower rate, it would have fetched ₹ 150 less. Find the sum.
   (a)   ₹ 1000   (b) ₹ 1500   (c)   ₹ 1800   (d) ₹ 2000

Sol. (b)

$$\text{Sum} = \left[\frac{A \times 100}{t \times x} \right] = \left[\frac{150 \times 100}{5 \times 2} \right] = ₹\, 1500$$

If a person deposits ₹ x_1 in a bank at r_1% per annum and ₹ x_2 in another bank at r_2% per annum, then the rate of interest for the whole sum is

$$\left[\frac{x_1 r_1 + x_2 r_2}{x_1 + x_2} \right].$$

5.   A man deposits ₹ 1350 in a bank at 5% per annum and ₹ 1150 in another bank at 6% per annum. Find the rate of interest for the whole sum.
   (a)   5.40%   (b) 6.40%   (c)   5.46%   (d) 11%

Sol. (c)

$$\text{Rate of Interest} = \left[\frac{x_1 r_1 + x_2 r_2}{x_1 + x_2} \right]$$

$$= \left[\frac{1350 \times 5 + 1150 \times 6}{1350 + 1150}\right] = \left[\frac{6750 + 6900}{2500}\right] = 5.46\%$$

Shortcut Approach - 5

A certain sum is invested for certain time. It amounts to ₹ A_1 at $r_1\%$ per annum. But when invested at $r_2\%$ per annum, it amounts to ₹ A_2, then the

sum is given by ₹ $\left[\dfrac{A_2 r_1 - A_1 r_2}{r_1 - r_2}\right]$ and the time is given

by $\left[\dfrac{A_1 - A_2}{A_2 r_1 - A_1 r_2}\right] \times 100$ years.

6. A certain sum is invested for certain time. It amounts to ₹ 500 at 8% per annum. But when invested at 3 % per annum, it amounts to ₹ 200. Find the sum.
   (a) ₹ 20   (b) ₹ 50   (c) ₹ 25   (d) ₹ 35

Sol (a)

$$\text{Sum} = \left[\frac{A_2 r_1 - A_1 r_2}{r_1 - r_2}\right] = \left[\frac{200 \times 8 - 500 \times 3}{8 - 3}\right]$$

$$= \frac{100}{5} = \quad ₹ \, 20$$

7. A certain sum is invested for certain time. It amounts to ₹ 450 at 7% per annum. But when invested at 5% per annum, it amounts to ₹ 350. Find the time.
   (a) 50 years   (b) 60 years   (c) 45 years   (d) 40 years

Sol. (a)

$$\text{Time} = \left[\frac{A_1 - A_2}{A_2 r_1 - A_1 r_2}\right] \times 100$$

$$= \left[\frac{450 - 350}{350 \times 7 - 450 \times 5}\right] \times 100 = \left[\frac{100 \times 100}{200}\right] = 50 \text{ years.}$$

Shortcut Approach - 6

If a certain sum of money at simple interest amounts to ₹ A_1 in t_1 years

and to ₹ A_2 in t_2 years, then the sum is given by $\left[\dfrac{A_2 t_1 - A_1 t_2}{t_1 - t_2}\right]$.

8. A certain sum of money amounts to ₹ 625 in 4 years and to ₹ 680 in 5 years. Find the sum.

   (a) ₹ 505   (b) ₹ 305   (c) ₹ 405   (d)   ₹ 504

Sol. (c)

$$\text{Sum} = \left[\frac{A_2 t_1 - A_1 t_2}{t_1 - t_2}\right] = \left[\frac{680 \times 4 - 625 \times 5}{4 - 5}\right]$$

$$= \left[\frac{2720 - 3125}{-1}\right] = ₹\,405$$

⊕ Shortcut Approach - 7

If a sum of money becomes 'n' times in 't' years at a simple interest, then the time in which it will amount to 'm' times itself is given by

$$\left[\frac{m-1}{n-1}\right] t \ \text{ years.}$$

9. A sum of money becomes 5 times itself in 5 years at a simple interest. In how many years will it amount to 7 times itself?

   (a) 7 years   (b) 6 years 6 months
   (c) 6 years   (d) 7 years 6 months

Sol. (d)

$$\text{Time} = \left[\frac{m-1}{n-1}\right] t \ \text{years} \ = \left[\frac{7-1}{5-1}\right] \times 5 \ \text{years}$$

$$= \frac{6}{4} \times 5 \ \text{years} \ = 7.5 \ \text{years} = 7 \ \text{years, 6 months.}$$

⊕ Shortcut Approach - 8

If the difference between the simple interest received from two different banks on Rs X for t years is ₹ I_d, then the difference between their rates

is given by $\left[\dfrac{I_d \times 100}{X \times t}\right]$ per cent.

10. The difference between the interest received from two different banks on ₹ 600 for 6 years is ₹ 72. Find the difference between their rates.

    (a) 3%   (b) 3.5%   (c) 4%   (d) 2%

Sol. (d)

$$\text{Difference between their rates} = \left[\dfrac{I_d \times 100}{X \times t}\right]$$

$$= \left[\dfrac{72 \times 100}{600 \times 6}\right] = 2\%$$

Shortcut Approach - 9

A certain sum of money at SI amounts to ₹ A_1 in t years at r% per annum, then the time in which it will amount to ₹ A_2 at the same rate of interest

is given by $\left[\dfrac{A_2}{A_1}\left(t + \dfrac{100}{r}\right) - \dfrac{100}{r}\right]$ years.

11. A certain sum of money amounts to ₹ 5000 in 5 years at 10% per annum. In how many years will it amount to ₹ 6000 at the same rate?
   (a) 8 years   (b) 6 years   (c) 10 years   (d) 9 years

Sol. (a)

$$\text{Time} = \left[\dfrac{A_2}{A_1}\left(t + \dfrac{100}{r}\right) - \dfrac{100}{r}\right]$$

$$= \left[\dfrac{6000}{5000}\left(5 + \dfrac{100}{10}\right) - \dfrac{100}{10}\right] = \left[\dfrac{6}{5} \times 15 - 10\right] = 8 \text{ years.}$$

Shortcut Approach - 10

If a sum of money becomes 'n' times at the simple interest rate of r% per annum, then it will become 'm' times at the simple interest rate of

$\left[\left(\dfrac{m-1}{n-1}\right) \times r\right]$ per cent

12. A sum of money becomes two times at the simple interest rate of 2% per annum. At what rate per cent will it become five fold?
   (a) 10%   (b) 8%   (c) 6%   (d) 9%

Sol. (b)

$$\text{Rate of Interest} = \left[\left(\dfrac{m-1}{n-1}\right) \times r\right]$$

$$= \left[\left(\dfrac{5-1}{2-1}\right) \times 2\right] = 8\%$$

Shortcut Approach - 11

₹ X is divided into two parts such that if one part be invested at r_1% and the other at r_2%, the annual interest from both the investments is ₹ A.

Then the first part is given by $\left[\dfrac{100A - r_2 X}{r_1 - r_2} \right]$.

13. Aniket deposited two parts of a sum of ₹ 25000 in different banks at the rates of 15% per annum and 18% per annum respectively. In one year he got ₹4050 as the total interest. What was the amount deposited at the rate of 18% per annum?

   (a) ₹ 9000   (b) ₹ 18000

   (c) ₹ 15000   (d) None of these

Sol. (d)

Applying the formula, we have the amount deposited at the rate of 15% per annum

$$= \dfrac{100 \times 4050 - 18 \times 25000}{15 - 18} = ₹15000$$

∴ Amount deposited at the rate of 18% per annum

$$= ₹ 25000 - ₹15000 = ₹10000.$$

⊕ Shortcut Approach - 12

Some amount out of ₹ P was lent at r_1% per annum and the remaining at r_2% per annum. If the total simple interest from both the fractions in t years was ₹ 'A' then the sum lent at r_1% per annum was given by ₹

$$\left[\dfrac{100A - P r_2 t}{\left(r_1 - r_2 \right) t} \right]$$

14. Some amount out of ₹ 950 was lent at 6% per annum and the remaining at 4% per annum. If the total simple interest from both the fractions in 5 years was ₹ 200, find the sum lent at 6% per annum.

   (a) ₹ 700   (b) ₹ 100   (c) ₹ 250   (d) ₹ 450

Sol. (b)

$$\text{Sum} = \left[\dfrac{100A - P r_2 t}{(r_1 - r_2)t} \right] = \left[\dfrac{100 \times 200 - 950 \times 4 \times 5}{(6 - 4) \times 5} \right] = ₹100$$

⊕ Shortcut Approach - 13

If a person borrows ₹ X from a bank at simple interest and after t_1 years he paid ₹ x_1 to the bank and at the end of t_2 years from the date of borrowing he paid $\overline{\tau}\, x_2$ to the bank to settle the account, then the rate of interest is

given by $\left[\dfrac{x_1 + x_2 - X}{x_1 t_1 + t_2\left(X - x_1\right)}\right] \times 100\%$

15. Uday borrows ₹ 5000 from a bank at SI. After 5 years he paid ₹ 1700 to the bank and at the end of 5 years from the date borrowing he paid ₹ 3550 to the bank to settle the account. Find the rate of interest.

    (a) 1%   (b) 1.5%   (c) 2%   (d) 10%

Sol. (a)

$$\text{Rate of Interest} = \left[\dfrac{x_1 + x_2 - X}{x_1 t_1 + t_2(X - x_1)}\right] \times 100\%$$

$$= \left[\dfrac{1700 + 3550 - 5000}{1700 \times 5 + 5(5000 - 1700)}\right] \times 100\%$$

$$= \dfrac{250}{25000} \times 100\% = 1\%$$

Shortcut Approach - 14

A person invested $\dfrac{1}{n_1}$ of his capital at $x_1\%$, $\dfrac{1}{n_2}$ at $x_2\%$ and the

remainder $\dfrac{1}{n_3}$ at $x_3\%$. If his annual income is ₹A, the capital is given

by ₹ $\left[\dfrac{A \times 100}{\dfrac{x_1}{n_1} + \dfrac{x_2}{n_2} + \dfrac{x_3}{n_3}}\right]$.

16. Out of a certain sum, $\dfrac{1}{3}$rd is invested at 3%, $\dfrac{1}{6}$th at 6% and the rest at 8%. If the simple interest for 2 years from all these investments amounts to ₹ 600, find the original sum.

    (a) ₹ 5000   (b) ₹ 6000   (c) ₹ 5200   (d) ₹ 5500

Sol. (a)

$$\text{Here A} = \text{Annual income} = ₹\, \dfrac{600}{2} = ₹\, 300$$

$$\text{Original sum} = \left[\frac{A \times 100}{\dfrac{x_1}{n_1} + \dfrac{x_2}{n_2} + \dfrac{x_3}{n_3}}\right] = \left[\frac{300 \times 100}{\dfrac{3}{3} + \dfrac{6}{6} + \dfrac{8}{2}}\right]$$

$$= \left[\frac{30000}{6}\right] = ₹\,5000$$

Shortcut Approach - 15

Let, Amount $= ₹\,A$
   Principal $= ₹\,P$
     Time $= t$ years

$$\text{Rate of interest}\,(r) = n \times 100\left[\left(\frac{A}{P}\right)^{\frac{1}{t} \times n} - 1\right]\%\ \text{per annum.}$$

Where, $n = 1$, when the interest is compounded yearly
$n = 2$, when the interest is compounded half-yearly
$n = 4$, when the interest is compounded quaterly
$n = 12$, when the interest is compounded monthly
If the interest is compounded yearly, then $n = 1$

$$\therefore\ r = 100\left[\left(\frac{A}{P}\right)^{1/t} - 1\right]\%\ \text{per annum}$$

17.   At what rate per cent compound interest will ₹ 625 amount to ₹ 676 in 2 years?
    (a) 3 %   (b) 2 %   (c) 4 %   (d) 5 %

Sol. (c)

$$\text{Rate of Interest} = 100\left[\left(\frac{A}{P}\right)^{1/t} - 1\right]\%$$

$$= 100\left[\left(\frac{676}{625}\right)^{\frac{1}{2}} - 1\right] = 100\left[\frac{26}{25} - 1\right] = 4\%$$

Shortcut Approach - 16

A sum of money, placed at compound interest, becomes n times in t years and m times in x years. We calculate the value of x from the equation given below $\left(n^{1/t} = m^{1/x}\right)$.

18. A sum of money placed at compound interest doubles itself in 6 years. In how many years will it amount to 16 times itself?
    (a) 24 years   (b) 26 years   (c) 22 years   (d) 20 years

Sol. (a)

We can calculate the value of x by the given equation $(n)^{1/t} = (m)^{1/x}$

From question, putting the values of n, m and t

$$\Rightarrow (2)^{1/6} = (16)^{1/x} \Rightarrow (2)^{1/6} = (2)^{4/x}$$

By comparing both side

$$\Rightarrow \left[\frac{1}{6} = \frac{4}{x}\right] \Rightarrow x = 24$$

⊕ Shortcut Approach - 17

If a certain sum becomes 'm' times in 't' years, the rate of compound interest

r is equal to $\left[(m)^{1/t} - 1\right] \times 100.$

19. At what rate per cent will the compound interest, does a sum of money become 27 times in 3 years?
    (a) 100%   (b) 150%   (c) 75%   (d) 200%

Sol. (d)

Rate of compound interest $= \left[(m)^{1/t} - 1\right] \times 100\%$

$$= \left[(27)^{1/3} - 1\right] \times 100\% = \left[(3) - 1\right] \times 100\%$$

$$= 2 \times 100 = 200\%$$

⊕ Shortcut Approach - 18

Let Principal   = P
        Rate   = r% per annum
     Amount   = A and

Note: Time must be given in the form of fraction like $2\frac{1}{2}$ years.

$$\text{Amount (A)} = P\left[1 + \frac{r}{100}\right]^2 \times \left[1 + \frac{\frac{r}{2}}{100}\right]$$

20. On what sum will the compound interest for $2\dfrac{1}{2}$ years at 10% amount to ₹ 6352.50 ?

(a) ₹ 4900   (b) ₹ 5500

(c) ₹ 5000   (d) ₹ 5800

Sol. (c)

$$A = P\left[1+\frac{r}{100}\right]^2 \times \left[1+\frac{\frac{r}{2}}{100}\right]$$

$$\Rightarrow 6352.50 = P\left[1+\frac{10}{100}\right]^2 \times \left[1+\frac{10}{2\times100}\right]$$

$$\Rightarrow 6352.50 \times \left(\frac{10}{11}\right)^2 \times \frac{20}{21} = P \Rightarrow P = ₹\,5000$$

⊕ Shortcut Approach - 19

On a certain sum of money, the difference between compound interest and simple interest for 3 years at r% per annum is given by

$P\left(\dfrac{R}{100}\right)^2\left(\dfrac{R}{100}+3\right)$ and the difference between CI and SI for 2 years =

$$P\left(\frac{R}{100}\right)^2 = \frac{SI \times R}{200}$$

> **Note :** SI and CI are given on the same sum, at the same rate and for the same time duration.

21. Find the difference between the simple and compound interest on ₹ 10000 for 3 years at 3 per cent.

(a) ₹ 27.8   (b) ₹ 27.27

(c) ₹ 37.27   (d) ₹ 37.8

Sol. (b)

$$\text{Difference} = \frac{\text{Sum} \times r^2 (300+r)}{(100)^3}$$

$$= \frac{10000 \times (3)^2 (300+3)}{(100)^3} = 27.27$$

22. On a certain sum of money, the simple interest for 2 years is ₹ 160 at the rate of 5 % per annum. Find the difference in CI and SI.
  (a) ₹ 4
  (b) ₹ 5
  (c) ₹ 6
  (d) ₹ 8

Sol. (a)

$$\text{Difference in C.I and S.I} = \left(\frac{xr}{200}\right) = \left(\frac{160 \times 5}{200}\right) = ₹\, 4.$$

Shortcut Approach - 20

To find the ratio of Compound Interest (CI) to Simple Interest (SI) on a certain sum at r% for 2 years, we use the following formula

$$\frac{CI}{SI} = \frac{r}{200} + 1.$$

Note : This formula is applicable only for 2 years.

23. Find the ratio of CI to SI on a certain sum at 10% per annum for 2 years.
  (a) 7 : 5
  (b) 21 : 20
  (c) 8 : 5
  (d) 20 : 19

Sol. (b)

$$\text{Ratio of CI to SI} = \frac{r}{200} + 1 = \left[\frac{10}{200} + 1\right] = \frac{210}{200}$$

$$= 21 : 20$$

Shortcut Approach - 21

If the compound interest on a certain sum for 2 years is ₹ 'C' and simple interest is ₹ 'S', then the rate of interest per annum is

$$\left[\frac{2 \times (C - S)}{S} \times 100\right]\% \text{ per or } \frac{2 \times \text{Diff.} \times 100}{SI} \text{ and sum} = \frac{\text{Diff.} \times (100)^2}{r^2}$$

24. The compound interest on a certain sum for 2 years is ₹ 105 and simple interest is ₹ 100. Find the rate of interest per annum and the sum.
  (a) 10%, ₹ 500
  (b) 10%, ₹ 1000
  (c) 20%, ₹ 1000
  (d) None of these

Sol. (a)

$$\text{Rate of Interest} = \left[\frac{2(C - S)}{S} \times 100\right]\%$$

$$= \left[\frac{2(105-100)}{100} \times 100\right] = \left[\frac{2 \times 5}{100} \times 100\right] = 10\% \text{ p.a.}$$

$$\text{and Sum} = \frac{\text{Diff} \times 10000}{r^2} = \frac{5 \times 10000}{(10)^2} = ₹ 500$$

⊕ Shortcut Approach - 22

If an amount of money grows upto ₹ A_1 in n years and upto ₹ A_2 in $(n+1)$ years on compound interest, then the sum is given by ₹ $\left[A_1\left(\dfrac{A_1}{A_2}\right)^n\right]$ and

the rate $= \left(\dfrac{A_2 - A_1}{A_1} \times 100\right)\%$

25. An amount of money grows upto ₹ 2750 in 2 years and upto ₹ 3125 in 3 years on compound interest. Find the sum
    (a) ₹ 2129.6   (b) ₹ 1229.6
    (c) ₹ 2219.6   (d) Data inadequate

Sol. (a)

$$\text{Sum} = \left[A_1\left(\frac{A_1}{A_2}\right)^n\right] = \left[2750\left(\frac{2750}{3125}\right)^2\right]$$

$$= 2750 \times \left[\frac{7562500}{9765625}\right] = ₹ 2129.60.$$

⊕ Shortcut Approach - 23

If the compound rate of interest for the first t_1 years is $r_1\%$, for the next t_2 year is $r_2\%$, for the next t_3 years is $r_3\%$... and the last t_n years is $r_n\%$, then compound interest on ₹ x for $(t_1 + t_2 + t_3 + ... t_n)$ years is

$$\left[x\left(1+\frac{r_1}{100}\right)^{t_1}\left(1+\frac{r_2}{100}\right)^{t_2} ... \left(1+\frac{r_n}{100}\right)^{t_n}\right] - x.$$

26. Find the compound interest on ₹ 8000 in 2 years, the rate of interest being 5% for the first year and 10% for the second year.
    (a) ₹ 1340   (b) ₹ 1420
    (c) ₹ 1240   (d) None of these

Sol. **(c)**

Compound Interest

$$= \left[x\left(1+\frac{r_1}{100}\right)^{t_1} \cdot \left(1+\frac{r_2}{100}\right)^{t_2} \ldots \left(1+\frac{r_n}{100}\right)^{t_n} \right] - x$$

$$= \left[8000\left(1+\frac{5}{100}\right)^{1} \cdot \left(1+\frac{10}{100}\right)^{1} \right] - 8000$$

$$= 9240 - 8000 = ₹\,1240$$

Shortcut Approach - 24

Let an article of ₹ P is purchased on cash down payment of ₹ X and n equal montly instalments of ₹ x. If r% simple interest is charged in this instalment scheme, then the value of each instalment is given by

$$(P-X)+\frac{(P-X)\times r\times n}{100\times 12} = x + \left(x+\frac{x\times r\times 1}{100\times 12}\right)$$

$$+ \left(x+\frac{x\times r\times 2}{100\times 12}\right) + \ldots + \left(x+\frac{x\times r\times(n-1)}{100\times 12}\right)$$

or

$$\text{Remaining amount} \left[1+\frac{r\times\text{no. of instalments}}{12\times 100}\right]$$

$$= (\textbf{Value of each instalments} \times \textbf{Number of instalments}) +$$

$$\frac{\text{Value of each instalments}}{12\times 100}(r+2r+3r+\ldots+(n-1)r)$$

or

$$(P-X)\left[1+\frac{r\times n}{1200}\right] = (x\times n)+\frac{x}{1200}[r+2r+3r+\ldots+(n-1)r]$$

27. The price of a television is ₹ 10,000. It can be purchased on a down payment of ₹ 3000 and 6 equal monthly instalment of ₹ 1300. Find the rate of interest.

(a)   42%

(b) $42\frac{2}{3}\%$

(c) $42\frac{1}{3}\%$

(d) $42\frac{1}{2}\%$

Sol. (b) $(P-X)\left[1+\dfrac{r\times n}{100\times 12}\right]=x\times n+\dfrac{x}{100\times 12}$

$$\left[r+2r+3r+(n-1)r\right]$$

$$(10000-3000)\left[1+\dfrac{r\times\cancel{6}}{\cancel{1200}}\right]=1300\times 6+$$

$$\dfrac{1300}{1200}\left[r+2r+3r+4r+5r\right]$$

$$7000+35r=7800+\dfrac{13}{12}\left[15r\right]$$

$$7000+35r=7800+\dfrac{65}{4}r$$

$$35r-\dfrac{65}{4}r=7800-7000$$

$$\dfrac{75r}{4}=800$$

$$r=\dfrac{800\times 4}{75}$$

$$r=\dfrac{128}{3}\%=42\dfrac{2}{3}\%$$

⊕ Shortcut Approach - 25

The annual payment that will discharge a debt of ₹ P due in t years at the

rate of simple interest r% per annum $=\dfrac{100P}{100t+\dfrac{rt(t-1)}{2}}$

28. What annual payment will discharge a debt of ₹1092 due in 2 years at 12% simple interest?

    (a) ₹725   (b) ₹325   (c) ₹515   (d) ₹900

Sol. (c)   Annual payment $=\dfrac{100P}{100t+\dfrac{rt(t-1)}{2}}$

$$= \frac{100 \times 1092}{100(2) + \dfrac{12(2)(2-1)}{2}}$$

$$= \frac{100 \times 1092}{200 + 12} = ₹\,515.09 = ₹\,515$$

29.　The annual payment of ₹160 in 5 years at 5% per annum simple interest will discharge a debt of

(a)　₹980　　　　　　(b)　₹880
(c)　₹440　　　　　　(d)　₹220

Sol. (b)　Annual payment $= \dfrac{100P}{100t + \dfrac{rt(t-1)}{2}}$

$$\Rightarrow 160 = \frac{100P}{100(5) + \dfrac{5(5)(5-1)}{2}}$$

$$\Rightarrow 160 = \frac{100P}{500 + 50} \Rightarrow ₹\,880 = P$$

A sum of ₹ P is to be paid back in n equal annual instalments. If the interest is compounded annually at r% per annum, then the value of each instalment

$$= \frac{P}{\left(\dfrac{100}{100+r}\right) + \left(\dfrac{100}{100+r}\right)^{2} + \,.... + \left(\dfrac{100}{100+r}\right)^{n}}$$

30.　Kamal took ₹ 6800 as a loan which along with interest is to be repaid in two equal annual instalments. If the rate of interest is

$12\dfrac{1}{2}\%$, compounded annually, then the value of each instalment is :

(a) ₹8100　　　　　(b) ₹4150
(c) ₹4050　　　　　(d) ₹4000

Sol. (c) Each instalment $= \dfrac{6800}{\left(\dfrac{100}{100+\dfrac{25}{2}}\right)+\left(\dfrac{100}{100+\dfrac{25}{2}}\right)^2}$

$$= \dfrac{6800}{\left(\dfrac{8}{9}\right)+\left(\dfrac{8}{9}\right)^2} = 6800 \times \dfrac{81}{136} = ₹\,4050$$

31. A man borrows ₹ 1820 and undertakes to pay back with compound interest @ 20% pa in 3 equal yearly instal ments at the end of first, second and third years. What is the amount of each instalment?

    (a) ₹500   (b) ₹560

    (c) ₹750   (d) ₹864

Sol. (d) Each instalment

$$= \dfrac{1820}{\left(\dfrac{100}{100+20}\right)+\left(\dfrac{100}{100+20}\right)^2+\left(\dfrac{100}{100+20}\right)^3}$$

$$= \dfrac{1820}{\left(\dfrac{5}{6}\right)+\left(\dfrac{5}{6}\right)^2+\left(\dfrac{5}{6}\right)^3} = \dfrac{1820}{455} \times 216 = ₹\,864$$

⊕ Shortcut Approach - 27

If a man borrows some money on compound interest at r% per annum compounded annually and returns it in n yearly equal instalments of ₹ x, then

(i) Amount borrowed

$$= x\left[\left(\dfrac{100}{100+r}\right)+\left(\dfrac{100}{100+r}\right)^2+...+\left(\dfrac{100}{100+r}\right)^n\right]$$

(ii) Total interest charged

$$= x\left[n-\left\{\left(\dfrac{100}{100+r}\right)+\left(\dfrac{100}{100+r}\right)^2+...+\left(\dfrac{100}{100+r}\right)^n\right\}\right]$$

32. A man borrows a certain sum and pays it back in two equal annual instalments. If he pays back ₹ 676 annually and rate of interest is 4%, what is the sum borrowed?

    (a) ₹1352   (b) ₹1300

    (c) ₹1275   (d) ₹1250

Sol. (c)   Amount borrowed

$$= 676\left[\left(\frac{100}{100+4}\right)+\left(\frac{100}{100+4}\right)^2\right]$$

$$= 676\left[\frac{25}{26}+\left(\frac{25}{26}\right)^2\right]$$

$$= 676\left[\frac{625+650}{676}\right]$$

$$= ₹\,1275$$

⊕ Shortcut Approach - 28

A sum of ₹ P is to be paid back in n annual instalments. If the interest is compounded annually on the balance at r% per annum and is to be included in each instalment, then

$$\text{Value of } m^{\text{th}} \text{ instalment } = \frac{P}{n}\left[1+\frac{r(n-m+1)}{100}\right]$$

$$\text{i.e. Value of } 1^{\text{st}} \text{ instalment } = \frac{P}{n}\left[1+\frac{rn}{100}\right]$$

$$\text{Value of } 2^{\text{nd}} \text{ instalment } = \frac{P}{n}\left[1+\frac{r(n-1)}{100}\right] \text{ and so on.}$$

33. A sum of ₹ 7200 has to be paid in three annual instalments of ₹ 2400 with interest. If the rate of interest is 8% per annum, then what amount will be paid at the end of every year?

    (a) ₹2976, ₹2784, ₹2592

    (b) ₹2782, ₹2529, ₹2425

    (c) ₹2594, ₹2463, ₹2218

    (d) ₹1800, ₹1712, ₹1690

Sol. (a) Value of 1st instalment $= \dfrac{7200}{3}\left[1+\dfrac{8\times 3}{100}\right]$

$$= 2400\left(1+\dfrac{24}{100}\right) = ₹\ 2976$$

Value of 2nd instalment

$$= \dfrac{7200}{3}\left[1+\dfrac{8\times 2}{100}\right] = 2400\left(1+\dfrac{16}{100}\right) = ₹\ 2784$$

Value of 3rd instalment

$$= \dfrac{7200}{3}\left[1+\dfrac{8\times 1}{100}\right] = 2400\left(1+\dfrac{8}{100}\right) = ₹\ 2592$$

Exercise

1. Rahim barrows ₹ 2730 and undertakes to pay back with C.I. of 20% p.a. in three equal yearly instalments at the end of first, second and third years. What is the amount each instalments?
   (a) ₹1096   (b) ₹1296
   (c) ₹864
   (d) None of these

2. What will be the ratio of simple interest earned by certain amount at the same rate of interest for 6 years and that for 9 years?
   (a) 1 : 3   (b) 1 : 4
   (c) 2 : 3
   (d) None of these

3. What will be the difference in simple and compound interest on ₹ 2000 after three years at the rate of 10 percent per annum?
   (a) ₹160   (b) ₹42
   (c) ₹62   (d) ₹20

4. The difference between interest received by A and B is ₹ 18 on ₹ 1500 for 3 year. What is the difference in rate of interest?
   (a) 1%   (b) 2.5 %
   (c) 0.5%   (d) 0.4%

5. Nitin borrowed some money at the rate of 6% p.a. for the first three years, 9% p.a. for the next five years and 13% p.a. for the period beyond eight years If the total interest paid by him at the end of eleven years is ₹ 8160, how much money did he borrow?
   (a) ₹ 8000
   (b) ₹ 10,000
   (c) ₹ 12,000
   (d) Data inadequate

6. Akram Ali left an amount of ₹ 340000 to be divided between his two sons aged 10 years and 12 years such that both of them would get an equal amount when each attain 18 years age. What is the share of elder brother if the whole amount was invested at 10% simple interest ?
   (a) 120000   (b) 140000
   (c) 160000   (d) 180000

7. If the difference between S.I and C.I for 2 years on a sum of money lent at 5% is ₹ 6, then the sum be.
   (a) ₹2200   (b) ₹2400
   (c) ₹2600   (d) ₹2000

8. A man borrows ₹ 12,500 at 20% compound interest. At the end of every year he pays ₹ 2000 as part repayment. How much does he still owe after three such instalments?
   (a) ₹ 12,000   (b) ₹ 12,864
   (c) ₹ 15,600
   (d) None of these

9. A person lent a certain sum of money at 4% simple interest; and in 8 years the interest amounted to ₹ 340 less than the sum lent. Find the sum lent.
   (a) 500   (b) 600
   (c) 1000   (d) 1500

10. The CI on ₹ 5000 for 3 years at 8% for first year, 10% for second year and 12% for third year will be:

(a) ₹ 1750   (b) ₹ 1652.80

(c) ₹ 1575   (d) ₹ 1685.20

11. The difference between simple and compound interest for the fourth years is ₹ 7280 at 20% p.a. What is the principal sum?

(a) ₹ 10000   (b) ₹ 50000

(c) ₹ 1 lakh   (d) ₹ 40000

12. The ratio of CI for 3 years and SI for 1 year for a fixed amount at a rate of r% is 91:25. What is the value of r?

(a) 10%

(b) 15%

(c) 20%

(d) None of these

Hints & Solution

1. **(b)** Use Short Approach -26

2. **(c)** Let the principal be P and rate of interest be R%.

∴ Required ratio

$$= \left[\frac{\left(\dfrac{P \times R \times 6}{100} \right)}{\left(\dfrac{P \times R \times 9}{100} \right)} \right]$$

$$= \frac{6PR}{9PR} = \frac{6}{9} = 2:3.$$

3. **(c)** Use Short Approach -19

4. **(d)** $\dfrac{1500 \times 3}{100}(r_1 - r_2) = 18$

$\Rightarrow r_1 - r_2 = 0.4\%$

5. **(a)** Use Short Approach -1

6. **(d)** Go through options

$$1.8 + \frac{1.8 \times 6 \times 10}{100}$$

$$= 1.6 + \frac{1.6 \times 8 \times 10}{100}$$

Hence (d) is correct.

Alternatively :

$$P_1 + \frac{P_1 \times 6 \times 10}{100}$$

$$= P_2 + \frac{P_2 \times 8 \times 10}{100}$$

$$\Rightarrow \frac{P_1}{P_2} = \frac{9}{8}$$

Share of elder brother

$$= \frac{340000 \times 9}{17}$$

$$= ₹180000$$

7. **(b)** Use Short Approach -19

8. **(d)** Balance =

$$₹ \left[\left\{ 12500 \times \left(1 + \frac{20}{100} \right)^3 \right\} - \right.$$

$$\left\{ 2000 \times \left(1 + \frac{20}{100} \right)^2 + 2000 \times \left(1 + \frac{20}{100} \right) + 2000 \right\} \right]$$

$$= ₹ \left[\left(12500 \times \frac{6}{5} \times \frac{6}{5} \times \frac{6}{5} \right) - \right.$$

$$\left. \left(2000 \times \frac{6}{5} \times \frac{6}{5} + 2000 \times \frac{6}{5} + 2000 \right) \right]$$

$$= ₹ [21600 - (2880 + 2400 + 2000)]$$

$$= ₹14320.$$

9. **(a)** Let the sum be ₹ x.

∴ Interest

$$= \frac{x \times 8 \times 4}{100} = \frac{32x}{100}$$

$$x - \frac{32x}{100} = \frac{68x}{100}$$

When interest is $\dfrac{68x}{100}$ less, the sum is ₹ x.

∴ When interest is ₹ 340 less, the sum is

$$\frac{x}{68x} \times 100 \times 340$$

$$= ₹ 500$$

Direct Formula: Sum

$$= \frac{100}{100 - 8 \times 4} \times 340$$

$$= \frac{100 \times 340}{68} = ₹ 500$$

10. (b) Use Short Approach -23

11. (b) Difference between CI and SI for n^{th} year

$$= \frac{Pr}{100}\left[\left(1+\frac{r}{100}\right)^{n-1}-1\right]$$

$$7280 = \frac{P \times 20}{100}\left[(1.2)^3 - 1\right]$$

$$\Rightarrow P = ₹\,50000$$

Alternatively :

	Initially	I^{st} year	IInd year	IIIrd year	IVth year
SI	10000	12000	14000	16000	18000
CI	10000	12000	14400	17280	20736

CI for 4th year
$= 20736 - 17280$
$= 3456$
SI for 4th year $= 2000$
Difference between CI and SI $= 1456$ for ₹ 10000
So, the difference of ₹7280 is for ₹ 50000

12. (c)

$$\frac{P\left[\left(1+\dfrac{r}{100}\right)^3 - 1\right]}{\dfrac{pr}{100}}$$

$$= \frac{\left(1+\dfrac{r}{100}\right)^3 - 1}{\dfrac{r}{100}} = 3.64$$

By taking the option (c),
$r = 20\%$

Now,

$$\frac{\left(1+\dfrac{20}{100}\right)^3 - 1}{\dfrac{20}{100}} = \frac{(1.2)^3 - 1}{0.2}$$

$$= \frac{0.728}{0.2} = 3.64$$

Hence, $r = 20\%$

Sequence and Series

Chapter 13

$a, b, c, d, \ldots\ldots$ are in A.P., if $a - b = b - c = c - d = \ldots\ldots$

1. **Check whether the series 0.6, 1.7, 2.8, 3.9, ... is**

 (a) an A.P   (b) a G.P

 (c) an H.P   (d) None of these

Sol. **(a)** Here $0.6 - 1.7 = -1.1$, $1.7 - 2.8 = -1.1$, $2.8 - 3.9 = -1.1$

   Hence, given series is an A.P.

In an A.P., the sum of terms equidistant from the beginning and end is constant and equal to the sum of first term and last term.

2. **Determine the sum of 6th and 19th term of A.P. 4, 9, 14, ..., 119 with 24 terms.**

 (a) 124   (b) 123

 (c) 120   (d) 122

Sol. **(b)** Since the given A.P. series has 24 terms.

   $\therefore$ 6th term from beginning is the 19th term from end.

   $\therefore$ Sum of 6th and 19th terms = 6th term from the beginning + 6th term from end

   $= 4 + 119$

   $= 123$

   $= $ 1st term + last term $= 4 + 119 = 123$

If in an A.P., sum of first p terms is equal to sum of first q terms, then sum of $(p + q)$ terms is zero.

3. **In a certain A.P, if the sum of m terms is the same as the sum of its n terms, then find the sum of its (m + n) terms.**

 (a) $-(m + n)$ (b) mn

 (c) $\dfrac{1}{mn}$ (d) 0

Sol. **(d)**   Sum of m terms = Sum of its n terms

$\therefore$ Sum of its (m + n) terms = 0.

If in an A.P., p^{th} term is q and q^{th} term is p, then n^{th} term is $(p + q - n)$.

4.   **In an A.P, it the 23th term is 40 and 40th term is 23, then find its 326th term.**

(a) -163 (b) -263

(c) -363 (d) -63

Sol. **(b)** $(23 + 40 - 326) = -263$

Shortcut Approach - 5

$a, b, c, d, \ldots\ldots$ are in G.P., if $\dfrac{a}{b} = \dfrac{b}{c} = \dfrac{c}{d} = \ldots\ldots$

5.   **Find the correct option for the given series. 5, 10, 20, 40, ...**

(a) A. P with difference 5

(b) G.P with ratio 2

(c) G.P with ratio $\left(\dfrac{1}{2}\right)$

(d) A.P. with difference 2

Sol. **(b)**   Here, $\dfrac{10}{5} = \dfrac{20}{10} = \dfrac{40}{20} = \ldots\ldots$

$\therefore$ Given series is a G.P with the ratio of (2).

6.   **Find the correct option for the given series.**

$3, 9, 27, 81, \ldots\ldots$

(a) A. P with difference (3)

(b) A.P with difference (6)

(c) G.P with ratio (3)

(d) G.P with difference $\left(\dfrac{1}{3}\right)$

Sol. **(c)**   Here, $\dfrac{9}{3} = \dfrac{27}{9} = \dfrac{81}{27}\ldots\ldots$

$\therefore$ Given series is G.P with the ratio of (3).

Shortcut Approach - 6

If each term of a G.P. be multiplied or divided by the same quantity, the resulting sequence will be also in G.P. with the same common ratio as before.

7. **Find the correct option for the given statement. If 4, 12, 36, 108, 324 ...... is a G.P, with common ratio 3. Then, 1, 3, 9, 27, 81 .... is**

    (a) G. P with common ratio 4

    (b) G.P with common ratio $\left(\dfrac{1}{3}\right)$

    (c) G.P with common ratio 3

    (d) None of these

Sol. (c) It is clear that every element of 1st series is divided by 4, then the 2nd series is obtained.

    $\therefore$ 2nd series is also a G.P with common ratio 3.

Shortcut Approach 7

If $a_1, a_2, a_3, \ldots\ldots$ and $b_1, b_2, b_3, \ldots\ldots$ are two geometric progressions, then the sequence $a_1 b_1, a_2 b_2, a_3 b_3, \ldots\ldots$ is also G.P.

8. **Find the correct option for the given statement consider two GP's 6, 12, 24, 48 .... and 1, 2, 4, 8 .... then. 6, 24, 96, 384, ... is**

    (a) an A.P

    (b) both A.p and G.P

    (c) a G.P

    (d) neither an AP nor a G.P

Sol. (c) Here, 3rd series is obtained by multiplying corresponding terms of 1st & 2nd series.

    $\therefore$ Third series is a G.P.

Shortcut Approach - 8

Sum of first n natural numbers $= \dfrac{n(n+1)}{2}$

i.e. $1 + 2 + 3 + 4 + 5 + \ldots\ldots + n = \dfrac{n(n+1)}{2}$

9. **Find the sum of the given series**

   $1 + 2 + 3 + 4 + \ldots\ldots\ldots 120.$

   (a) 5260 (b) 6260

   (c) 7260 (d) 8260

Sol. (c) $1 + 2 + 3 + 4 + \ldots\ldots 120.$

   We know that

   The sum of n natural number $= \dfrac{n(n+1)}{2}$

   Since the given series is a set of 1st 120 natural number

   $$\text{Sum} = \dfrac{120(120+1)}{2} = 7260$$

10. **Find the sum of the gvien series.**

   $1 + 2 + 3 + 4 + 5 + \ldots\ldots 5600$

   (a) 15682600 (b) 15682800

   (c) 15682700 (d) 15682900

Sol. (b) $1 + 2 + 3 + 4 + \ldots\ldots 5600$

   Since the given series is a set of 1st 5600 natural numbers.

   $$\text{So,} \quad \text{Sum} = \dfrac{5600(5600+1)}{2} = 15682800$$

Shortcut Approach - 9

Sum of first n odd natural numbers $= n^2$

i.e. $1 + 3 + 5 + 7 + \ldots\ldots + (2n-1) = n^2$

11. **Find the sum of the given series.**

   $1 + 3 + 5 + 7 + \ldots\ldots$ **upto 100 terms.**

   (a) 10000 (b) 9000

   (c) 8000 (d) 11000

Sol. (a) Since the given series is a set of first 100 odd natural numbers

   $\therefore \quad \text{Sum} = (100)^2 = 10000$

Shortcut Approach - 10

Sum of first n even natural numbers $= n(n+1)$

i.e. $2+4+6+8+\ldots+2n = n(n+1)$

12. Find the sum of the given series:

$2+4+6+8+\ldots$ upto 50 terms.

(a) 2450   (b) 2560

(c) 2460   (d) 2550

Sol. (d) Since the givcen series is a set of first 50 even natural numbers

$\therefore$ Sum $= 50(50+1) = 2550$

Shortcut Approach - 11

Sum of squares of first n natural numbers

$$= \frac{n(n+1)(2n+1)}{6}$$

i.e. $1^2+2^2+3^2+\ldots+n^2 = \dfrac{n(n+1)(2n+1)}{6}$

13. If $1^2+2^2+3^2+\ldots+x^2 = \dfrac{x(x+1)(2x+1)}{6}$

then $1^2+3^2+5^2+\ldots+19^2$ is equal to:

(a) 1330   (b) 2100

(c) 2485   (d) 2500

Sol. (a) $(1^2+3^2+5^2+\ldots+19^2) = (1^2+2^2+3^2+\ldots+20^2)$

$$- (2^2+4^2+6^2+\ldots+20^2)$$

$$= \left[\frac{20(20+1)(40+1)}{6}\right] - 2^2 \times \left(1^2+2^2+3^2+\ldots+10^2\right)$$

$$= \left(\frac{20\times21\times41}{6}\right) - 4\times\left(\frac{10\times11\times21}{6}\right)$$

$$= 2870 - (4\times385) = 2870 - 1540 = 1330$$

Sum of cubes of first n natural numbers $= \left[\dfrac{n(n+1)}{2}\right]^2$

i.e. $1^3 + 2^3 + 3^3 + 4^3 + \ldots + n^3 = \left[\dfrac{n(n+1)}{2}\right]^2$

14. Find the sum of the given series:
$1^3 + 2^3 + 3^3 + 4^3 + \ldots (30)^3 =$

(a) 206225   (b) 226225

(c) 236225   (d) 216225

Sol. (d) Here, $n = 30$,

$$\therefore \quad \text{Sum} = \left[\dfrac{30(30+1)}{2}\right]^2 = 216225$$

15. Find the value of $5^3 + 6^3 + \ldots + 10^3$.

(a) 2295   (b) 2425

(c) 2495   (d) 2925

Sol. (d) Required sum $= (5^3 + 6^3 + \ldots 10^3)$

$$= \left(1^3 + 2^3 + 3^3 + \ldots + 10^3\right) - \left(1^3 + 2^3 + 3^3 + 4^3\right)$$

$$= \left[\dfrac{10(10+1)}{2}\right]^2 - \left[\dfrac{4(4+1)}{2}\right]^2$$

$$= (5 \times 11)^2 - (2 \times 5)^2$$
$$= 3025 - 100 = 2925$$

16. If $1^3 + 2^3 + 3^3 + \ldots + 10^3 = 3025$, then $4 + 32 + 108 + \ldots + 4000$ is equal to:

(a) 12000   (b) 12100   (c) 12200   (d) 12400

Sol. (b) $4 + 32 + 108 + \ldots + 4000$

$$= 4 \times (1 + 8 + 27 + \ldots + 1000)$$
$$= 4 \times (1^3 + 2^3 + 3^3 + \ldots + 10^3)$$

$$= 4 \times \left[\dfrac{10(10+1)}{2}\right]^2 = 4 \times 3025 = 12100$$

If $m_1, m_2, m_3, \ldots\ldots, m_k$ and $n_1, n_2, n_3, \ldots, n_k$ are in A.P., then $(m_1 - n_1)$, $(m_2 - n_2)$, $(m_3 - n_3)$, $\ldots\ldots (m_k - n_k)$ are also an A.P.

17. Find the correct option for the given statement consider two AP's

    15   19   23 27   31 .....

    2   5   8   11   14 .....

    then 13, 14, 15, 16, 17 .....

    (a)   an A.P   (b) a G.P

    (c)   both A.P and G.P   (d) None of these

Sol. (a)   Here 3rd given series is obtained by substracting terms of the 2nd series from the corresponding elements of 1st series.

        $\therefore$ Third series is : 13, 14, 15, 16, 17.....is also in an A.P.

Exercise

1. What is the sum of all the two-digit numbers which when divided by 7 gives a remainder of 3?
   (a) 94
   (b) 676
   (c) 696
   (d) None of these

2. The sum of an infinite GP is 162 and the sum of its first n terms is 160. If the inverse of its common ratio is an integer, then how many values of common ratio is/are possible, common ratio is greater than 0?
   (a) 0
   (b) 1
   (c) 2
   (d) 3

3. The 4th and 10th term of a GP are 1/3 and 243 respectively. Find the 2nd term.
   (a) 3
   (b) 1
   (c) 1/27
   (d) 1/9

4. Find the sum of the integers between 1 and 200 that are multiples of 7?
   (a) 2742
   (b) 2842
   (c) 2642
   (d) 2546

5. Find the number of terms in the A.P. 22, 28, 34, ...616:
   (a) 80
   (b) 78
   (c) 99
   (d) 100

6. Find the sum of the first hundred even natural numbers divisible by 5 :
   (a) 50500
   (b) 55000
   (c) 50050
   (d) 50005

7. How many terms of the series 20 + 16 + 12 + ... amounts to 48?
   (a) 3
   (b) 5
   (c) 8
   (d) both (a) and (c)

8. What is the sum of 100 terms of the series
   $1 - 2 + 3 - 4 + 5 - 6 + ...$?
   (a) 100
   (b) 50
   (c) 550
   (d) None of these

9. Complete the series 5, 19, 41, 71, ?, 155
   (a) 106
   (b) 125
   (c) 115
   (d) 109

10. In a geometric progression the sum of the first and the last term is 66 and the product of the second and the last but one term is 128. Determine the first term of the series.
    (a) 64
    (b) 64 or 2
    (c) 2 or 32
    (d) 32

11. Find the sum of all odd numbers of four digits which are divisible by 9 :
    (a) 2784491
    (b) 2478429
    (c) 2754000
    (d) 2448729

12. The sum of the infinite series
    $$\frac{1}{1.4} + \frac{1}{4.7} + \frac{1}{7.10} + ...\infty$$
    is equal to :
    (a) $\frac{1}{3}$
    (b) $\frac{1}{4}$
    (c) $\frac{38}{27}$
    (d) None of these

Hints & Solution

1. **(b)** Two digits smallest number that gives remainder 3 when divided by $7 = 10$

Two digits largest number that gives remainder 3 when divided by $7 = 94$.

$\therefore$ Series sum $= 10 + 17 + 24 + ... + 94$

$\therefore$ Required sum

$$= \frac{n(a+b)}{2}$$

$$= \frac{13(10+94)}{2}$$

$$= 676.$$

2. **(c)** $a/(1-r) = 162$ and $a(1-r^n)/(1-r) = 160$

$\Rightarrow 1 - r^n = 160/162$

$\Rightarrow r^n = 1/81$

Hence, there will be only two values of n, *i.e.*, 2 and 4.

3. **(c)** $T_4 = ar^3 = \dfrac{1}{3}$ ...(i)

$T_{10} = ar^9 = 243$ ...(ii)

From (i) and (ii)

$$\frac{T_{10}}{T_4} = \frac{ar^9}{ar^3} = \frac{243}{\frac{1}{3}}$$

$\Rightarrow r^6 = 243 \times 3 \Rightarrow r^6 = 3^6$

$r = 3$

$\Rightarrow a(3)^3 = \dfrac{1}{3}, \quad a = \dfrac{1}{81}$

$$T_2 = ar = \frac{1}{81} \cdot 3 = \frac{1}{27}$$

4. **(b)** Use Short Approach - 8

5. **(d)** Number of terms

$$= \left(\frac{616-22}{6}\right) + 1$$

$$= \frac{594}{6} + 1 = 100$$

Alternatively :

$22, 28, 34, ... 616 = (4, 10, 16, 22, 28 ,....., 616) - (4, 10, 16)$

$\Rightarrow (6, 12, 18, 24, 30, ..., 618) - (6, 12, 18)$

$\Rightarrow (1, 2, 3, 4, 5, ..., 103) - (1, 2, 3)$

$\Rightarrow 103 - 3 = 100$

Alternatively :

$22, 28, 34, ..., 616$

$\Rightarrow 24, 30, 36, ..., 618$

$\Rightarrow 4, 5, 6, ..., 103$

$\Rightarrow 103 - 3 = 100$

6. **(a)** Use Short Approach - 8

7. **(d)** $20 + 16 + 12 = 48$

Hence number of terms $= 3$

Again $20 + 16 + 12 + 8 + 4 + 0 + (-4) + (-8) = 48$

Hence number of terms $= 8$

Alternatively :

$S_n = 48$

$$= \frac{n}{2}\big[2 \times 20 + (n-1)(-4)\big]$$

$$\Rightarrow 96 = 40n - 4n^2 + 4n$$

$$\Rightarrow n^2 - 11n + 24 = 0$$

$$\Rightarrow (n-8)(n-3) = 0$$

$$\Rightarrow n = 8 \text{ or } n = 3$$

8. **(d)** Use Short Approach - 9, 10

9. **(d)** The series is as follows:

$$1 + 2^2 = 5$$

$$3 + 4^2 = 19$$

$$5 + 6^2 = 41$$

$$7 + 8^2 = 71$$

$$9 + 10^2 = 109$$

$$11 + 12^2 = 155$$

10. **(b)** Let a be the first term and r be the common ratio of the G.P.

Also assume that n^{th} term is the last term of the GP.

Then, $a + ar^{n-1} = 66$

$$\quad\quad\quad\quad\quad ...(1)$$

and $ar.ar^{n-2} = 128$

or $a^2 r^{n-1} = 128$

$$\quad\quad\quad\quad\quad ...(2)$$

From (1) and (2),

$$a + \frac{128}{a} = 66$$

or $a^2 - 66a + 128 = 0$

$\therefore \quad a = 64, 2.$

11. **(c)** Use Short Approach - 8

12. **(a)** Let

$$S = \frac{1}{1.4} + \frac{1}{4.7} + \frac{1}{7.10} + ...\infty$$

$$\Rightarrow S = \frac{1}{3}\left[\frac{3}{1.4} + \frac{3}{4.7} + \frac{3}{7.10} + ...\infty\right]$$

$$\Rightarrow S = \frac{1}{3}\left[\left(\frac{1}{1} - \frac{1}{4}\right) + \left(\frac{1}{4} - \frac{1}{7}\right) + \left(\frac{1}{7} - \frac{1}{10}\right) + ...\infty\right]$$

$$\Rightarrow S = \frac{1}{3}[1] \quad \therefore S = \frac{1}{3}$$

Allegation and Mixture

The proportion in which rice at ₹ x per kg must be mixed with rice at ₹ y per kg, so that the mixture be worth ₹ z a kg, is given by $\left(\dfrac{y-z}{z-x}\right)$

1. **In what proportion, must wheat at ₹ 6.20 per kg be mixed with wheat at ₹ 7.20 per kg, so that the mixture be worth ₹ 6.50 per kg?**
    (a) 4 : 7   (b)   2 : 5   (c)   3 : 4   (d)   7 : 3

Sol. (d)   Required ratio $= \dfrac{7.20 - 6.50}{6.50 - 6.20} = \dfrac{0.70}{0.30} = 7 : 3$

The quantity of salt m kg at ₹ x per kg that a man must mix with n kg of salt at ₹ y per kg, so that he may, on selling the mixture at ₹ z per kg, gain p% on the outlay is given by

$$n \times \left[\frac{100z - y\,(100 + p)}{x\,(100 + p) - 100z}\right] kg.$$

> **Note: If we suppose that the quantity of salt at ₹x be m, then we have**

$$\frac{m}{n} = \frac{100z - y\,(100 + p)}{x\,(100 + p) - 100z}.$$

2. **A shopkeeper buys 50 kg sugar at the rate of 40/kg and 100kg sugar at the rate 70/kg. At what price per kg should he sell the mixture to earn 20% profit on cost price?**
    (a) 72/kg   (b)   75/kg   (c)   84/kg   (d)   90/kg

Sol. (a) $\dfrac{m}{n} = \dfrac{100z - y(100 + P)}{x(100 + P) - 100z}$

$\dfrac{50}{100} = \dfrac{100z - 70(100 + 20)}{40(100 + 20) - 100z}$

$$\frac{1}{2} = \frac{100z - 8400}{4800 - 100z}$$

$$200z - 16800 = 4800 - 100z$$

$$300z = 21600$$

$$\therefore z = 72/\text{kg}$$

⊕ Shortcut Approach - 3

n gm of sugar solution has $x\%$ sugar in it. The quantity of sugar should be added to make it $y\%$ in the solution is given by $n\left(\dfrac{y - x}{100 - y}\right)$ gm or quantity of sugar added =

$$\text{Solution} \times \frac{(\text{required\% value} - \text{present\% value})}{(100 - \text{required\% value})}$$

3. **If 50 litres of milk solution has 40% milk in it, then how much milk should be added to make it 60% in the solution?**
   (a) 25 L   (b) 30 L
   (c) 35 L   (d) 40 L

Sol. (a)

$$\frac{\text{Amount of A left}}{\text{Amount of A Originally Present}} = \left[1 - \frac{R}{50}\right]$$

$$\Rightarrow \frac{15}{60} = \left[1 - \frac{R}{50}\right]^{n}$$

$$\Rightarrow \frac{1}{4} = \left(1 - \frac{R}{50}\right)^{2}$$

$$\Rightarrow \frac{1}{2} = 1 - \frac{R}{50}$$

$$\Rightarrow R = 25 \text{ litres}$$

⊕ Shortcut Approach - 4

A trader has N kg of certain item, part of which he sells at $x\%$ profit and the rest at $y\%$ profit. He gains $P\%$ on the whole. The quantity of item sold at $x\%$ profit is $\left[\left(\dfrac{y - P}{y - x}\right)N\right]$ kg and the quantity of item sold at $y\%$ profit is given by $\left[\left(\dfrac{P-x}{y-x}\right)N\right]kg.$.

4. **A shopkeeper has 180 kg of sugar. Some sugar he sells at 10% profit and rest of sugar at 15% profit. If his overall profit is 12%, then what is quantity of sugar sold at 15% discount?**

    (a) 72 kg   (b)   75 kg   (c) 90 kg   (d)   108 kg

Sol. **(a)** Required quantity

$$= \left(\dfrac{P-x}{y-x}\right)n\,kg = \dfrac{12-10}{15-10}\times180 \ = \dfrac{2}{5}\times180 = 72$$

Shortcut Approach - 5

A trader has N kg of a certain item, a part of which he sells at $x\%$ profit and the rest at $y\%$ loss. He gains P % on the whole. Then the quantity

sold at x% profit is given by $\left[\left(\dfrac{P+y}{x+y}\right)N\right]$ kg and the quantity sold

at y% loss is given by $\left[\left(\dfrac{x-P}{x+y}\right)N\right]$ kg

5. **A person has 216 books in his stock. He sells some books at 24% profit and remaining books at 8% loss. If he got a profit of 12% on whole stock then what is number of books sold at 24% profit and 8% loss?**

    (a) 116, 100 (b) 120, 96

    (c) 135, 81   (d) 132, 84

Sol. **(c)** Number of books sold at 24 % profit

$$= \left(\dfrac{P+y}{x+y}\right)N = \dfrac{8+12}{24+8}\times216 \ = \dfrac{20}{32}\times216 = 135$$

Number of books sold at 8 % loss

$$= \left(\dfrac{x-P}{x+y}\right)N = \dfrac{24-12}{24+8}\times216 \ = \dfrac{12}{32}\times216 = 81$$

Shortcut Approach - 6

A trader has N kg of a certain item, a part of which he sells at $x\%$ profit and the rest at $y\%$ loss. On the whole his loss is $P\%$. Then the quantity

sold at x% profit is $\left(\dfrac{y-P}{x+y}\right)N$ kg and the quantity sold at y % loss is given by $\left(\dfrac{x+P}{x+y}\right)$ N kg.

6. **A person has 200 litres of milk. He sold some quantity of milk at 20% profit and some quantity at 30% loss. If his loss was 6% on whole stock then what quantity of milk is sold at 20% profit and 30% loss?**
   (a) 100 litres, 100 litres
   (b) 96 litres, 104 litres
   (c) 80 litres, 120 litres
   (d) 125 litres, 75 litres

Sol. (b) Quantity of milk sold at 20 % profit

$$= \frac{30-6}{20+30} \times 200 = \frac{24}{50} \times 200$$

$= 96$ litres

Quantity of milk sold at 30 % loss

$$= \frac{20+6}{20+30} \times 200 = \frac{26}{50} \times 200$$

$= 104$ litres

⊕ Shortcut Approach - 7

If a person buys n kg of an item at the rate of ₹ P per kg. If he sells m kg at a profit of $x\%$, then the rate per kg, at which he should sell the remaining to get a profit of $y\%$ on the total deal, is given by ₹

$$P\left[1+\frac{ny-mx}{(n-m)100}\right]$$

7. **A person buys 100 kg of sugar at the rate of ₹ 40/kg. He sells 30 kg sugar at 8% profit. Then what is rate per kg of sugar is he need 10% overall profit?**
   (a) 34.44   (b) 37.84
   (c) 40.84   (d) 44.34

Sol. (d) Required rate

$$= P\left[1+\frac{ny-mx}{(n-m)100}\right] = \left[1+\frac{100\times10-30\times8}{(100-30)100}\right]40$$

$$= \left[1+\frac{760}{70\times100}\right]40 = \frac{776}{700}\times40 = \frac{1552}{35} = 44.34$$

⊕ Shortcut Approach - 8

Amount of liquid A left after n operations, when the container originally contains x units of liquid A from which y units is taken out and replaced by liquid B each time is $x\left(\dfrac{x-y}{x}\right)^n$ units.

8. From a container full of milk 20 % is drawn and the container filled with water and this process is performed two times more. What would be the ratio of milk in the mixture in present and original?

(a) 64 : 125 (b) 216 : 125

(c) 125 : 64 (d) 64 : 81

Sol. (a) Required ratio

$$= \left(1-\frac{y}{x}\right)^n = \left(\frac{x-y}{x}\right)^n = \left(\frac{100-20}{100}\right)^3 = \left(\frac{80}{100}\right)^3 = 64:125$$

⊕ Shortcut Approach - 9

Consider a container containing only ingredient 'A' of x_0 unit. From this, x_r unit is taken out and replaced by an equal amount of ingredient B. This process is repeated n times, then after n operations.

$$\frac{\text{Amount of A left}}{\text{Amount of B left}} = \frac{\left(1-\dfrac{x_r}{x_0}\right)^n}{1-\left(1-\dfrac{x_r}{x_0}\right)^n}$$

9. In a drum there is 100 litres of milk. From this 10 litres of milk taken out and replaced with water this process is repeated one more time then what is respective ratio of milk and water in new mixture?

(a) 19 : 81 (b) 81 : 19

(c) 81 : 100 (d) 100 : 8 1

Sol. (b) Required ratio

$$= \frac{\left(1-\dfrac{x_r}{x_0}\right)^n}{1-\left(1-\dfrac{x_r}{x_0}\right)^n} = \frac{\left(1-\dfrac{10}{100}\right)^2}{1-\left(1-\dfrac{10}{100}\right)^2} = \frac{81}{100}\times\frac{100}{19} = 81:19$$

⊕ Shortcut Approach - 10

A person's expenditure and savings are in the ratio $a : b$. His income increases by $x\%$. His expenditure also increases by $y\%$. His percentage increase in saving is given by

$$\left[\left(\frac{a}{b}+1\right)x - \frac{a}{b}y\right]\%$$

10. Respective ratio of expenditure and saving of Ravi is 7 : 3. His income is increases by 12% and his expenditure is increases by 15% then what is increament in his saving?

    (a) 15%   (b) 8%   (c) 5%   (d) 7%

Sol. **(c)** Required increment

$$=\left\{\left(\frac{a}{b}+1\right)x - \frac{a}{b}y\right\} = \left\{\left(\frac{7}{3}+1\right)12 - \frac{7}{3}\times15\right\}$$

$$=\frac{120}{3}-\frac{105}{3} = 40 - 35 = 5\%$$

⊕ Shortcut Approach - 11

In a group, there are some 4-legged creatures and some 2-legged creatures. If heads are counted, there are x and if leggs are counted there are y, then the no. of 4 – legged creatures are given by $\left(\dfrac{y-2x}{2}\right)$

or

$\left(\dfrac{\text{Total legs} - 2\times \text{Total heads}}{2}\right)$ and the no. of

2– legged creatures are given by $\left(\dfrac{4x-y}{2}\right)$ or

$\left(\dfrac{4\times \text{Total heads} - \text{Total legs}}{2}\right)$

11. On a place some persons and some horses are moving. If heads are counted, there are 60 and if legs are counted there are 190. What is number of persons?

    (a) 40   (b) 20   (c) 35   (d) 25

Sol. **(d)** Required number of persons

$$=\frac{4x-y}{2} = \frac{4\times60-190}{2} = \frac{50}{2} = 25$$

Exercise

1. The average weight of girls is 15 and the average weight of boys is 30 and the average weight of boys and girls both is 25. If the number of boys are 12, then the number of girls is:
   (a) 4　　(b) 6
   (c) 10　　(d) 18

2. In what ratio must water be mixed with milk costing ₹12 per litre in order to get a mixture worth of ₹ 8 per litre?
   (a) 1 : 3　　(b) 2 : 2
   (c) 1 : 2　　(d) 3 : 1

3. 5 kg of superior quality of sugar is mixed with 25 kg of inferior quality sugar. The price of superior quality and inferior quality sugar is ₹ 18 and ₹ 12 respectively. The average price per kg of the mixture is:
   (a) ₹ 13　　(b) ₹ 15
   (c) ₹ 18　　(d) ₹ 21

4. If the average weight of a class of students is 15 and the average weight of another class of students is 30, then find the ratio of the students of the first class to the another class of 30 students when the average weight of both the classes is 25 :
   (a) 1 : 2　　(b) 2 : 1
   (c) 1 : 3　　(d) 3 : 4

5. In what ratio should freely available water be mixed with the wine worth ₹ 60 per litre so that after selling the mixture at ₹ 50 per litre, the profit will be 25%?
   (a) 1 : 2　　(b) 2 : 3
   (c) 3 : 4　　(d) 4 : 5

6. There are three types of milk, Parag. Amul and Nestle. The ratio of fat to the non–fat contents in milk is 4 : 5, 5 : 6, 6 : 7 respectively. If all these three types of milk is mixed in equal quantity, the ratio of fat to the non-fat contents in the mixture will be :
   (a) 1751 : 2110
   (b) 175 : 543
   (c) 3 : 5
   (d) 10 : 18

7. Find the ratio in which rice at ₹ 7.20 a kg be mixed with rice at ₹ 5.70 a kg to produce a mixture worth ₹ 6.30 a kg.
   (a) 4 : 3　　(b) 3 : 4
   (c) 2 : 3　　(d) 3 : 2

8. The diluted wine contains only 8 litres of wine and the rest is water. A new mixture whose concentration is 30% is to be formed by replacing wine. How many litres of mixture shall be replaced with pure wine if there was initially 32 litres of water in the mixture?
   (a) 4　　(b) 5
   (c) 8
   (d) None of these

9. We have a 630 ml mixture of milk and water in the ratio 7:2. How much water must be added to make the ratio 7:3?
   (a) 70 ml　　(b) 60 ml
   (c) 80 ml　　(d) 50 ml

10. A container contains 40 litres of milk. From this container 4 litres of milk was taken out and replaced by water. This process was repeated further two times. How much milk is now contained by the container?
 (a) 26 litres
 (b) 29.16 litres
 (c) 28 litres
 (d) 28.2 litres
11. A can contains a mixture of two liquids A and B is the ratio 7 : 5. When 9 litres of mixture are drawn off and the can is filled with B, the ratio of A and B becomes 7 : 9. How many litres of liquid A were contained by the can initially?
12. A dishonest milkman sells his milk at cost price but he mixes it with water and thereby gains 25%. What is the percentage of water in the mixture?
 (a) 25% (b) 20%
 (c) 22% (d) 24%

Hints & Solution

1. **(b)** Let number of girls = n
 then, ATQ,
 $15n + 30 \times 12 = 25(12 + n)$
 $15n + 360 = 300 + 25n$
 $10n = 60 \Rightarrow n = 6.$

2. **(c)** By rule of alligation,

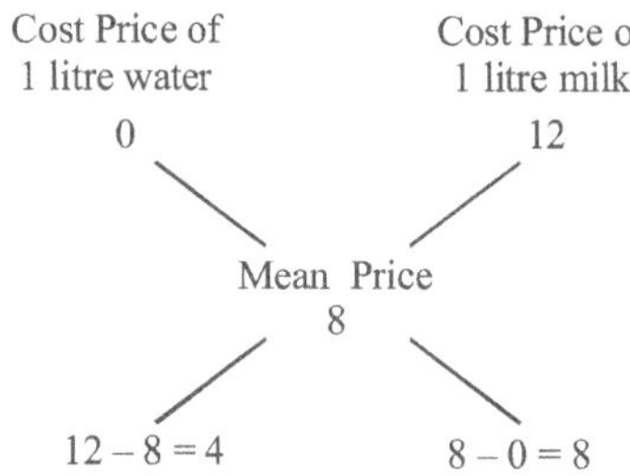

3. **(a)** Average price of the mixture

$$= \frac{5 \times 18 + 25 \times 12}{(5 + 25)}$$

$$= \frac{90 + 300}{30}$$

$$= \frac{390}{30} = ₹13.$$

4. **(a)** Let the ratio of the students with 15 students to 30 students be $x : y$, then

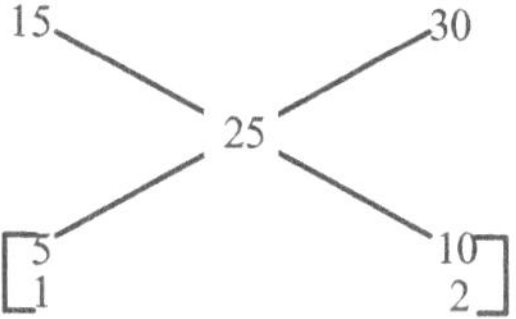

Here we know that the averages of individual classes is 15 and 30. Again we know that the averages of both the combined classes is 25. So the difference between 25 and 15 i.e., 10 and 30 & 25, i.e., 5 is written diagonally opposite. Thus the required ratio

$$= \frac{5}{10} = \frac{1}{2}$$

5. **(a)** Use Short Approach - 2
6. **(a)** In this type of questions, we consider only one item (viz, either fat or non-fat) as the fraction of the total quantity. Again we

equate the denominators. Let us consider fraction of fat

	Parag	Amul	Nestle
Fraction of fat →	$\dfrac{4}{9}$	$\dfrac{5}{11}$	$\dfrac{6}{13}$
	$\dfrac{4\times11\times13}{9\times11\times13}$	$\dfrac{5\times9\times13}{11\times9\times13}$	$\dfrac{6\times9\times11}{13\times9\times11}$
	$\dfrac{572}{1287}$	$\dfrac{585}{1287}$	$\dfrac{594}{1287}$

So the total fat in the total mixture

$$= \frac{572+585+594}{1287+1287+1287}$$

$$= \frac{1751}{3861}$$

Hence, the ratio of fat to the non-fat contents in the mixture

$$= 1751 : 2110$$

$$\because \quad (3861 - 1751 = 2110)$$

7. (c) Use Short Approach - 1

8. (b)

Wine		Water
8L		32L
1	:	4
20%		80% (original ratio)
30%		70% (required ratio)

In this case, the percentage of water being reduced when the mixture is being replaced with wine.

So the ratio of left quantity to the initial quantity is 7 : 8.

Therefore

$$\frac{7}{8} = \left[1 - \frac{K}{40}\right]$$

$$\Rightarrow \frac{7}{8} = \left[\frac{40-K}{40}\right]$$

$$\Rightarrow K = 5 \text{ litres}$$

9. (a) Use short approach - 3

10. (b) Suppose a container contains x units of a liquid from which y units are taken out and replaced by water. After n operations, quantity of pure liquid

$$= x\left(1 - \frac{y}{x}\right)^n \text{ units.}$$

milk contained by the container now

$$= 40\left(1 - \frac{4}{40}\right)^3$$

$$= 40\left(1 - \frac{1}{10}\right)^3$$

$$= 40 \times \frac{9}{10} \times \frac{9}{10} \times \frac{9}{10}$$

$$= \frac{4\times9\times9\times9}{100} = 29.16$$

11. (c) Suppose the can initially contains $7x$ and $5x$ of mixtures A and B respectively.

Quantity of A in mixture left

$$= \left(7x - \frac{7}{12} \times 9\right) \text{ litres}$$

$$= \left(7x - \frac{21}{4}\right) \text{ litres.}$$

Quantity of B in mixture left

$$= \left(5x - \frac{5}{12} \times 9 \right) \text{litres}$$

$$= \left(5x - \frac{15}{4} \right) \text{litres.}$$

$$\therefore \quad \frac{\left(7x - \frac{21}{4} \right)}{\left(5x - \frac{15}{4} \right) + 9} = \frac{7}{9} \quad \Rightarrow$$

$$\frac{28x - 21}{20x + 21} = \frac{7}{9}$$

$$\Rightarrow \quad 252x - 189 = 140x + 147$$

$$\Rightarrow \quad x = 3.$$

So, the can contained 21 litres of A

12. (b) Gain % =

$$\left[\frac{\text{Error}}{(\text{True Value-Error})} \times 100 \right] \%$$

Here Gain = 25%
error = quantity of water he mixes in the milk = x
true value = true quantity of milk = T
So the formula becomes,

$$25 = \frac{x}{(T-x)} \times 100$$

$$\Rightarrow 1 = \frac{x}{(T-x)} \times 4$$

$$\Rightarrow T - x = 4x$$

$$\Rightarrow T = 5x$$

Percentage of water in the mixture

$$= \frac{x}{T} \times 100 = \frac{x}{5x} \times 100$$

$$= \frac{1}{5} \times 100 = 20\%$$

Time, Work and Wages

If A and B can do a piece of work in x days, B and C in y days, C and A in z days, then $(A + B + C)$ working together will do the same work in

$$\left[\frac{2xyz}{xy + yz + xz}\right] \text{ days.}$$

1. A and B can do a piece of work in 12 days, B and C in 8 days, C and A in 6 days. How long would B take to do the same work alone?
   (a) 24 days
   (b) 32 days
   (c) 40 days
   (d) 48 days

Sol. (d) $\therefore (A + B + C)$ will work together for

$$= \left[\frac{2ABC}{AB + BC + AC}\right]\text{days} = \left[\frac{2 \times 12 \times 8 \times 6}{12 \times 8 + 8 \times 6 + 6 \times 12}\right]\text{days}$$

$$= \frac{1152}{216} = \frac{16}{3}\text{days}$$

Now, work done by B in one day
= Work done by $(A + B + C)$ in one day
$\qquad\qquad\qquad$ – Work done by $(A + C)$ in one day.

$$= \frac{3}{16} - \frac{1}{6} = \frac{9 - 8}{48} = \frac{1}{48}$$

Hence, B take 48 days to do the same work alone.

A certain number of men can do a work in 'D' days. If there were 'x' men less it could be finished in 'd' days more, then the number of men originally are $\left[\dfrac{x(D + d)}{d}\right]$.

2. A certain number of women can do a work in 12 days. If there were 4 women less it could be finished in 16 days more. How many women are there?

   (a) 5 women   (b) 6 women

   (c) 7 women   (d) None of these

Sol. **(c)** $\therefore$ No. of women

$$= \left[\frac{x(D+d)}{d}\right] = \left[\frac{4(12+16)}{16}\right] = \frac{4\times 28}{16} = 7 \text{ women}$$

If A is 'n' times as fast (or slow) as B, and is therefore able to finish a work in 'D' days less (or more) than B, then the time in which they can do it working together is given by $\left(\dfrac{Dn}{n^2-1}\right)$ **days.**

3. Two men A and B started a job in which A was thrice as good as B and therefore took 60 days less than B to finish the job. How many days will they take to finish the job if they start working together?

   (a) 15 days   (b) 20 days

   (c) $22\dfrac{1}{2}$ days   (d) 25 days

Sol. **(c)** $\therefore$ Number of days

$$= \left(\frac{Dn}{n^2-1}\right)\text{days} = \left[\frac{60\times 3}{(3)^2-1}\right]\text{days}$$

$$= \frac{180}{8} = \frac{90}{4} = 22\frac{1}{2}\text{days}$$

If x_1 men or y_1 women can reap a field in 'D' days, then x_2 men and y_2 women take to reap it $\left[\dfrac{D(x_1 y_1)}{x_2 y_1 + x_1 y_2}\right]$ **days.**

4. 12 men or 15 women can reap a field in 14 days. Find the number of days that 7 men and 5 women will take to reap it.

(a) $12\dfrac{3}{11}$ days

(b) $13\dfrac{3}{11}$ days

(c) $14\dfrac{3}{11}$ days

(d) $15\dfrac{3}{11}$ days

Sol. **(d)** $\therefore$ Number of days

$$= \left[\frac{D(x_1 y_1)}{x_2\, y_1 + x_1\, y_2}\right] = \left[\frac{14\times(12\times15)}{7\times15+12\times5}\right]$$

$$= \frac{168}{11} = 15\frac{3}{11}\,\text{days}$$

If a_1 men and b_1 boys can do a piece of work in x days and a_2 men and b_2 boys can do it in y days, then the following relationship is obtained.

$$1\ man = \left[\frac{yb_2 - xb_1}{xa_1 - ya_2}\right]\text{boys}$$

5. If 5 men and 8 boys can complete a piece of work in 8 days and 3 men and 12 boys can complete same work in 10 days then what is respective ratio of the work efficiency of a man to that of a boy?

(a) $5:24$ (b) $5:28$ (c) $28:5$ (d) $14:5$

Sol. **(c)** $\therefore$ 1 man

$$= \left[\frac{yb_2 - xb_1}{xa_1 - ya_2}\right]\text{boys}$$

$$= \left[\frac{10\times12 - 8\times8}{8\times5 - 10\times3}\right]\text{boys}$$

$$\frac{\text{A man work}}{\text{A boy's work}} = \left[\frac{120 - 64}{40 - 30}\right]$$

$$= \frac{28}{5} = 28:5$$

Shortcut Approach - 6

If A and B can do a work in x and y days respectively, they began the work together, but A left after some time and B finished the remaining work in z days; then the no. of days after which A left is given by $\left(\dfrac{xy}{x+y}\right)\left(\dfrac{y-z}{y}\right)$ days.

6. A and B can separately complete a piece of work in 20 days and 30 days respectively. They worked together for sometime, then B left the work. If A completed the rest of the work in 10 days, then B worked for:

    (a) 6 days   (b) 8 days

    (c) 12 days   (d) 16 days

Sol. (a) Number of days

$$= \left(\frac{xy}{x+y}\right)\left(\frac{x-z}{x}\right) = \left(\frac{20\times30}{20+30}\right)\left(\frac{20-10}{20}\right)$$

$$= \frac{600}{50}\times\frac{1}{2} = 6 \text{ days}$$

Shortcut Approach - 7

A certain number of men can do a work in 'D' days. If there were 'x' men more it could be finished in 'd' days less, then the number of men originally are $\left[\dfrac{x(D-d)}{d}\right]$

7. A certain number of men can do a work in 60 days. If there were 8 men more it could be finished in 10 days less. How many men are there?

    (a) 40   (b) 45

    (c) 50   (d) 55

Sol. **(a)** Number of worker $= \left[\dfrac{x(D-d)}{d}\right]$

$$= \left[\dfrac{8(60-10)}{10}\right] = \dfrac{8 \times 50}{10} = 40 \text{ men}$$

Shortcut Approach - 8

A builder decided to build a farmhouse in 'D' days. He employed 'x' men in the beginning and 'y' more men after 'd' days and completed the construction in stipulated time. If he had not employed the additional men, then the men in the beginning would have finished it in

$$\left[\dfrac{D(x+y)-yd}{x}\right] \textbf{ days and it would have been } \left[\dfrac{y(D-d)}{x}\right] \textbf{ days behind}$$

the schedule.

8. A builder decided to build a farmhouse in 40 days. He employed 100 men in the beginning and 100 more after 35 days and completed the construction in stipulated time. If he had not employed the additional men, how many days behind schedule would it have been finished?
   (a) 2 days (b) 4 days (c) 5 days (d) 6 days

Sol. **(c)** No. of days $= \left[\dfrac{D(x+y)-yd}{x}\right]$

$$= \left[\dfrac{40(100+100)-100 \times 35}{100}\right] = \dfrac{4500}{100} = 45 \text{ days}$$

Therefore, the work would have lasted
$= 45 - 5 = 5$ days before scheduled time

OR

$\therefore$ No. of days

$$= \left[\dfrac{y(D-d)}{x}\right] = \left[\dfrac{100(40-35)}{100}\right]$$

$= 5$ days before scheduled time

Shortcut Approach - 9

A team of x persons is supposed to do a work in 'D' days. After 'd_1' days, 'y' more persons were employed and the work was finished 'd_2' days earlier, then the number of days it would have been delayed if 'x' more persons were not employed is given by $\left[\dfrac{y\{D-(d_1+d_2)\}-d_2x}{x}\right]$ days

and the number of days in which the work would have been finished is given by $\left[\dfrac{(x+y)(D-d_2)-d_1y}{x}\right]$ days

9. A contractor employed 30 men to do a work in 38 days. After 25 days, he employed 5 men more and the work was finished 1 day earlier. How many days he would have behind, if he had not employed additional men?

(a) 1   (b) 1.5   (c) 2   (d) 2.5

Sol. **(a)** No. of days

$$= \left[\frac{(x+y)(D-d_2)-d_1y}{x}\right]\text{days} = \left[\frac{(30+5)(38-1)-25\times5}{30}\right]$$

$= 39$ days

$\therefore$ Required number of days $= (39 - 38) = 1$ day after the scheduled time.

Shortcut Approach - 10

A group of men decided to do a work in x days, but 'n' of them became absent. If the rest of the group did the work in 'y' days, then the original number of men is given by $\left(\dfrac{ny}{y-x}\right)$ men.

10. A team of workers decided to finish a work in 100 days. But due to some reason, 10 of them became absent, and the remaining work finished the whole work in 110 days. Then the original number of workers was _________.

(a) 100   (b) 110   (c) 120   (d) None of these

Sol. **(b)**　∴ Number of men

$$= \left[\frac{ny}{y-x}\right] = \left[\frac{10 \times 110}{110 - 100}\right]$$

$$= \left[\frac{10 \times 110}{10}\right] = 110 \text{ men}$$

⊕ Shortcut Approach - 11

A can do a work in x days and B can do the same work in y days. If they work together for 'd' days and A goes away, then the number of days in which B finishes the work is given by $y - \left(1 + \dfrac{y}{x}\right)d$ days.

11.　A can do a piece of work in 20 days and B can do the same work in 30 days. They start work together but A left after 10 days. How many days required to B for remaining work?
　　(a)　10 days　　　　　　(b) 2.5 days
　　(c)　15 days　　　　　　(d) 5 days

Sol. **(d)**　No. of days $= \left[y - \left(1 + \dfrac{y}{x}\right)d\right]$ days

$$= \left[30 - \left(1 + \frac{30}{20}\right) \times 10\right] = \left[30 - \frac{50}{20} \times 10\right] = 5 \text{ days}$$

⊕ Shortcut Approach - 12

A and B can do a piece of work in x and y days respectively and both of them starts the work together. If A leaves the work 'a' days before the completion of the work, then the total time in which

$$\text{the whole work is completed} = \frac{(x+a)y}{(x+y)} \text{days.}$$

A and B can do a piece of work in x and y days respectively and both of them starts the work together. If B leaves the work 'a' days before the completion of work, then the total time, in which the whole work is

$$\text{completed} = \left[\frac{(y+a)x}{x+y}\right] \textbf{ days}$$

12. A and B can complete a piece of work in 30 days and 40 days respectively. Both of them start the work together but A left the work 10 days before the completion of work then what is total time?

(a) $21\dfrac{4}{5}$ days

(b) $22\dfrac{1}{7}$ days

(c) $22\dfrac{6}{7}$ days

(d) 25 days

Sol. (c) No. of days

$$= \left[\dfrac{(x+a\ y)}{(x+y\ )}\right]\text{days}$$

$$= \left[\dfrac{(30+10)40}{(30+40)}\right]$$

$$= \dfrac{1600}{70} = 22\dfrac{6}{7}(\text{days }\,)$$

Shortcut Approach - 13

If A working alone takes 'x' days more than A and B, and B working alone takes 'y' days more than A and B together then the number of days taken by A and B

working together is given by $\left[\sqrt{xy}\right]$ days.

13. A takes 18 days more than A and B together to complete a piece of work and B takes 50 days more than A and B together. What is time required to complete the work for A and B together?

(a) 30 days   (b) 45 days

(c) 15 days   (d) 50 days

Sol. (a) No. of days $= \sqrt{xy}$

$$= \sqrt{18\times50}\ = 30\text{ days}$$

Shortcut Approach - 14

There is a sufficient food for 'M' men for 'D' days. If after 'd' days 'm' men leave the place, then the rest of the food will last for the rest of the men for $\left[\dfrac{D-d}{M-m} \times M\right]$ days.

There is a sufficient food for 'M' persons for 'D' days. If after 'd' days 'm' more men join them the food will last in $\dfrac{D-d}{M+m} \times M$ days.

14. There is a sufficient rice for 280 men for 20 days. After 18 days 200 men leave the place. For how many days will the rest of the rice last for the rest of the men?

    (a) 6 days (b) 7 days (c) 9 days (d) 11 days

Sol. (b) No. of days

$$= \left[\frac{D-d}{M-m} \times M\right]$$

$$= \left[\frac{20-18}{280-200} \times 280\right]$$

$$= \frac{2}{80} \times 280 = 7 \text{ days}$$

Shortcut Approach - 15

A can do a work in x days and B can do the same work in y days. If the contract for the work is ₹ X, and both of them work together, then the share of A and B is given by ₹ $\left(\dfrac{X}{x+y} \times y\right)$ and $\left(\dfrac{X}{x+y} \times x\right)$ respectively.

15. A and B can do a piece of work in 20 days and 45 days respectively. If the total of ₹ 910 is paid for the work then what is the share of B?

    (a) 420   (b) 390

    (c) 280   (d) 260

Sol. **(c)** Share of B $= \dfrac{X}{x+y} \times x = \dfrac{910}{45+20} \times 20$

$$= \dfrac{910 \times 20}{65} = 280$$

⊕ Shortcut Approach - 16

A person A can do a work in *x* days. With the help of another person B, he can do the same work in *y* days. If they get ₹ X for that work, then the share of A and

B is given by ₹ $\left[\dfrac{Xy}{x}\right]$ and ₹ $\left[\dfrac{X(x-y)}{x}\right]$ repsectively.

16. Rakesh can complete a piece of work in 40 days. He can complete same piece of work with help of Ranjan in 30 days. If they are paid ₹ 1200 for the work then what is share of Ranjan

    (a) 900   (b) 300   (c) 600   (d) 400

Sol. **(b)** Share of Ranjan

$$= \dfrac{X(x-y)}{x} = \dfrac{1200(40-30)}{40} = 300$$

⊕ Shortcut Approach - 17

If a pipe can fill a tank in *x* hours and another can fill the same tank in

y hours, then time taken to fill the tank $= \left[\dfrac{xy}{x+y}\right]$ hours.

Or

A tap 'A' can empty a cistern in *x* hours and the other tap 'B' can empty is in y hours. If both emptying taps are opened together, then the time

taken to empty the full cistern is given by $\left[\dfrac{xy}{x+y}\right]$ hrs.

17. Two pipes A and B can fill a tank in 18 h and 12 h, repectively. If both the pipes are opened simultaneously, how much time will be taken to fill the tank:

    (a) $7\dfrac{1}{5}$ hr   (b) $6\dfrac{1}{5}$ hr   (c) $7\dfrac{2}{5}$ hr   (d) $6\dfrac{2}{5}$ hr

Sol. **(a)** $\text{Time} = \left[\dfrac{xy}{x+y}\right] = \dfrac{18 \times 12}{18+12} = \dfrac{216}{30} = \dfrac{36}{5} = 7\dfrac{1}{5}$ hr.

Shortcut Approach - 18

A, B and C are three pipes connected to a tank. A and B together fill the tank in x hours. B and C together fill the tank in y hours. A and C together fill the tank in z hours.

(i) Time taken by A to fill the tank $= \left(\dfrac{2xyz}{xy+yz-xz}\right)$ **hrs,**

(ii) Time taken by B to fill the tank $= \left(\dfrac{2xyz}{yz+xz-xy}\right)$ **hrs,**

(iii) Time taken by C to fill the tank $= \left(\dfrac{2xyz}{xz+xy-yz}\right)$ **hrs**

18. Three pipes are connected with a tank. A and B can fill the tank in 40 hrs and B and C in 50 hrs. If A and C can fill the tank in 30 hrs then find the time required for each pipe?

    (a) $\dfrac{400}{11}$ hrs, $\dfrac{1200}{7}$ hrs, $\dfrac{1200}{17}$ hrs

    (b) $\dfrac{500}{3}$ hrs, $\dfrac{200}{3}$ hrs, $\dfrac{700}{17}$ hrs

    (c) 60 hrs, 50 hrs, 80 hrs

    (d) 90.5 hrs, 83.3 hrs, 62.5 hrs

Sol. **(a)** Required time of A

$$= \frac{2xyz}{xy+yz-xz} = \frac{2 \times 40 \times 50 \times 30}{40 \times 50 + 50 \times 30 - 40 \times 30}$$

$$= \frac{2 \times 40 \times 50 \times 30}{3300} = \frac{400}{11} \text{ hrs}$$

Time of B

$$= \frac{2xyz}{yz+xz-xy} = \frac{2 \times 40 \times 50 \times 30}{50 \times 30 + 40 \times 30 - 40 \times 50}$$

$$= \frac{2 \times 40 \times 50 \times 30}{700} = \frac{1200}{7} \text{ hrs}$$

Time of C

$$= \frac{2xyz}{xz + xy - yz} = \frac{2 \times 40 \times 50 \times 30}{40 \times 30 + 40 \times 50 - 30 \times 50}$$

$$= \frac{2 \times 40 \times 50 \times 30}{1700} = \frac{1200}{17} \text{ hrs}$$

⊕ Shortcut Approach - 19

One filling pipe A is *n* times faster than the other filling pipe B. If B can fill a cistern in *x* hours, then the time in which the cistern will be full, if both the filling pipes are opened together, is $\left(\dfrac{x}{n+1} \right)$ hours.

Note: Value of the slower filling pipe is given.

19. Two inlet pipes A and B are connected with a tank. A is 4 times faster than B. If B can fill the tank in 20 hrs then find the time when tank will be full if both A and B are opened together?

   (a) 4 hrs   (b) 5 hrs   (c) 16 hrs   (d) $6\dfrac{2}{3}$ hrs

Sol. (a)   Required time $= \dfrac{x}{n+1} = \dfrac{20}{4+1} = 4\text{hrs}$

⊕ Shortcut Approach - 20

One filling pipe A is *n* times faster than the other filling pipe B. If A can fill a cistern in *x* hours, then the time in which the cistern will be full, if both the filling pipes are opened together, is $\left(\dfrac{n}{n+1} \right) x$ hours.

Note: Value of the faster filling pipe is given.

20. Two inlet pipes A and B are connected with a tank. A is 3 times faster than B. If A can fill the tank in 24 minutes, then what is time required for A and B together to fill the tank?

   (a) 15 minutes   (b) 20 minutes
   (c) 18 minutes   (d) 12 minutes

Sol. (c) Required time

$$= \left(\frac{n}{n+1}\right)x = \left(\frac{3}{3+1}\right)24 = \frac{3}{4} \times 24 = 18 \text{ min}$$

Shortcut Approach - 21

If one filling pipe A is n times faster and takes x minutes less time than the other filling pipe B, then the time, they will take to fill a cistern, if both the pipes are opened together, is $\left[\dfrac{nx}{\left(n^2-1\right)}\right]$ minutes.

21. Two inlets pipes A and B are connected with a tank. A is 6 times faster than B. A takes 35 minutes less than B to fill the tank then what is time required for A and B together to fill the tank?
    (a) 35 minutes (b) 6 minutes
    (c) 10 minutes (d) 7.5 minutes

Sol. (b) Required time

$$= \frac{nx}{n^2-1} = \frac{6 \times 35}{6^2-1} = \frac{6 \times 35}{35} = 6 \text{ min}$$

Shortcut Approach - 22

If a pipe A fills a cistern in x hours and suddenly a leak develops through which every hour n part of the water filled by the pipe A leaks out, then the time in which tank is full $= \left(\dfrac{x}{1-n}\right)$ hours.

22. Pipe A can fill the tank in 35 minutes. Due to some leakage 40% water is leaks out. What is time required to fill the tank?

    (a) 40 minutes (b) 30 minutes
    (c) 60 minutes (d) 45 minutes

Sol. (c) Required time

$$= \frac{x}{1-n} = \frac{36}{1-\dfrac{40}{100}} = \frac{36 \times 100}{60} = 60 \text{ min}$$

A cistern is normally filled in x hrs but takes t hrs longer to fill because of

a leak in its bottom. If the cistern is full, the leak will empty it in $\left[\dfrac{x \times (x+t)}{t}\right]$

hrs.

23. A pipe can fill a tank in 15 hrs. Due to a leak it takes 5 hrs more to fill it. If tank is full the leak will empty it in:

(a) 20 hrs   (b) 40 hrs
(c) 45 hrs   (d) 60 hrs

Sol. **(d)** Required time

$$= \left\{\dfrac{x \times (x+t)}{t}\right\} = \dfrac{15 \times (15+5)}{5} = \dfrac{15 \times 20}{5} = 60 \text{ hrs}$$

If a pipe fills a tank in x hours and another fills the same tank in y hours, but a third one empties the full tank in z hours when all of them are opened

together, then the time taken to fill the tank $= \left[\dfrac{xyz}{yz + xz - xy}\right]$ **hours.**

24. Two inlet pipes A and B and outlet pipe C is connected with a tank. A and B can fill the tank in 30 hrs and 40 hrs and C can empty it in 20 hrs. If all pipes are opened together then what is time required to fill the tank?

(a) 100 hrs (b) 120 hrs (c) 60 hrs (d) 80 hrs

Sol. **(b)** Required time

$$= \dfrac{xyz}{yz + xz - xy} = \dfrac{30 \times 40 \times 20}{40 \times 20 + 30 \times 20 - 30 \times 40}$$

$$= \dfrac{30 \times 40 \times 20}{200} = 120$$

A pipe can fill a tank in x hours. Due to a leak in the bottom it is filled in y hours. If the tank is full, the time taken by leak to empty the tank

$= \left(\dfrac{xy}{y-x}\right)$ **hrs.**

25. A pipe can fill the tank in 20 hrs. Due to a leak it takes 25 hrs to fill the tank then what is time required for leak to empty the full tank?

(a) 100 hrs (b) 80 hrs (c) 75 hrs (d) 50 hrs

Sol. (a) Required time

$$= \frac{xy}{y-x} = \frac{20 \times 25}{25-20} = \frac{500}{5} = 100 \text{ hrs}$$

Shortcut Approach - 26

A cistern has a leak which would empty it in x hours. If a tap is turned on which admits water at the rate of w litres per hour into the cistern, and the cistern is now emptied in *y* hours, then the capacity of the cistern is

$$w \times \left(\frac{xy}{y-x} \right) \text{ litres.}$$

26. A outlet can empty the tank in 20 hrs. A inlet pumps 5 litres water in 1 hr and it is now emptied in 30 hrs then what is capacity of tank?
    (a) 600 litres   (b) 200 litres
    (c) 300 litres   (d) 500 litres

Sol. (c) Required capacity

$$= w \left(\frac{xy}{y-x} \right) = 5 \left(\frac{20 \times 30}{30-20} \right) = 5 \times \frac{600}{10} = 300 \text{ litres}$$

Exercise

1. *A* is 30% more efficient than *B*. How much time will they take working together, to complete a job which *A* alone could have done in 23 days?
   (a) 11 days
   (b) 13 days
   (c) $20\dfrac{3}{17}$ days
   (d) None of these

2. If *m* man can do a work in *r* days, then the number of days taken by $(m + n)$ men to do it is:
   (a) $\dfrac{m+n}{mn}$
   (b) $\dfrac{m+n}{mr}$
   (c) $\dfrac{mr}{(m+n)}$
   (d) $\dfrac{(m+n)r}{mn}$

3. 12 men complete a work in 18 days. Six days after they had started working, 4 men joined them. How many days will all of them take to complete the remaining work ?
   (a) 10 days
   (b) 12 days
   (c) 15 days
   (d) 9 days

4. 6 children and 2 men complete a certain piece of work in 6 days. Each child takes twice the time taken by a man to finish the work. In how many days will 5 men finish the same work?
   (a) 6   (b) 8
   (c) 9   (d) 15

5. X can do a piece of work in 15 days. If he is joined by Y who is 50% more efficient, in what time will X and Y together finish the work?
   (a) 10 days
   (b) 6 days
   (c) 18 days
   (d) Data insufficient

6. Chandni and Divakar can do a piece of work in 9 days and 12 days respectively. If they work for a day alternatively, Chandni beginning, in how many days, the work will be completed?
   (a) $10\dfrac{1}{4}$ (b) $9\dfrac{1}{5}$
   (c) 11.11   (d) 10

7. If 20 persons complete one–third of a work in 20 days then how many more persons will be required to complete the rest work in 25 days?
   (a) 6   (b) 12
   (c) 18   (d) 24

8. A contractor undertakes to built a walls in 50 days. He employs 50 peoples for the same. However after 25 days he finds that only 40% of the

work is complete. How many more man need to be employed to complete the work in time?

(a)　25　　(b)　30
(c)　35　　(d)　20

9. A cistern has two taps which fill it in 12 minutes and 15 minutes respectively. There is also a waste pipe in the cistern. When all the three are opened, the empty cistern is full in 20 minutes. How long will the waste pipe take to empty the full cistern ?

(a) 10 min
(b) 12 min
(c) 15 min
(d) None of these

10. A construction farm undertakes to built a bridge in 75 days. He employs 75 peoples for the same. However after 37 days he finds that only 40% of the work is complete. How many more man need to be employed to complete the work in time?

(a) 25　　(b) 30
(c) 35　　(d) 20

11. One hundred men in 10 days do a third of a piece of work. The work is then required to be completed in another 13 days. On the next day (the eleventh day) 50 more men are employed, and on the day after that, another 50. How many men must be discharged at the end of the 18th day so that the rest of the men, working for the remaining time, will just complete the work ?

(a) 100　　(b) 105
(c) 110　　(d) 115

12. A pump can be operated both for filling a tank and for emptying it. The capacity of tank is 2400 m^3. The emptying capacity of the pump is 10 m^3 per minute higher than its filling capacity. Consequently, the pump needs 8 minutes less to empty the tank to fill it. Find the filling capacity of pump.

(a) 50 m^3/min
(b) 60 m^3/min
(c) 58 m^3/min
(d) None of these

Hints & Solution

1. **(b)** Time required to complete the work by B

$$= 23 \times \frac{130}{100} = 30 \text{ days}$$

Time required to complete the work, when two work together

$$= \frac{23 \times 30}{23 + 30} = \frac{23 \times 30}{53} = 13 \text{ days}$$

2. **(c)** $M_1 \times D_1 = M_2 \times D_2$

$$m \times r = (m + n) \times D_2$$

$$D_2 = \frac{mr}{(m+n)}$$

3. **(d)** Use Short Approach - 8

4. **(a)** $6C + 2M = 6$ days

5. **(b)** X do the work in 15 days, then Y do the same work in

$$15 \times \frac{100}{(100 + 50)} = 10 \text{ days}$$

time required to complete the same work when they work together $= \dfrac{15 \times 10}{(15 + 10)} = 6$ days.

6. **(a)** Work done in two days

$$= \frac{1}{9} + \frac{1}{12} = \frac{7}{36}$$

Work done in 10 days

$$= \frac{7 \times 5}{36} = \frac{35}{36}$$

Remaining work $= \dfrac{1 - 35}{36} = \dfrac{1}{36}$

Time required to complete $\dfrac{1}{36}$

work by A $= \dfrac{1}{36} \times 9 = \dfrac{1}{4}$ days

Total days $= 10 + \dfrac{1}{4} = 10\dfrac{1}{4}$ days.

7. **(b)** $\dfrac{M_1 D_1}{W_1} = \dfrac{M_2 D_2}{W_2}$,

$$\frac{20 \times 20}{\dfrac{1}{3}} = \frac{(20 + x) \times 25}{\dfrac{2}{3}}$$

or, $2 \times 20 \times 20 = (20 + x) \times 25$

or, $x = 12$

8. **(a)** 50 men complete 0.4 work in 25 days.

Applying the work rule,

$$m_1 \times d_1 \times w_2 = m_2 \times d_2 \times w_1$$

we have,

$$50 \times 25 \times 0.6 = m_2 \times 25 \times 0.4$$

or m_2

$$= \frac{50 \times 25 \times 0.6}{25 \times 0.4} = 75 \text{ men}$$

Number of additional men required $= (75 - 50) = 25$

9. **(a)** Use Short Approach - 24

10. **(c)** 75 men complete 0.4 work in 37 days.

Applying the work rule,

$$m_1 \times d_1 \times w_2$$

$$= m_2 \times d_2 \times w_1$$

we have, $75 \times 37 \times 0.6 =$

$m_2 \times 38 \times 0.4$ or m_2

$$= \frac{75 \times 37 \times 0.6}{38 \times 0.4} = 110 \text{ men}$$

Number of additional men required $= (110 - 75) = 35$

11. **(c)** Suppose that X men must be discharged at the end of the 18th day.

$100 \times 10 + 150 \times 1 + 200 \times 7 + (200 - X) \times 5 = 100 \times 30$

$5X = 550 \Rightarrow X = 110 \text{ men}$

12. **(a)** Let the filling capacity of pump be x m³/min.

Then, emptying capacity of pump $= (x + 10)$ m³ /min.

$$\therefore \quad \frac{2400}{x} - \frac{2400}{x + 10} = 8$$

$$\Rightarrow x^2 + 10x - 3000 = 0$$

$$\Rightarrow (x - 50)(x + 60) = 0$$

$$\Rightarrow x = 50 \text{ m}^3/\text{min.}$$

Time, Speed and Distance

Shortcut Approach - 1

A man takes x hours to walk to a certain place and ride back. However, if he walks both ways he needs t hours more, then the time taken by him to ride both ways is $(x - t)$ hours.

1. I walk a certain distance and ride back and take $6\frac{1}{2}$ hours altogether. I could walk both ways in $7\frac{3}{4}$ hours. How long would it take me to ride both ways?
    (a) 4 hr 25 min   (b) 5 hr 25 min
    (c) 4 hr 15 min   (d) 5 hr 15 min

1. **(d)** Difference $= 7\frac{3}{4} - 6\frac{1}{2} = \frac{5}{4}$ hours

He, need 5/4 hour more to walk both ways
∴   Time taken to ride both ways $= (X - t)$ hours

$$= \left(6\frac{1}{2} - \frac{5}{4}\right) = \left(\frac{13}{2} - \frac{5}{4}\right)$$

$$= \frac{21}{4} = 5\frac{1}{4} \text{ hours} = 5 \text{ hours } 15 \text{ minute}$$

Shortcut Approach - 2

A person goes to a destination at a speed of x km/hr and returns to his place at a speed of y km/hr. If he takes T hours in all, the distance between his place and destination is $\left(\dfrac{xy}{x+y} \times T\right)$ km. In other words, Required distance

$$= \text{Total time taken} \times \frac{\text{Product of the two speeds}}{\text{Addition of the two speeds}}$$

2. A man rode out a certain distance by train at the rate of 25 km per hour and walked back at the rate of 4 km per hour. The whole journey took 5 hours 48 minutes. What distance did he ride?

    (a) 20 km   (b) 29 km   (c) 24 km   (d) 25 km

Sol. **(a)** Distance

$$= T\left[\frac{x\,y}{x+y}\right]$$

$$= \left(5 + \frac{48}{60}\right)\left[\frac{25 \times 4}{25 + 4}\right]$$

$$= \left[\frac{29}{5} \times \frac{25 \times 4}{29}\right] = 20 \text{km}$$

⊕ Shortcut Approach - 3

If a certain distance is covered at x km/hr and the same distance is covered at y km/hr, then the average speed during the whole journey is

$$\frac{2xy}{x+y} \text{ km/hr.}$$

3. Sahil covers a certain distance by car driving at 35 km/h and he returns back to the starting point riding on a scooter with a speed of 25 km/hr. Find the average speed for the whole journey.

    (a) 57.1 km/hr   (b) 16.41 km/hr

    (c) 29.16 km/hr (d)   23.14 km/hr

Sol. **(c)** Speed $= \dfrac{2xy}{x+y} \text{ km/hr}$

$$= \frac{2 \times 35 \times 25}{35 + 25}$$

$$= \frac{1750}{60} = 29.16 \text{ km/hr}$$

Shortcut Approach - 4

If a person does a journey in T hours and the first half at S_1 km/hr and the second half at S_2 km/hr, then the distance $= \dfrac{2 \times T \times S_1 \times S_2}{S_1 + S_2}$

4. A bus covers a certain distance in 16 hours. It covers half the distance at 40 km/hr and the rest at 60 km/hr. Find the length of the journey.
   - (a) 528 km
   - (b) 408 km
   - (c) 314 km
   - (d) 768 km

Sol. **(d)** Distance

$$= \left[\frac{2T\left(S_1 \times S_2\right)}{S_1 + S_2} \right]$$

$$= \left[\frac{2 \times 16 \times 40 \times 60}{40 + 60} \right] = 768 \text{ km}$$

Shortcut Approach - 5

A person covers a certain distance between two points. Having an average speed of x km/hr, he is late by x_1 hours. However, with a speed of y km/hr he reaches his destination y_1 hours earlier. The distance between the two points is given by $\left[\dfrac{xy\left(\left(x_1 + y_1\right)\right)}{\left(y - x\right)} \right] km.$

5. A man riding a bicycle from his house at 10 km/ hr and reaches his office late by 6 min. He increases his speed by 2 km/hr and reaches 6 min before. How far is the office from his house?
   - (a) 6 km
   - (b) 7 km
   - (c) 12 km
   - (d) 16 km

Sol. **(c)** Distance

$$= \left[\frac{xy\left(x_1 + y_1\right)}{\left(y - x\right)} \right] km$$

$$= \left[\frac{10 \times 12 \left(\dfrac{6}{60} + \dfrac{6}{60} \right)}{\left(12 - 10\right)} \right] km = \left[\frac{120 \times 12}{2 \times 60} \right] = 12 \text{ km}$$

⊕ Shortcut Approach - 6

A person walking at a speed of x km/hr reaches his destination x_1 hrs late. Next time he increases his speed by y km/hr, but still he is late by y_1 hrs. The distance of his destination from his house is given by

$$\left[(x_1 - y_1)(x+y)\frac{x}{y}\right] \text{ km.}$$

6. If a train runs at 40 km/hr, it reaches its destination late by 11 min, but if it runs at 50 km/hr, it is late by 5 min only. Find the correct time for the train to complete its journey.
   (a) 19 min   (b) 20 min
   (c) 21 min   (d) 18 min

Sol. (a) $\text{Distance} = \left[(x_1 - y_1)(x+y)\frac{x}{y}\right] \text{km}$

$$= \left[\left(\frac{11}{60} - \frac{5}{60}\right)(40+10)\frac{40}{10}\right]\text{km} = \left[\frac{6}{60} \times 50 \times \frac{40}{10}\right] = 20 \text{ km}$$

$$\text{Time taken @ 40 km/hr} = 20 \times \frac{60}{40} = 30 \text{ minutes}$$

$\Rightarrow$ Normal time = $(30 - 11)$ min = 19 minutes
or   Time taken @ 50 km/hr
     = $20 \times 60/50 = 24$ minutes
$\Rightarrow$ Normal time = $(24 - 5)$ min = 19 min

⊕ Shortcut Approach - 7

If a train travelling x km an hour leaves a place and t hours later another train travelling y km an hour, where $y > x$, in the same direction, then they will be together after travelling $\left[\frac{t(xy)}{y-x}\right]$ km from the starting place.

7. Amit walks at a uniform speed of 4 km/hr and 4 hr after his start Brijesh cycles after him at the uniform rate of 20 km/hr. How far from the starting point will Brijesh catch Amit?
   (a) 15 km   (b) 18 km   (c) 13 km   (d) 20 km

Sol. (d) Distance

$$= \left[\frac{t(xy)}{y-x}\right] km$$

$$= \left[\frac{4 \times 4 \times 20}{20-4}\right] km$$

$$= \left[\frac{16 \times 20}{16}\right] km = 20 \text{ km}$$

Shortcut Approach - 8

A person has to cover a distance of x km in t hours. If he covers n^{th} part of the journey in m^{th} of the total time, then his speed should be

$$\left(\frac{x}{t} \times \frac{1-n}{1-m}\right)$$ **km/hr to cover the remaining distance in the remaining time.**

8. A bullockcart has to cover a distance of 80 km in 10 hr. If it covers half of the journey in $\frac{3}{5}$ th time, what should be its speed to cover the remaining distance in the left time?

(a) 5 km/hr.   (b) 10 km/hr.
(c) 15 km/hr.   (d) 20 km/hr.

Sol. (b) Speed

$$= \left[\frac{x}{t}\frac{(1-n)}{(1-m)}\right] km/hr$$

$$= \left[\frac{80\left(1-\frac{1}{2}\right)}{10\left(1-\frac{3}{5}\right)}\right]$$

$$= \frac{80 \times \frac{1}{2}}{10 \times \frac{2}{5}} = \frac{40}{4} = 10 \text{ km/hr}$$

⊕ Shortcut Approach - 9

A thief is spotted by a policeman from a distance of d km. When the policeman starts the chase, the thief also starts running. Assuming the speed of the thief x kilometres an hour, and that of the policeman y kilometres an hour, then the thief will run before he is overtaken

$$= d\left[\frac{x}{y-x}\right] \text{ km.}$$

9.   A thief is spotted by a policeman from a distance of 200 m. When the policeman starts chasing, the thief also starts running. If the speed of the thief be 16 km/hr and that of the policeman be 20 km/hr. How far the thief will have run before he is overtaken?

   (a) 800 m   (b) 900 m
   (c) 1000 m   (d) 700 m

Sol. **(a)** Distance

$$= d\left[\frac{x}{y-x}\right] \text{km}$$

$$= \frac{200}{1000} \times \left[\frac{16}{20-16}\right]$$

$$= \frac{4}{5}\,\text{km} = \frac{4}{5} \times 1000 = 800\,\text{m}$$

⊕ Shortcut Approach - 10

A person covers a certain distance on scooter. Had he moved x_1 km/hr faster, he would have taken t_1 hours less. If he had moved x_2 km/hr slower, he would have taken t_2 hours more, then the original speed

(S) is $\left[\dfrac{x_1 x_2 (t_1 + t_2)}{t_2 x_1 - t_1 x_2}\right]$ km/hr and the distance is given by

$$\left[\frac{t_1 \times S(S + x_1)}{x_1}\right] \text{km.}$$

10. A train covered a certain distance at a uniform speed. If the train had been 6 km/hr faster, it would have taken 4 hours less than the scheduled time. And, if the train were slower by 6 km/hr, the train would have taken 6 hours more than the scheduled time. The length of the journey is:

(a) 700 km (b) 720 km
(c) 740 km (d) 760 km

Sol. (b) $\text{Speed} = \left[\dfrac{x_1 x_2 \left(t_1 + t_2\right)}{t_2 x_1 - t_1 x_2} \right] \text{km/hr}$

$$= \left[\frac{6 \times 6 (4+6)}{6 \times 6 - 4 \times 6} \right] = \frac{36 \times 10}{12} = 30 \text{ km/hr}$$

$$\text{Distance} = \left[\frac{t_1 \times s \left(s + x_1\right)}{x_1} \right] = \left[\frac{4 \times 30 (30 + 6)}{6} \right] = 720 \text{ km}$$

⊕ Shortcut Approach - 11

One aeroplane starts t hours later than the scheduled time from a place D km away from its destination. To reach the destination at the scheduled time the pilot has to increase the speed by $'p'$ km/hr.

Then the plane takes $\left[\dfrac{\sqrt{t^2 + \dfrac{4Dt}{p}} + t}{2} \right]$ hours in the normal case. And the

normal speed of the aeroplane is $\left[\dfrac{2D}{\sqrt{t^2 + \dfrac{4Dt}{p}} + t} \right]$ km/hr.

11. One aeroplane started 30 minutes later than the scheduled time from a place 1500 km away from its destination. To reach the destination at the scheduled time the pilot had to increase the speed by 250 km/hr. What was the speed of the aeroplane during the journey?

(a) 750 km/hr (b) 500 km/hr
(c) 350 km/hr (d) 1000 km/hr

Sol. (a) speed

$$= \left[\frac{2 \times 1500}{\sqrt{\left(\dfrac{30}{60}\right)^2 + \left[\dfrac{4 \times 1500 \times \dfrac{1}{2}}{250}\right]} + \left(\dfrac{30}{60}\right)} \right]$$

$$= \left[\frac{3000}{\sqrt{\dfrac{1}{4} + \left(\dfrac{3000}{250}\right)} + \dfrac{1}{2}} \right] = \left[\frac{3000}{\left(\sqrt{\dfrac{49}{4}} + \dfrac{1}{2}\right)} \right]$$

$$= \frac{3000}{4} = 750 \text{ km / hr}$$

⊕ Shortcut Approach - 12

A goods train and a passenger train are running on parallel tracks in the same or in the opposite direction. The driver of the goods train observes that the passenger train coming from behind overtakes and crosses his train completely in T_1 seconds. Whereas a passenger on the passenger train marks that he crosses the goods train in T_2 seconds. If the speeds of the trains be in the ratio of a : b, then the ratio

of their lengths is given by $\left[\dfrac{T_2}{T_1 - T_2}\right]$.

12. A goods train and a passenger train are running on the parallel tracks in the same direction. The driver of the goods train observes that the passenger train coming from behind overtakes and crosses his train completely in 1 min whereas a passenger on

the passenger train marks that he crosses the goods train in $\dfrac{2}{3}$ min.

If the speeds of the train is in the ratio of 1 : 2, then find the ratio of their lengths.

(a) 4 : 1   (b) 3 : 1   (c) 1 : 4   (d) 2 : 1

Sol. **(d)** The ratio of their lengths $= \left(\dfrac{T_2}{T_1 - T_2}\right)$

$$= \left[\dfrac{\dfrac{2}{3} \times 60}{\left(60 - \dfrac{2}{3} \times 60\right)}\right] = \dfrac{40}{20} = 2:1$$

Shortcut Approach - 13

Two trains start at the same time from A and B and proceed towards each other at the rate of x km/hr and y km/hr respectively. When they meet it is found that one train has travelled d km more than the other.

Then the distance between A and B is $\left[\dfrac{x+y}{x-y}\right] d$ km.

13. From stations M and N, two trains start moving towards each other at speed 125 km/hr and 75 km/hr, respectively. When the two trains meet each other, it is found that one train covers 50 km more than another. Find the distance between M and N.

    (a) 190 km   (b) 200 km

    (c) 145 km   (d) 225 km

Sol. **(b)** The distance between A and B is

$$= \left(\dfrac{x+y}{x-y}\right) d = \left(\dfrac{125+75}{125-75}\right) \times 50 = \dfrac{200}{50} \times 50 = 200 \text{ km}$$

Shortcut Approach - 14

A train meets with an accident 't_1' hours after starting, which detains it for 't' hours, after which it proceeds at $\dfrac{x}{y}$ of its original speed. It arrives at the destination 't_2' hours late. Had the accident taken place 'd' km farther along the railway line, the train would have arrived only 't_3' hours late. The original speed of the train is given by

$$\left[\frac{d\left(1-\dfrac{x}{y}\right)}{\dfrac{x}{y}\left(t_2 - t_3\right)}\right]$$ km/hr and the length of the trip is given by

$$\left(\frac{d}{t_2 - t_3}\right)\left[t_2 + t_1\left(\frac{y}{x} - 1\right)\right]$$ km.

14. A train left station A for station B at a certain speed. After travelling for 2 hours, the train meets with an accident and could travel at $\dfrac{4}{5}$th of the original speed and reaches 45 minutes late at station B. Had the accident taken place 50 km further on, it would have reached 30 minutes late at station B. What is the distance between station A and B?

(a) 200 km   (b) 250 km

(c) 300 km   (d) 350 km

Sol. **(b)** Distance between A and B

$$= \frac{d}{\left(t_2 - t_3\right)}\left[t_2 + t_1\left(\frac{y}{x} - 1\right)\right]$$

$$= \frac{50}{\left(\dfrac{45}{60} - \dfrac{30}{60}\right)}\left[\frac{45}{60} + 2\left(\frac{5}{4} - 1\right)\right]$$

$$= \frac{50 \times 60}{15}\left[\frac{3}{4} + 2 \times \frac{1}{4}\right]$$

$$= \frac{50 \times 60}{15} \times \frac{5}{4} = 250 \text{ km}$$

⊕ Shortcut Approach - 15

Two trains of the length l_1 m and l_2 m respectively with different speeds pass a static pole in t_1 seconds and t_2 seconds respectively. When they are moving in the opposite direction they will cross each other in

$$\left[\frac{(l_1 + l_2)t_1 t_2}{t_2 l_1 + t_1 l_2)}\right] \text{ seconds.}$$

15. Two trains of equal length running in opposite directions, pass a student standing by the side of railway line in 18 sec, and 12 sec respectively. The time that the two trains take to cross each other, is

(a) 7.2 sec   (b) 9.6 sec
(c) 10.8 sec   (d) 14.4 sec

Sol. (d) Time $= \left[\dfrac{(l_1 + l_2)t_1 t_2}{t_2 l_1 + t_1 l_2}\right]$

$$= \left[\frac{(l + l) \times 18 \times 12}{12l + 18l}\right]$$

$$\Rightarrow \quad \frac{432l}{30l} = 14.4 \text{ sec}$$

Two trains of the length l_1 and l_2 m respectively with different speeds pass a static pole in t_1 seconds and t_2 seconds respectively. When they are moving in the same direction, they will cross each other in

$$\left[\frac{(l_1 + l_2)t_1 t_2}{t_2 l_1 - t_1 l_2}\right] \text{ seconds.}$$

16. A man standing on a railway platform notices that a train going in one direction takes 6 seconds to pass him and other train of the same length takes 9 seconds to pass him. Find the time taken by the two trains to cross each other when they are running in the same direction.

(a) 12 seconds   (b) 24 seconds
(c) 36 seconds   (d) 48 seconds

Sol. (c) Time $l = \left[\dfrac{(l_1 + l_2)t_1 t_2}{t_2 l_1 - t_1 l_2}\right]$

$$= \left[\frac{(l+l)9 \times 6}{9 \times l - 6l} \right]$$

$$= \frac{108l}{3l} = 36 \text{ seconds}$$

⊕ Shortcut Approach - 17

A train after travelling d_1 km meets with an accident and then proceeds

at $\dfrac{x}{y}$ of its former speed and arrives at its destination t_1 hours late. Had

the accident occurred d_2 km further, it would have reached the

destination only t_2 hours late. The speed of the train is $\left[\dfrac{d_2\left(1 - \dfrac{x}{y}\right)}{\dfrac{x}{y}(t_1 - t_2)} \right]$ **km/**

hr and the distance which train travels is $\left(d_1 + \dfrac{d_2 t_1}{t_1 - t_2} \right)$ **km.**

17.   A train left station A for station B at a certain speed. After travelling for 100 km, the train meets with an accident and could travel at

$\dfrac{4}{5}$ th of the original speed and reaches 45 minutes late at station B.

Had the accident taken plain 50 km further on, it would have reached 30 minutes late at station B. What is the distance between station A and B?

(a) 100 km   (b) 150 km

(c) 200 km   (d) 250 km

Sol. **(d)**   Speed $= \left[\dfrac{d_2\left(1 - \dfrac{x}{y}\right)}{\dfrac{x}{y}(t_1 - t_2)} \right]$ km/hr

$$\therefore \quad \text{Distance} = \left[d_1 + \frac{d_2 t_1}{t_1 - t_2} \right] \text{km}$$

$$= \left[100 + \frac{50 \times \dfrac{45}{60}}{\left(\dfrac{45}{60} - \dfrac{30}{60} \right)} \right] \text{km} \quad = \left[100 + \frac{2250}{15} \right] \text{km} = 250 \, \text{km}$$

Shortcut Approach - 18

A train covers a distance between station A and B in T_1 hours. If the speed is reduced by x km/hr, it will cover the same distance in T_2 hours, then the distance between the two stations A and B is

$\left(\dfrac{x T_1 T_2}{T_2 - T_1} \right)$ km and the speed of the train is given by $\left(\dfrac{x T_2}{T_2 - T_1} \right)$ km/hr.

18. A train can complete its journey from P to Q in 6 hrs with its uniform speed. If speed of train is reduced by 20 km/h it takes 2 hrs more to reach from P to Q. What is distance between P and Q? Also find the speed of train?

(a) 420 km, 70 km/h   (b) 360 km, 60 km/h
(c) 240 km, 40 km/h   (d) 480 km, 80 km/h

Sol. (d) $\quad \text{Distance} = \left[\dfrac{x(T_1 T_2)}{T_2 - T_1} \right] \text{km}$

$$= \left[\frac{20(6 \times 8)}{(8 - 6)} \right]$$

$$= \frac{960}{2} = 480 \text{ km}$$

$$\therefore \quad \text{Speed} = \left[\frac{x.T_2}{T_2 - T_1} \right]$$

$$= \left[\frac{20 \times 8}{8-6}\right] = 80 \, \text{km/hr}$$

⊕ Shortcut Approach - 19

Two trains A and B start from P and Q towards Q and P respectively. After passing each other they take T_1 hours and T_2 hours to reach Q and P respectively. If the train from P is moving x km/hr, then the

speed of the other train is $\left(x\sqrt{\dfrac{T_1}{T_2}} \right)$ km/hr.

19. Two trains x and y start from Mumbai and Delhi towards Delhi and Mumbai, respectively. After passing each other, they take 12 hours 30 minutes and 8 hours to reach Delhi and Mumbai, respectively. If the train from Mumbai is moving at 60 km/hr, then find the speed of the other train.

    (a) 75 km/hr   (b) 68 km/hr

    (c) 72 km/hr   (d) 62 km/hr

Sol. **(a)** $\quad \text{Speed} = \left[x\sqrt{\dfrac{T_1}{T_2}} \right] \text{km/hr}$

$$= \left[60 \times \sqrt{\dfrac{12.5}{8}} \right] \text{km/hr}$$

$$= \left[60 \times \sqrt{1.5625} \right] \text{km/hr}$$

$$= \left[60 \times 1.25 \right] \text{km/hr}$$

$$= 75 \, \text{km/hr}$$

⊕ Shortcut Approach - 20

A man rows a certain distance downstream in x hours and returns the same distance in y hrs. If the stream flows at the rate of z km/hr then

the speed of the man in still water is given by $\left[\dfrac{z(x+y)}{y-x} \right]$.

20. Ramesh can row a certain distance downstream in 6 hours and return the same distance in 9 hours. If the speed of Ramesh in still water be 12 km/hr, find the speed of the stream.

    (a) 2.2 km/hr
    (b) 3 km/hr
    (c) 2.4 km/hr
    (d) 3.2 km/hr

Sol. (c) Speed $= \left[\dfrac{z(x+y)}{(y-x)}\right]$ km/hr

$$12 = \left[\dfrac{z(6+9)}{9-6}\right] \text{ km/hr}$$

$$12 = \left[\dfrac{z \times 15}{3}\right] \text{ km/hr}$$

$$z = \dfrac{36}{15} = 2.4 \text{ km/hr}$$

Shortcut Approach - 21

If x km be the rate of stream and a man takes n times as long to row up as to row down the river, then the rate of the man in still water is

given by $x\left[\dfrac{n+1}{n-1}\right]$ **km/hr.**

21. A boat goes 6 km an hour in still water. It takes thrice as much time going upstream as much time going downstream. The speed of the current is:

    (a) 4 km/hr
    (b) 5 km/hr
    (c) 3 km/hr
    (d) 2 km/hr

Sol. (c) Speed $= x\left[\dfrac{n+1}{n-1}\right]$ km/hr

$$6 = x\left[\dfrac{3+1}{3-1}\right]$$

$$x = \dfrac{6 \times 2}{4} = 3 \text{ km/hr.}$$

⊕ Shortcut Approach - 22

A man can row x km/hr in still water. If in a stream which is flowing at y km/hr, it takes him z hrs to row to a place and back, the distance

between the two places is $\left(\dfrac{z\left(x^2-y^2\right)}{2x}\right)$.

22. In a stream, running at 2 km/hr, a motorboat goes 10 km upstream and back again to the starting point in 55 minutes. Find the speed of the motorboat in still water.

(a) 22 km/hr   (b) 12 km/hr   (c) 6 km/hr   (d) 16 km/hr

Sol. (a) Distance $=\dfrac{z\left(x^2-y^2\right)}{2x}$

$$10=\dfrac{\dfrac{55}{60}\left(x^2-4\right)}{2x}$$

$$\Rightarrow \quad 20x=\dfrac{55}{60}\left(x^2-4\right)\Rightarrow \dfrac{1200x}{55}=x^2-4$$

$$\Rightarrow \quad 11x^2-44-240x=0$$
$$\Rightarrow \quad (x-22)(11x+2)=0$$
$$\therefore \quad x=22 \text{ km/hr}$$

⊕ Shortcut Approach - 23

If a man can row at a speed of x km/hr in still water to a certain upstream point and back to the starting point in a river which flows at y km/hr, then the average speed for total journey (up + down) is given

by $\left(\dfrac{(x+y)(x-y)}{x}\right)$ km/hr.

23. Speed of a boat is 5 km/hr in still water and the speed of the stream is 3 km/hr. If the boat takes 3 hours to go to a place and come back, the distance of the place is:

(a) 3.75 km   (b) 4 km
(c) 4.8 km   (d) 4.25 km

Sol. **(c)** Average speed $= \left[\dfrac{(x+y)(x-y)}{x}\right]$ km/hr

$$= \left[\dfrac{(5+3)(5-3)}{5}\right] \text{km/hr} \ = \dfrac{8\times2}{5} \text{ km/hr} = \dfrac{16}{5} \text{ km/hr}$$

Given time, t = 3 hours.

Two way distance (D) = Time (t) × Speed

$$= 3\times\dfrac{16}{5} = \dfrac{48}{5} = 9.6$$

Hence, distance of the place (D)

$$= \dfrac{9.6}{2} = 4.8 \text{ km}$$

Shortcut Approach - 24

In 'd' metre race, *A* runs at '*x*' km/hr. *A* gives *B* a start of *y* metres and still beats him by '*t*' seconds, then the speed of *B* is given by

$$\dfrac{18x(d-y)}{18d+5xt} \text{ km/hr.}$$

24. In a 400 m race, A runs at a speed of 16 m/s. If A gives B a start of 16 m and still beats him by 40s, what will be the speed of B?

   (a) 6 m/s   (b) 8 m/s

   (c) 15 m/s   (d) 5.9 m/s

Sol. **(d)** Speed

$$= \left[\dfrac{18x(d-y)}{18d+5xt}\right]$$

$$= \left[\dfrac{18\times16\times\dfrac{18}{5}(400-16)}{18\times400+5\times16\times\dfrac{18}{5}\times40}\right] = 21.26 \text{ km/hr}$$

$$= 21.25\times\dfrac{5}{18} \text{ m/sec.} = 5.9 \text{ m/sec.}$$

Exercise

1. Two runner start running together for a certain distance, one at 8 km/h and another at 5 km/h. The former arrives one and half an hour, before the latter. The distance (in km) is:
   (a) 12 (b) 20
   (c) 25 (d) 36

2. A dog starts chasing to a cat 2 hours later. It takes 2 hours to dog to catch the cat. If the speed of the dog is 30 km/h, what is the speed of cat?
   (a) 10 km/h
   (b) 15 km/h
   (c) 20 km/h
   (d) Can't be determined

3. Excluding stoppages, the speed of a train is 45 km/h and including stoppages, it is 36 km/h. For how many minutes does the train stop per hour ?
   (a) 10 min. (b) 12 min.
   (c) 15 min. (d) 18 min.

4. If I walk at 4 km/h, I miss the bus by 10 minutes. If I walk at 5 km/h, I reach 5 minutes before the arrival of the bus. How far I walk to reach the bus stand ?
   (a) 5 km
   (b) 4.5 km
   (c) $5\dfrac{1}{4}$ km
   (d) Cannot be determined

5. A car travels 25 km an hour faster than a bus for a journey of 500 km. If the bus takes 10 hours more than the car, then the speeds of the bus and the car are
   (a) 25 km/h and 40 km/h respectively
   (b) 25 km/h and 60 km/h respectively
   (c) 25 km/h and 50 km/h respectively
   (d) None of these

6. A bullockcart has to cover a distance of 80 km in 10 hr. If it covers half of the journey in $\dfrac{3}{5}$ th time, what should be its speed to cover the remaining distance in the left time?
   (a) 5 km/hr   (b) 10 km/hr
   (c) 15 km/hr (d) 20 km/hr

7. A thief goes away with a Maruti car at a speed of 40 km/h. The theft has been discovered after half an hour and the owner sets off in another car at 50 km/h. When will the owner overtake the thief from the start.
   (a) $2\dfrac{1}{2}$ hours
   (b) 2 hr 20 min
   (c) 1 hr 45 min
   (d) Cannot be determined

8. A car driver travels from the plains to a hill station, which are 200 km apart at an average speed of 40 km/h. In the return trip he covers the same distance at an average speed of 20 km/h. The average speed of the car over the entire distance of 400 km is
(a) 16.56 km/h (b) 17.89 km/h
(c) 26.67 km/h (d) 35 km/h

9. Two people A and B start from P and Q (distance = D) at the same time towards each other. They meet at a point R, which is at a distance 0.4 D from P. They continue to move to and fro between the two points. Find the distance from point P at which the fourth meeting takes place.
(a) 0.8 D   (b) 0.6 D
(c) 0.3 D   (d) 0.4 D

10. A student rides on a bicycle at 8 km/h and reaches his school 2.5 minutes late. The next day he increases his speed to 10 km/h and reaches the school 5 minutes early. How far is the school from his house?
(a) 1.25 km   (b) 8 km
(c) 5 km   (d) 10 km

11. A gives both B and C a start of 60 m in a 1500 m race. However, while B finishes with him, C is 15 m behind them when A and B cross the finishing line. How much start can B give C for the 1500 m race course?

(a) $7\dfrac{6}{23}$ m   (b) $15\dfrac{5}{8}$ m

(c) $7\dfrac{11}{16}$ m   (d) $5\dfrac{5}{24}$ m

12. The driver of an ambulance sees a school bus 40 m ahead of him. After 20 second, the school bus is 60 metre behind. If the speed of the ambulance is 30 km/h, what is the speed of the school bus?
(a) 10 km/h (b) 12 km/h
(c) 15 km/h (d) 22 km/h

Hints & Solution

1. **(b)** Required distance

$$= \frac{S_1 S_2}{\left(S_1 - S_2\right)} \times \text{Time difference}$$

$$= \frac{8 \times 5}{3} \times \frac{3}{2} = 20 \text{ km}$$

2. **(b)** Use Shortcut approch-10

3. **(b)** Due to stoppges the train travels $(45 - 36) = 9$ km less in an hour than it could have travelled without stoppages.

Thus train stops per hour for

$$\frac{9}{45} \times 60 = 12 \text{ min.}$$

4. **(a)** Use Shortcut approch-6

5. **(c)** Let the speed of the bus be x km / h.

then speed of the car $= (x + 25) \text{ km / h}$

$$\therefore \quad \frac{500}{x} = \frac{500}{x + 25} + 10$$

$$\Rightarrow x^2 + 25x - 1250 = 0$$

$$\Rightarrow x = 25$$

Thus speed of the bus = 25 km/h

Speed of the car = 50 km/h

Alternative:

Difference in speeds 25 km / hr is in only option (c).

6. **(b)** Use Shortcut Approach-3

7. **(a)** Distance to be covered by the thief and by the owner is same.

Let after time 't', owner catches the thief.

$$\therefore 40 \times t = 50\left(t - \frac{1}{2}\right)$$

$$\Rightarrow 10t = 25 \Rightarrow t$$

$$= \frac{5}{2} \text{hr} = 2\frac{1}{2} \text{hr}$$

8. **(c)** Use Shortcut approch-3

9. **(a)** The ratio of speeds of A to B would be $2 : 3$.

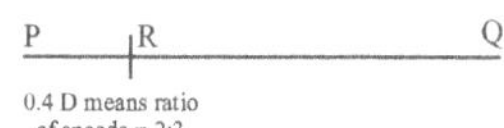

The 4th meeting would occur after a combined movement of $D + 6D = 7D$. 2/5th of this distance would be covered by A and 3/5th of this distance would be the distance covered by B. Thus, distance covered by A would be 2/5th of $7D$: distance covered by $A = 2.8D$ – which means that the 4th meeting occurs at a distance of $0.8\,D$ from P.

10. **(c)** Use Shortcut approch-6

11. **(b)**

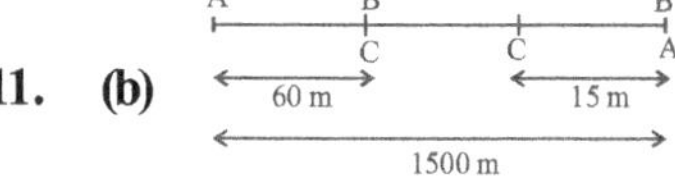

In the same time, when A covers 1500 m, B covers 1440 m and C covers 1425 m.

So, in 1440 m race B can give a start of 15 m.

$\therefore$ In 1500 m race B will give a start of

$$\frac{15}{1440}\times 1500 = 15\frac{5}{8}\,\text{m}$$

12. (b) Relative speed

$$=\frac{\text{Total distance}}{\text{Total time}}$$

$$=\frac{60+40}{20}=5\,\text{m}/\text{s}$$

$$\therefore\quad 5\,\text{m}/\text{s} = 5\times\frac{18}{5}$$

$$=18\,\text{km}/\text{h}$$

Now, relative speed = 18 km/h

So, speed of ambulance – Speed of school bus = 18

30 – speed of school bus = 18

Speed of school bus = 12 km/h

Clock and Calendar

Between x and $(x+1)$ o'clock the two hands are at right angle at $(5x \pm 15)$ $\times \dfrac{12}{11}$ minutes past x.

1. At what time between 9'O clock and 10'O clock will the hands of a clock are at right angle?

(a) $32\dfrac{8}{11}$ min past 9   (b) $32\dfrac{1}{11}$ min past 9

(c) $32\dfrac{3}{11}$ min past 9   (d) $16\dfrac{2}{11}$ min past 9

Sol. (a) The hands of a clock will be at right angles twice between 9'O clock and 10'O clock

$$\left((\because 5x \pm 15) * \dfrac{12}{11} \right) \text{ minutes past } x$$

$$\Rightarrow \left((5*9 \pm 15) * \dfrac{12}{11} \right) \text{ minute past } 9$$

$$= (45 \pm 15) * \dfrac{12}{11} \text{ minute past } 9$$

$$= \left(60 * \dfrac{12}{11} \text{minute past } 9 \right) \text{ or } \left(30 * \dfrac{12}{11} \text{minute past } 9 \right)$$

$$= \dfrac{720}{11} \text{ min past 9 or } \dfrac{360}{11} \text{ min past 9}$$

$$= 65\dfrac{5}{11} \text{ min past 9 or } 32\dfrac{8}{11} \text{ min past 9}$$

Between x and $(x+1)$ O' clock the two hands are in the same straight line

Case I : (a) When they are in opposite directions at

$(5x - 30)\dfrac{12}{11}$ minutes past x, [where $x > 6$]

(b) $(5x + 30)\dfrac{12}{11}$ minutes past x. [where $x < 6$]

Note : At 6 O' clock two hands will be in opposite direction.

Case II : When they coincide (or come together), at $5x\left(\dfrac{12}{11}\right)$ **minutes past**

x.

2. At what time between 3o' clock and 4o' clock will the hands of a clock be in opposite directions?

(a) $48\dfrac{2}{11}$ min past 3   (b) $49\dfrac{1}{11}$ min past 3

(c) $50\dfrac{1}{11}$ min past 4   (d) $50\dfrac{2}{11}$ min past 4

Sol. (b) Required time

$$= (5x + 30)\dfrac{12}{11} \text{ minutes past } x.$$

$$= (5 \times 3 + 30)\dfrac{12}{11} \text{ minutes past } 3$$

$$= \left(45 \times \dfrac{12}{11}\right) \text{ minutes past } 3.$$

$$= 49\dfrac{1}{11} \text{ minutes past } 3.$$

⊕ Shortcut Approach - 3

The minute hand of a clock overtakes the hour hand at certain intervals (given in minutes) of correct time. The clock lose or gain in a day is given by

$$\left[\frac{720}{11} - \text{given interval in minute}\right] \times \left[\frac{60 \times 24}{\text{given interval in minutes}}\right]$$

according as the sign in +ve or –ve.

3.   The minute hand of a clock overtakes the hour hand at the intervals of 63 min of the correct time. How much does a clock gain or lose in a day?

    (a) $56\dfrac{8}{77}$ min   (b) $44\dfrac{1}{11}$ min

    (c) $77\dfrac{4}{23}$ min   (d) $91\dfrac{1}{11}$ min

Sol. (a)   Required Time

$$\Rightarrow \quad \left[\frac{720}{11} - 63\right] \times \left[\frac{60 \times 24}{63}\right]$$

$$\Rightarrow \quad \frac{27}{11} \times \frac{60 \times 24}{63}$$

$$\Rightarrow \quad \frac{3 \times 60 \times 24}{77} = \frac{4320}{77} = 56\frac{8}{77} \text{ minute.}$$

Exercise

1. What will be the acute angle between hands of a clock at 2 : 30?
   (a) 105°   (b) 115°
   (c) 95°   (d) 135°

2. At what time between 8 and 9 o'clock will the hands of a watch be in straight line but not together?

   (a) $10\dfrac{11}{10}$ min. past 8

   (b) $10\dfrac{10}{11}$ min. past 8

   (c) $11\dfrac{10}{11}$ min. past 8

   (d) $12\dfrac{10}{11}$ min. past 8

3. The calendar for the year 2005 is the same as for the year :
   (a) 2010   (b) 2011
   (c) 2012   (d) 2013

4. Find the exact time between 7 am and 8 am when the two hands of a watch meet ?
   (a) 7 hrs 35 min
   (b) 7 hrs 36.99 min
   (c) 7 hrs 38.18 min
   (d) 7 hrs 42.6 min

5. When do the hands of a clock coincide between 5 and 6 ?
   (a) 5 : 30
   (b) 5 : 27 : 16
   (c) 5 : 32 : 16
   (d) 5 : 28 : 56

6. At what time between 9'O clock and 10'O clock will the hands of a clock point in the opposite directions?

   (a) $16\dfrac{4}{11}$ minutes past 9

   (b) $16\dfrac{4}{11}$ minutes past 8

   (c) $55\dfrac{5}{61}$ minutes past 7

   (d) $55\dfrac{5}{61}$ minutes to 8

7. At what point of time after 3 O' clock, hour hand and the minute hand are at right angles for the first time?
   (a) 9 O' clock

   (b) $4\text{ h }37\dfrac{1}{6}$ min

   (c) $3\text{ h }30\dfrac{8}{11}$ min

   (d) $3\text{ h }32\dfrac{8}{11}$ min

8. A clock gains 15 minutes per day. It is set right at 12 noon. What time will it show at 4.00 am, the next day?
   (a) 4 : 10 am
   (b) 4 : 45 am
   (c) 4 : 20 am
   (d) 5 : 00 am

9. If 5th March, 1999 was Friday, what day of the week was it on 9th March 2000?

(a) Wednesday

(b) Saturday

(c) Friday

(d) Thursday

10. What was the day of the week on 15th August, 1947 ?

(a) Wednesday

(b) Tuesday

(c) Friday

(d) Thursday

11. A watch which gains 5 seconds in 3 minutes was set right at 7 a.m. In the afternoon of the same day, when the watch indicated quarter past 4 O'clock, the true time is

(a) 4 p.m.

(b) $59\dfrac{7}{12}$ min past 3

(c) $58\dfrac{7}{11}$ min past 3

(d) $2\dfrac{3}{11}$ min past 4

12. A clock is set right at 1 p.m. If it gains one minute in an hour, then what is the true time when the clock indicates 6 p.m. in the same day?

(a) $55\dfrac{5}{61}$ min past 5

(b) 5 min past 6

(c) 5 min to 6

(d) $59\dfrac{1}{64}$ min past 5

Hints & Solution

1. **(a)** At 2'O Clock, Minute Hand will be $10 \times 6 = 60°$ behind the Hour Hand.

   In 30 minutes, Minute Hand will gain

   $$\left(5\frac{1}{2}\right)^{\circ} \times 30 = 150 + 15$$

   $$= 165°$$

   $\therefore$ Angle between Hour Hand and Minute Hand $= 165 - 60 = 105°$

2. **(b)** Use Short Approach -2

3. **(c)** Count the number of days from 2005 onwards to get 0 odd day.

Year	2005	2006	2007	2008	2009	2010
Odd days	1	1	1	2	1	1

   $= 7$ or 0 odd day.

   $\therefore$ Calendar for the year 2005 is the same as that for the year 2011.

4. **(c)** Use Short Approach -2

5. **(b)**

   $$\frac{5 \times 30}{11/2} = \frac{300}{11} = 27\frac{3}{11} \text{ min} = 27 \text{ min } 16\text{s}$$

   Therefore, required time $= 5 : 27 : 16$

6. **(a)** Use Short Approach -2

7. **(d)** Clock will make right angle at

   $$(5n + 15) \times \frac{12}{11} \text{ min past n.}$$

   Given that, $n = 3$

   $\therefore$ $(5 \times 3 + 15) \times \frac{12}{11}$ min past 3.

   $$= 30 \times \frac{12}{11} \text{ min past 3}$$

   $$= 32\frac{8}{11} \text{ min past 3}$$

   i.e., 3 h and $32\frac{8}{11}$ min.

8. **(a)** Use Short Approach -3

9. **(d)** 5th March, 1999 was Friday.

   Then, 5th March 2000

   $= \text{Friday} + 2 = \text{Sunday.}$

   $\{ \because 2000$ is a leap year and it crosses 29th Feb 2000, so 2 is taken as odd day$\}$

   Then, 9th March 2000 = Thursday.

10. **(c)** 15th August, 1947 = (1946 years + Period from 1st Jan., 1947 to 15th Aug., 1947)

    Counting of odd days :

    1600 years have 0 odd day. 300 years have 1 odd day.

    46 years = (11 leap years + 35 ordinary years)

    $= [(11 \times 2) + (35 \times 1)] = 57$ odd days

$\Rightarrow$ 1 odd day.

Jan.	Feb.	March	April	May
31	28	31	30	31

June	July	Aug.
30	31	15

$= 227$ days $= (32$ weeks $+3$ days$) = 3$ odd days.

Total number of odd days $= (0+1+1+3) = 5$

Hence, the required day was 'Friday'.

11. (a) Use Short Approach -3

12. (a) Time interval indicated by incorrect clock

$= 6$ p.m $- 1$ p.m $= 5$ hrs.

Time gained by incorrect clock in one hour

$= +1$ min $= +\dfrac{1}{60}$ hr.

Using the formula,

$$\dfrac{\text{True time interval}}{\text{Time interval in incorrect clock}}$$

$$= \dfrac{1}{1 + \text{hour gained in 1 hour by incorrect clock}}$$

$$\Rightarrow \dfrac{\text{True time interval}}{5} = \dfrac{1}{1 + \dfrac{1}{60}}$$

$\Rightarrow$ True time interval

$$= \dfrac{5 \times 60}{61} = 4\dfrac{56}{61}$$

$\therefore$ True time $= 1$ p.m. $+ 4\dfrac{56}{61}$ hrs.

$$= 5 \text{ p.m.} + \dfrac{56}{61} \text{ hrs.} = 5 \text{ p.m.} + \dfrac{56}{61} \times 60 \text{ min.}$$

$$= 55\dfrac{5}{61} \text{ minutes past 5.}$$

Permutation & Combination and Probability

Shortcut Approach - 1

Number of permutation of n different things taken all together when r particular things are to be place at some r given places $= (n-r)!$.

1. **How many different words can be formed with the letter of the word 'JAIPUR' which start with 'A' and end with 'T'.**

Sol. Required number of words
$$= (6-2)! = 4! = 4 \times 3 \times 2 = 24$$

Shortcut Approach - 2

Number of permutation of n different things, taken r at a time when m particular things are to be placed at m given places
$$= {}^{n-m}P_{r-m}$$

2. **In how many ways 8 different cycles out of 10 can be arranged when 2 particular cycles are always taken?**

Sol. Required number of arrangement
$$= {}^{10-2}P_{8-2} = {}^{8}P_{6}$$

$$= \frac{8!}{(8-6)!} = \frac{8 \times 7 \times 6 \times 5 \times 4 \times 3 \times 2 \times 1}{2 \times 1}$$

$$= 20160$$

Shortcut Approach - 3

Number of permutation of n particular things, taken r at a time when m particular things is never taken in each arrangement
$$= {}^{n-m}P_{r}$$

3. **How many different 3-letter words can be formed with the letter of word 'JAIPUR' when A and I are always to be excluded?**

Sol. Required number of words

$$= {}^{6-2}C_3 = {}^4C_3 = 4 \times 3 \times 2 = 24.$$

Shortcut Approach - 4

Number of permutation of n different things taken all at a time when m specified things always come together

$$= m! \times (n - m + 1)!$$

4. **Find the number of ways to arrange 8 students in a que when the tallest and smallest student always come together.**

Sol. Required number of arrangement

$$= 2!(8 - 2 + 1)! = 2! \times 7! = 10080$$

Shortcut Approach - 5

Number of arrangement of n beads or flowers (all different) around a circular necklace or garland

$$= \frac{1}{2}(n - 1)!$$

5. **In how many ways 11 different flowers be strong into a garland?**

Sol. Required number of ways

$$= \frac{1}{2} \times (11 - 1)! = \frac{1}{2} \times (10)! = 1814400$$

Shortcut Approach - 6

Number of arrangement of n beads or flowers (all different) taken r at a time around a circular necklace or garland

$$= \frac{{}^nP_r}{2r}$$

6. **In how many ways can 4 beads out of 6 different beads be strung into a ring?**

Sol. Required number of ways

$$= \frac{^6P_4}{2 \times 4} = \frac{\dfrac{6!}{2!}}{2 \times 4}$$

$$= \frac{6 \times 5 \times 4 \times 3}{2 \times 4} = 45$$

Shortcut Approach - 7

Sum of the total numbers which can be formed with the given n different digits $a_1, a_2, a_3, \ldots\ldots, a_n = (a_1 + a_2 + a_3 + \ldots + a_n)\,[(n-1!)]\,.\,(111\,\ldots.. n$ times$)$

7. **Find the sum of all 4 digits numbers formed with the digits 1, 2, 4 and 6.**

Sol. Required sum

$$= (1+2+4+6)\cdot(3!)\cdot(1111) = 13 \times 6 \times 1111 = 86658$$

Shortcut Approach - 8

Number of rectangles which can be formed on a grid with m rows and n

columns $= \dfrac{mn(m+1)(n+1)}{4}$

8. **Find the number of rectangles which can be form on a grid with 6 rows and 8 columns.**

Sol. Number of rectangles

$$= \frac{6 \times 8 \times (6+1) \times (8+1)}{4} = 756$$

Shortcut Approach - 9

Number of square which can be formed on a grid with m rows and n columns $(m > n)$

$$= \frac{2n^3 + 3n^2 + n}{6} + \frac{(m-n)\cdot n\cdot(n+1)}{2}$$

9.   Find the number of square on a grid with 6 rows and 5 columns.

Sol. Required number of square

$$= \frac{2 \times 5^3 + 3 \times 5^2 + 5}{6} + \frac{(6-5) \times 5 \times (5+1)}{2}$$

$$= 55 + 15 = 70$$

Shortcut Approach - 10

Number of rectangles which can be formed on a grid with n rows and n columns

$$= \left[\frac{n(n+1)}{2} \right]^2$$

10.   Find the number of rectangles formed on a grid with 8 rows and 8 columns.

Sol. Required number of rectangles formed

$$= \left(\frac{8 \times 9}{2} \right)^2 = 36 \times 36 = 1296$$

Shortcut Approach - 11

Number of squares which can be formed on a grid with n rows and n columns

$$= \frac{n(n+1)(2n+1)}{6}$$

11.   How many possible squares are there in a chess board?

Sol. Required number of squares in a chess board

$$= \frac{8(8+1)(2 \times 8+1)}{6} = \frac{8 \times 9 \times 17}{6} = 204$$

Shortcut Approach - 12

Let there are h number of horizontal steps and v number of vertical steps then number of ways to reach from one corner to another corner

$$= {}^{h+v}C_h \text{ or } {}^{h+v}C_v$$

12. Suppose a person is at south west corner in the following grid and he has to travel to north-east corner through the lines. Then, find the number of ways for the person to reach at north east corner from south west corner.

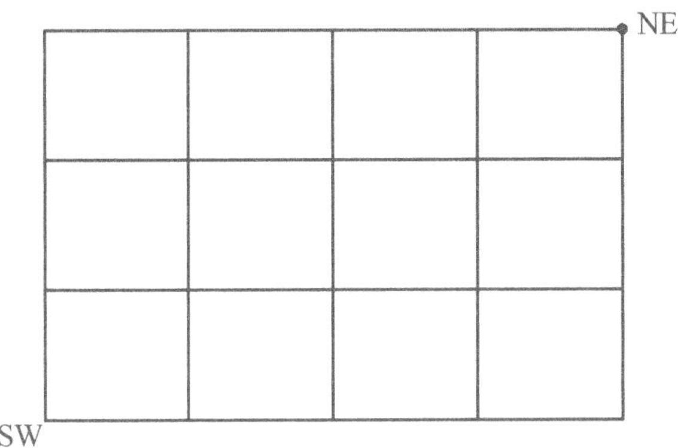

Sol. Required number of ways for the person to reach from south west corner to north east corner

$$= {}^{3+4}C_3 \text{ or } {}^{3+4}C_4 = 7 \times 5 = 35.$$

Shortcut Approach - 13

If a problem is given to r person $A, B, C, \ldots, R$ whose chances of solving it are $\dfrac{1}{a_1}, \dfrac{1}{b_1}, \dfrac{1}{c_1}, \ldots, \dfrac{1}{r_1}$ respectively. Then the probability that the problem will be solved

$$= 1 - \left(1 - \dfrac{1}{a}\right)\left(1 - \dfrac{1}{b}\right)\left(1 - \dfrac{1}{c}\right)\ldots\left(1 - \dfrac{1}{r}\right)$$

13. A problem of Chemistry is given to four students P, Q, R and S; whose chances of solving it are $\dfrac{1}{3}, \dfrac{1}{4}, \dfrac{1}{5}$ and $\dfrac{2}{15}$ respectively. Then find the probability that the problem will be solved.

Sol. Required probability

$$= 1 - \left(1 - \frac{1}{3}\right)\left(1 - \frac{1}{4}\right)\left(1 - \frac{1}{5}\right)\left(1 - \frac{2}{15}\right)$$

$$= 1 - \frac{2}{3} \times \frac{3}{4} \times \frac{4}{5} \times \frac{13}{15} = 1 - \frac{26}{75} = \frac{49}{75}$$

⊕ Shortcut Approach - 14

If two boys A and B are playing a game in which they throw a coin alternatively till one of them gets a 'head' and wine the game. Then the probability that A wins the game if he started the game, is $\frac{1}{2}$.

⊕ Shortcut Approach - 15

A fact is stated by two persons A and B. If probability of speaking the truth by A is a and by B is b, then the probability that they contradict each other is $a(1 - b) + (1 - a).b$.

⊕ Shortcut Approach - 16

The probability that a leap year selected at random will have 53 Tuesday (or any other particular days) is $\frac{2}{7}$.

⊕ Shortcut Approach - 17

The probability that a non-leap year selected at random will have 53 Thursday (or any other particular day) is $\frac{1}{7}$.

Exercise

1. If A and B are two independent events with $P(A) = 0.6$, $P(B) = 0.3$, then $P(A' \cap B')$ is equal to :
   (a) 0.18   (b) 0.28
   (c) 0.82   (d) 0.72

2. In tossing three coins at a time, what is the probability of getting at most one head?
   (a) $\dfrac{3}{8}$ (b) $\dfrac{7}{8}$
   (c) $\dfrac{1}{2}$ (d) $\dfrac{1}{8}$

3. How many words beginning with vowels can be formed with the letters of the word EQUATION?
   (a) 25200   (b) 15200
   (c) 25300   (d) 35200

4. If three vertices of a regular hexagon are chosen at random, then the chance that they form an equilateral triangle is:
   (a) $\dfrac{1}{3}$ (b) $\dfrac{1}{5}$
   (c) $\dfrac{1}{10}$ (d) $\dfrac{1}{2}$

5. Letters of the word DIRECTOR are arranged in such a way that all the vowels come together. Find out the total number of ways for making such arrangement.
   (a) 4320   (b) 2720
   (c) 2160   (d) 1120

6. Three squares of a chessboard are chosen at random, the probability that two are of one colour and one of another is :
   (a) $\dfrac{67}{992}$ (b) $\dfrac{16}{21}$
   (c) $\dfrac{31}{32}$
   (d) None of these

7. An old person forgets the last two digits of a telephone number, remembering only that these are different dialled at random. The probability that the number is dialled correctly is :
   (a) 1/90
   (b) 81/91
   (c) 2/99
   (d) None of these

8. Each of A and B tosses two coins. What is the probability that they get equal number of heads?
   (a) $\dfrac{3}{16}$ (b) $\dfrac{5}{16}$
   (c) $\dfrac{4}{16}$ (d) $\dfrac{6}{16}$

9. A speaks truth in 75% of the cases and B in 80% of the cases. In what percentage of cases are they likely to contradict each other in stating the same fact?
   (a) 15%   (b) 20%
   (c) 5%   (d) 35%

10. From eighty cards numbered 1 to 80, two cards are selected randomly. The probability that both the cards have the numbers divisible by 4 is given by

(a) $\dfrac{21}{316}$

(b) $\dfrac{19}{316}$

(c) $\dfrac{1}{4}$

(d) None of these

11. If A and B are two events such that P (A) = 0.5, P (B) = 0.6 and P (A $\cup$ B) = 0.8. Find $P\left(\dfrac{A}{B}\right)$.

(a) $\dfrac{1}{3}$

(b) $\dfrac{1}{2}$

(c) $\dfrac{1}{4}$

(d) None of these

12. A bag contains 3 black, 4 white and 2 red balls, all the balls being different. The number of at most 6 balls containing balls of all the colours is

(a) 36(4!)

(b) $2^6 \times 4!$

(c) $(2^6 - 1)(4!)$

(d) None of these

Hints & Solution

1. **(b)** Since, A and B are independent events
∴ A' and B' are also independent events
$$\Rightarrow P(A' \cap B') = P(A').P(B')$$
$$= (0.4)(0.7) = 0.28$$
$$[\because P(A') = 1 - P(A),\ P(B') = 1 - P(B)]$$

2. **(c)** Use Short Approach - 14

3. **(a)** Number of vowels in EQUATION = 5
∴ Required number
$$= 5 \times (8 - 1)! = 25200.$$

4. **(c)** Three vertices can be selected in $^6C_3$ ways.

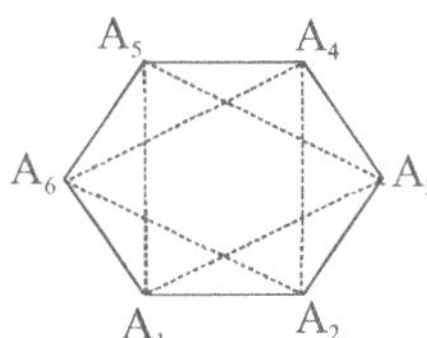

The only equilateral triangles possible are $A_1A_3A_5$ and $A_2A_4A_6$
$$p = \frac{2}{^6C_3} = \frac{2}{20} = \frac{1}{10}$$

5. **(a)** Use Short Approach - 4

6. **(b)** 3 squares on a chessboard can be chosen in $^{64}C_3$ ways. Two squares of one colour and third square of different colour can be chosen in two mutually exclusive way.
(i) 2 white and one black
(ii) 2 black and one white
Thus the favourable number of cases

$$= {}^{32}C_2 \times {}^{32}C_1 + {}^{32}C_1 \times {}^{32}C_2$$
$$= 2\,({}^{32}C_2 \times {}^{32}C_1)$$
Hence, the required probability

$$= \frac{2\left({}^{32}C_2 \times {}^{32}C_1\right)}{{}^{64}C_3} = \frac{16}{21}$$

7. **(a)** The last two digits can be dialled in
$^{10}P_2 = 90$ ways.
Out of these 90 cases only one case is favourable.
Hence, the required probability $= \dfrac{1}{90}$.

8. **(a)** Use Short Approach - 14

9. **(d)** Contradiction can occur if A speaks truth and B lies, B speaks truth and A lies.
So, required probability
$$= 0.75 \times 0.2 + 0.8 \times 0.25$$
$$= 0.35$$
Req% $= 0.35 \times 100$
$$= 35\%$$

10. **(b)** Total no. of divisible by 4 between 1 to 80
$$80 = 4 + (n - 1)4$$
$$80 = 4n \Rightarrow n = 20$$
∴ Required probability
$$= \frac{{}^{20}C_2}{{}^{80}C_2} = \frac{19}{316}$$

11. **(b)** $\because P(A \cap B) = P(A) + P(B) - P(A \cup B)$
$$= 0.5 + 0.6 - 0.8 = 0.3$$
$$\therefore P\left(\frac{A}{B}\right) = \frac{P(A \cap B)}{P(B)} = \frac{0.3}{0.6} = \frac{1}{2}$$

12. **(a)** Use Short Approach - 6

Geometry-I

Sum of all the interior angles of a polygon with 'n' sides $= (n-2) \times 180°$

1. **Sum of all interior angles of a regular polygon is 1440° then find the number of sides of the polygon**

    (a) 6   (b) 8   (c) 10   (d) 12

Sol. **(c)** $(n-2)\,180 = 1440$

$$\Rightarrow n - 2 = 8$$

$$\therefore n = 8 + 2 = 10$$

Each exterior angle of a regular polygon $= \dfrac{360}{n}$, where n is number of sides of the regular polygon.

2. **Each exterior angle of a regular polygon is 30° then find the number of its sides.**

    (a) 6   (b) 8   (c) 10   (d) 12

Sol. **(d)** $\dfrac{360}{n} = 30$

$$\therefore n = 12$$

Number of diagonals of a regular polygon with n sides $= \dfrac{n(n-3)}{2}$

3. **Find the is number of diagonals in a regular octagon.**

    (a) 20   (b) 18   (c) 12   (d) 15

Sol. **(a)**   Number of diagonals $= \dfrac{8(8-3)}{2} = 20$

If PB is a secant of a circle which intersects the circle at A and B and PQ is the circle, at point T and Q, then another secant which intersect.

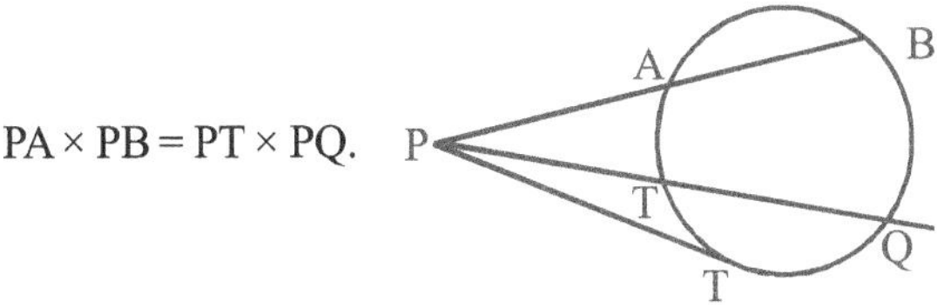

$$PA \times PB = PT \times PQ.$$

4. **In the given figure, chords AB and CD of a circle when produced intersect externally at P. If AB = 6cm, CD = 3cm and PD = 5cm then PB = ?**

   (a) 5 cm   (b) 6.25 cm   (c) 6 cm   (d) 4 cm

Sol. **(b)** $PA \times PB = PC \times PD$

$\Rightarrow (x+6)\,x = 8 \times 5$

$\Rightarrow x^2 + 6x - 40 = 0$

$\Rightarrow (x+10)(x-4) = 0 \Rightarrow x = 4$

$\therefore PB = 4$ cm

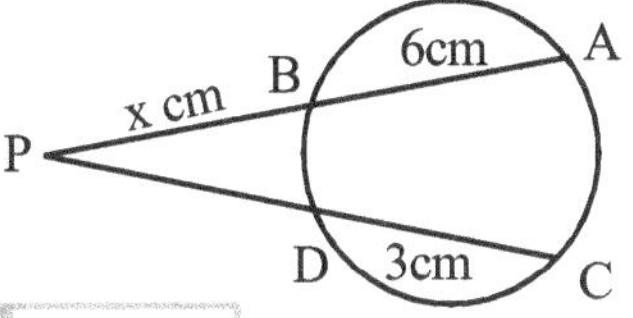

⊕ Shortcut Approach - 5

In the figure AB is chord of a circle PQ is a tangent at end point A of the chord AB to the circle. C is any point on arc AB and D is any point on arc BA

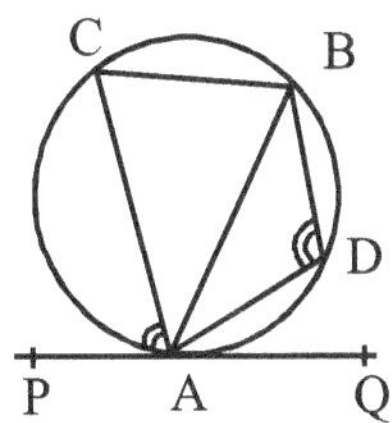

$\angle$ BAQ and $\angle$ ACB are angles in the alternate segments.

$\angle$ BAP and $\angle$ ADB are angles in the alternate segments.

Angles in the alternate segments of the circle are equal.

5. **In the given figure, PAQ is the tangent. BC is the diameter of the circle. m $\angle$BAQ = 60°, find m $\angle$ABC :**

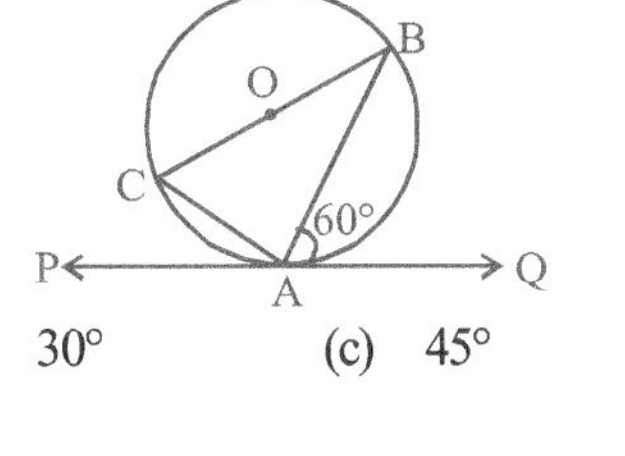

   (a) 25°   (b) 30°   (c) 45°   (d) 60°

Sol. **(b)** $\angle BAC = 90°$

$\angle BCA = 60°$ $(\because \angle BCA = BAQ)$

$\therefore \quad \angle ABC = 180° - (90° + 60°)$

$\angle ABC = 30°$

EXERCISE

1. Find the number of sides of a regular polygon whose interior angle measures 108°.
   (a) 5   (b) 6
   (c) 7   (d) 8

2. The interior angle of a regular polygon is 135°, find number of sides of the polygon.
   (a) 6   (b) 8
   (c) 10   (d) 15

3. Each interior angle of a regular polygon is 100° greater than each exterior angle. How many sides the polygon has ?
   (a) 9   (b) 10
   (c) 12   (d) 8

4. A polygon has 54 diagonals. The number of sides in the polygon is :
   (a) 7
   (b) 9
   (c) 12
   (d) None of these

5. There are two circles each with radius 5 cm. Tangent AB is 26 cm. The length of tangent CD is :

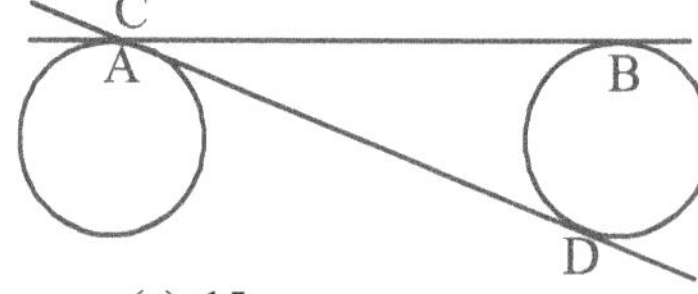

   (a) 15 cm
   (b) 21 cm
   (c) 24 cm
   (d) can't be determined

6. ABC be a rt. triangle with rt. angle at A. If AD ⊥ BC, then AD in terms of 'b' and 'c' provided AC = b and AB = c is

   (a) $\dfrac{b}{\sqrt{b^2 c}}$ (b) $\dfrac{bc}{\sqrt{b^2 c + c}}$

   (c) $\dfrac{bc}{\sqrt{b^2 + c^2}}$ (d) $\dfrac{c}{\sqrt{b^2 + 1}}$

7. With the vertices $\triangle ABC$ as centres, three circles are described, each touching the other two externally. If the sides of the triangle are 9 cm. 7 cm. and 6 cm, find the radii of the circle.
   (a) 3 cm, 6 cm, 9 cm
   (b) 4 cm, 5 cm, 2 cm
   (c) 2 cm, 3 cm 11 cm
   (d) 9 cm, 7 cm, $\sqrt{3}$ cm

8. Two concentric circles with centre O have A, B, C, D as the points of intersection with the line ℓ as shown in the figure. If AD = 12 cm and BC = 8 cm, the length of AB, CD, AC and BD are respectively.

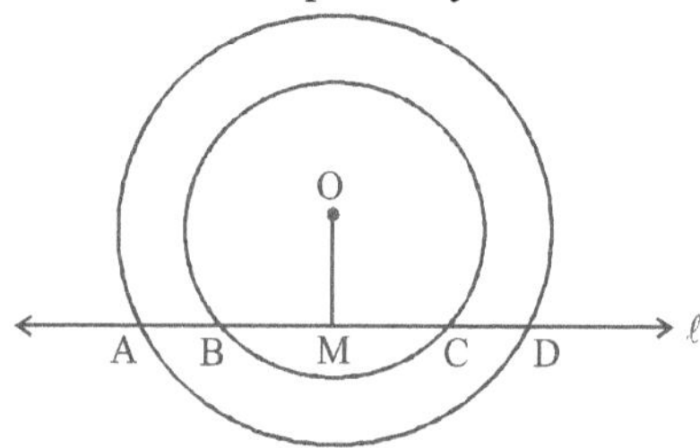

   (a) 2 cm, 2 cm, 10 cm, 10 cm
   (b) 10 cm, 10 cm, 2 cm, 2 cm
   (c) 10 cm, 2 cm, 10 cm, 2 cm
   (d) 2 cm, 10 cm, 2 cm, 10 cm

9. In the given figure, POQ is a diameter and PQRS is a cyclic quadrilateral. If $\angle PSR = 150°$, find $\angle RPQ$

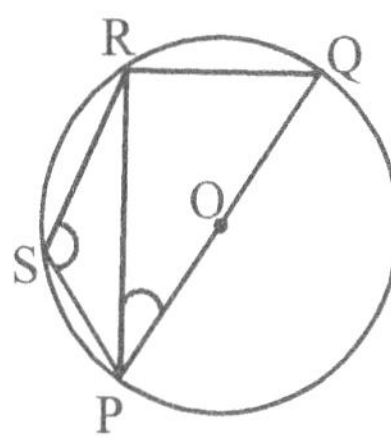

(a) 50°   (b) 60°
(c) 90°   (d) 45°

10. In the figure given below, PT is a tangent to the circle. Find PT if AT = 16 cm and AB = 12 cm.

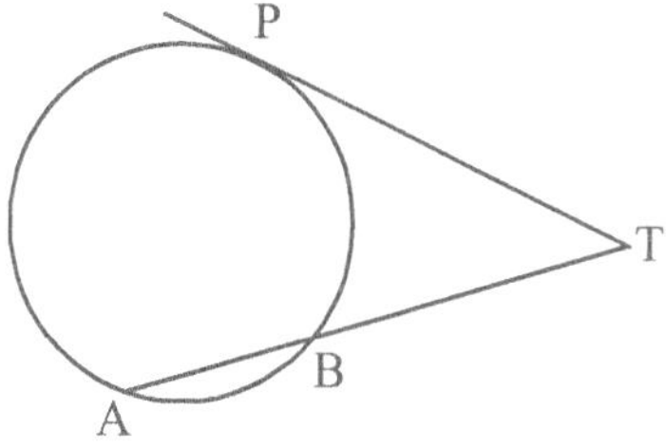

(a) 5 cm   (b) 6 cm
(c) 8 cm   (d) 10 cm

11. In the figure given below, radius of a greater circle is r cm. Find the area of non-shaded portion :

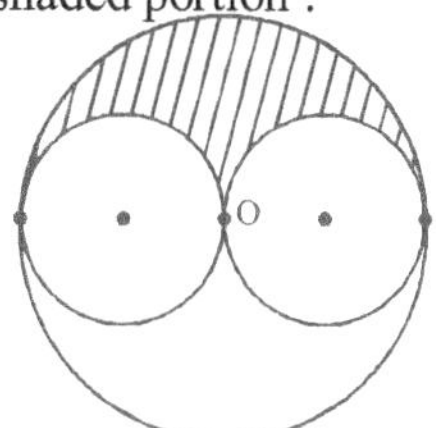

(a) $\dfrac{\pi r^2}{4}$ sq. cm

(b) $\dfrac{3\pi r^2}{4}$ sq. cm

(c) $2\pi r^2$ sq. cm

(d) $\dfrac{4\pi r^2}{3}$ sq. cm

12. Find the number of diagonals of a regular polygon of which each entiror angle is 36°?

(a) 30   (b) 27
(c) 35   (d) None of these

Hints & Solution

1. **(a)** Shortcut Approach -1
2. **(b)** Shortcut Approach -1
3. **(a)** Shortcut Approach -1, 2
4. **(c)** Use Shortcut Approach -3
5. **(c)** $AB = PQ = 26\,CM$
   $AND\ PO = OQ = 13\,CM$

   $$CO = \sqrt{(PO)^2 - (PC)^2}$$

   $$CO = \sqrt{(13)^2 - (5)^2}$$
   $$= CO = 12\,cm$$
   $$\therefore CD = 2\,CO = 24\,cm$$

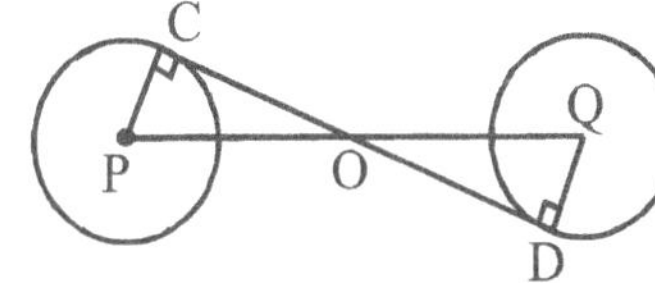

6. **(c)** In right angled $\triangle CAB$,
   BC^2
   $= AB^2 + AC^2 = c^2 + b^2$

   or $BC = \sqrt{b^2 + c^2}$

   Area of $\triangle ABC$ = 1/2
   base × height = 1/2 bc
   Also area of $\triangle ABC$ = 1/2 (BC) (AD)

   $$= \frac{1}{2}\sqrt{b^2 + c^2} \times AD$$

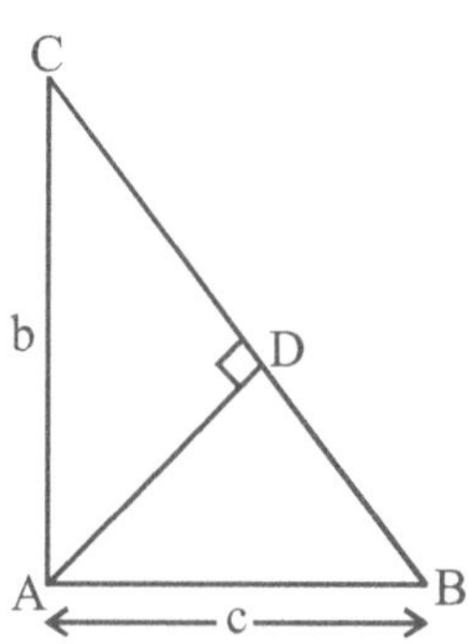

$$\therefore \frac{1}{2}\left(\sqrt{b^2 + c^2}\right)AD = \frac{1}{2}bc.$$

Hence

$$AD = \frac{bc}{\sqrt{b^2 + c^2}}$$

7. **(b)** Let $AB = 9$ cm, $BC = 7$ cm and $CA = 6$ cm
   Let, x, y, z be the radii of circles with centre A, B, C respectively.
   Then, $x + y = 9$, $y + z = 7$ and $z + x = 6$.
   Adding, we get $2(x + y + z) = 22$
   $\Rightarrow x + y + z = 11$

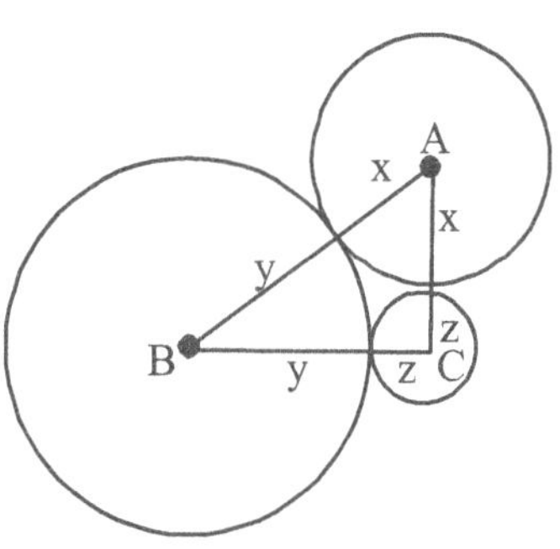

$\therefore x = [(x+y+z)-(y+z)]$
$= (11 - 7)\,cm = 4\,cm.$
Similarly, $y = (11 - 6)\,cm$
$= 5$ cm and z
$= (11 - 9)\,cm = 2\,cm.$
Hence, the radii of circle with centres A, B, C are 4 cm, 5 cm and 2 cm respectively.

8. (a) Since $OM \perp BC$, a chord of the circle.

$\therefore$ it bisects BC.

$\therefore \quad BM = CM = \dfrac{1}{2}(BC)$

$= \dfrac{1}{2}(8) = 4$ cm.

Since $OM \perp AD$, a chord of the circle.

$\therefore$ it bisects AD.

$\therefore \qquad AM = MD = \dfrac{1}{2}$

$AD = \dfrac{1}{2}(12) = 6$ cm.

Now, $AB = AM - BM = 6 - 4 = 2$ cm.

$CD = MD - MC = 6 - 4 = 2$ cm

$AC = AM + MC = 6 + 4 = 10$ cm

$BD = BM + MD = 4 + 6 = 10$ cm.

9. (b) Shortcut Approach-5

10. (c) Shortcut Approach-4

11. (b) Required area
= Area of 2 small semi-circles
+ Area of big semi circle

$\Rightarrow \dfrac{\pi\left(\dfrac{r}{2}\right)^2}{2} + \dfrac{\pi\left(\dfrac{r}{2}\right)^2}{2} + \dfrac{\pi r^2}{2}$

$\Rightarrow \pi\left(\dfrac{r}{2}\right)^2 + \dfrac{\pi r^2}{2}$

$\Rightarrow \dfrac{\pi r^2}{4} + \dfrac{\pi r^2}{2} = \dfrac{3\pi r^2}{4}$ sq.cm.

12. (c) Use shortcut Approach-1, 3

Geometry-II

 **Shortcut Approach - 1**

Sum of the lengths of any two sides of a triangle is greater than the length of the third side.

1. **Lengths of one of the two equal sides and third side of an isosceles triangle is 7 cm and 15 cm. Find the perimeter of the triangle?**
   (a) 29 cm (b) 37 cm   (c) 33 cm   (d) None of these

Sol. **(b) Case-I**
   Sides of triangle = 7, 7, 15
   Case-II
   Sides of triangle = 7, 15, 15
   Here case I is not possible because $7 + 7 < 15$
   $\therefore$ Perimeter of triangle = $7 + 15 + 15 = 37$ cm

 **Shortcut Approach - 2**

Difference between the tenths of any two sides of a triangle is smaller than the length of third side.

2. **Which one of the following is not a length of the sides of a triangle?**
   (a)   10, 17, 6   (b)   15, 22, 8
   (c)   11, 5, 15   (d)   8, 7, 14

Sol. **(a)**   Here $17 - 10 > 6$
   Which is not possible.

 **Shortcut Approach - 3**

In any triangle, line segment Joining the mid points of any two sides is Parallel to third side and half of the length of the third side.

3. **In the figure given below D and E are mid points of AB and AC respectively and BC = 20 cm then D E = ?**

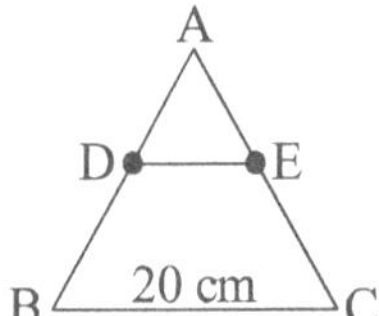

(a)   5 cm   (b) 8 cm   (c) 15 cm   (d) 10 cm

Sol. (d) $DE = \dfrac{1}{2}BC = \dfrac{1}{2} \times 20 = 10$ cm

Shortcut Approach - 4

Bisector of an angle (internal or external) of a triangle divides the opposite side (internally or eternally) in the ratio of the sides containing the angle.

4. **In the given figure AD is bisector of $\angle$ BAC which meets BC at D. AB = 10 cm, BD = 4 cm CD = 6 cm, them AC = ?**

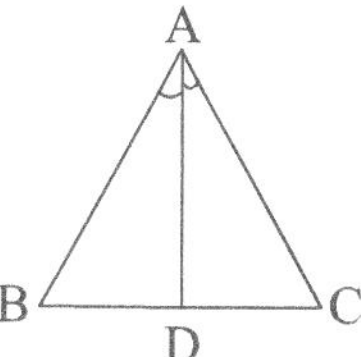

(a)   12 cm   (b) 15 cm   (c) 16 cm   (d) None of these

Sol. (b)   A D is Angle bisector then

$$\frac{AB}{AC} = \frac{BD}{CD}$$

$$\Rightarrow \frac{10}{AC} = \frac{4}{6} \qquad \therefore AC = \frac{10 \times 6}{4} = 15 \text{ cm}$$

Shortcut Approach - 5

If a line is drawn parallel to one side of a triangle which intersects the other two sides in distinct points, the other two sides are divide into same ratio.

5. **In triangle ABC, DE is parallel to BC. AB = 10 cm, BD = 6 cm and AE = 8 cm them what is length of AC?**

(a)   20 cm   (b) 18 cm   (c) 15 cm   (d) None of these

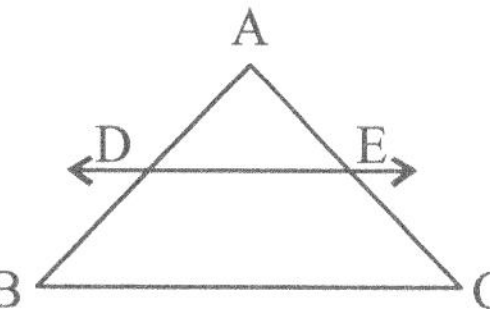

Sol. (a)   In $\triangle ABC$,

DE ∥ BC

$$\therefore \quad \frac{AD}{BD} = \frac{AE}{EC} \Rightarrow \frac{10-6}{6} = \frac{8}{EC} \Rightarrow EC = \frac{8 \times 6}{4} = 12 \text{cm}$$

Now AC = AE + EC = 8 + 12 = 20 cm

Shortcut Approach (Angle-Angle-Angle Similarity) - 6

6. Two triangles are said to be similar, if their all corresponding angles are equal.

Sol. For example:

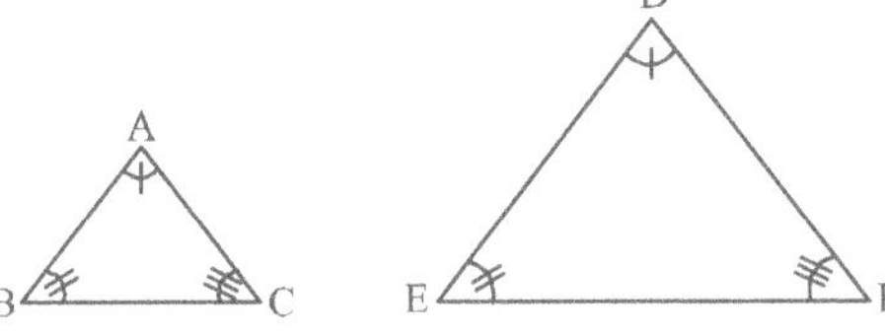

In $\triangle ABC$ and $\triangle DEF$, if

$$\angle A = \angle D$$
$$\angle B = \angle E$$
$$\angle C = \angle F$$

Then $\triangle ABC \sim \triangle DEF$ [By AAA Similarity]

If two triangles are similar, then their corresponding sides are in the smae ratios.

Shortcut Approach (Side-Side-Side Similarity) - 7

7. Two triangles are said to be similar, if sides of one triangle are proportional (or in the same ratio of) to the sides of the other triangle:

Sol. For example:

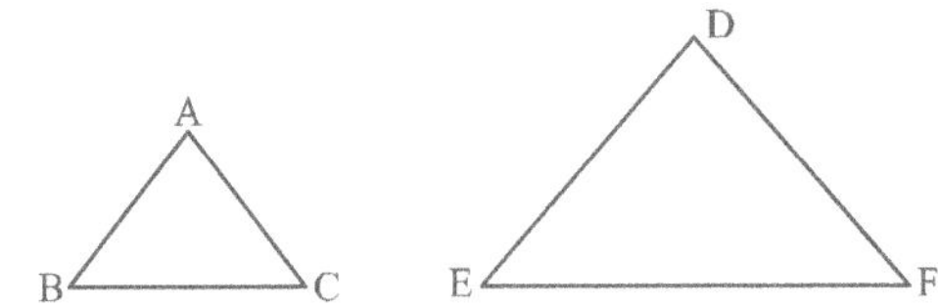

In $\triangle ABC$ and $\triangle DEF$, if

$$\frac{AB}{DE} = \frac{BC}{EF} = \frac{CA}{FD}$$

Then $\triangle ABC \sim \triangle DEF$ [By SSS Similarity]

Shortcut Approach (Side-Angle-Side Similarity) - 8

8. Two triangles are said to be similar if two sides of a triangle are proportional to the two sides of the other triangle and the angles included between these sides of two triangles are equal.

Sol. **For example:**

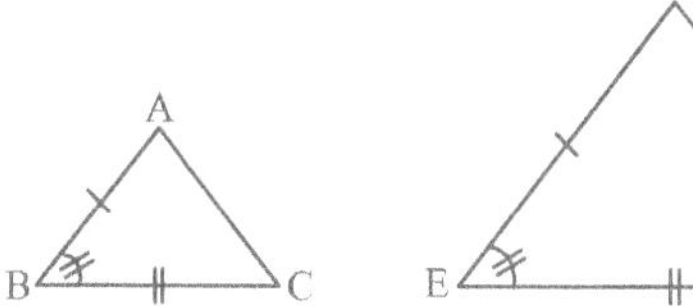

In $\triangle ABC$ and $\triangle DEF$, if

$$\frac{AB}{DE} = \frac{BC}{EF}$$

and $\qquad \angle B = \angle E$

Then, $\triangle ABC \sim \triangle DEF$ [By SAS Similarity]

9. **D and E are the points on the sides AB and AC respectively of a $\triangle ABC$ and AD = 8 cm, DB = 12 cm, AE = 6 cm and EC = 9 cm, then BC is equal to**

(a) $\dfrac{2}{5} DE$ (b) $\dfrac{5}{2} DE$

(c) $\dfrac{3}{2} DE$ (d) $\dfrac{2}{3} DE$

Sol. **(b)** As in $\triangle ADE$ and $\triangle ABC$

$$\frac{AD}{AB} = \frac{8}{20} = \frac{2}{5}, \frac{AE}{AC} = \frac{6}{15} = \frac{2}{5}$$

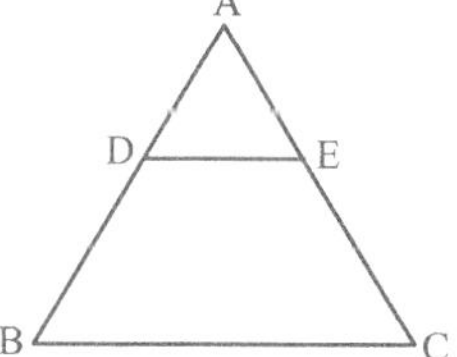

So, $\dfrac{AD}{AB} = \dfrac{AE}{EC}$

and $\qquad \angle A = \angle A \qquad$ (common)

$\triangle ADE \sim \triangle ABC$

$\therefore \qquad \dfrac{DE}{BC} = \dfrac{AD}{AB} \Rightarrow \dfrac{DE}{BC} = \dfrac{2}{5}$

$\Rightarrow BC = \dfrac{5}{2} DE$

10. Two triangles are said to be similar if one angle of both triangle is right angle and hypotenuse of both triangles are proportional to any one other side of both triangles respectively.

Sol. For example:

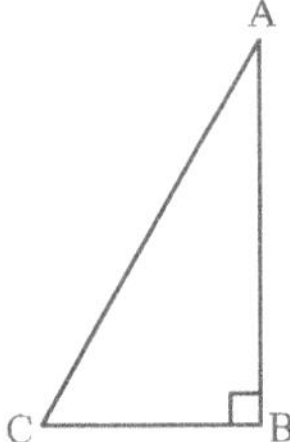 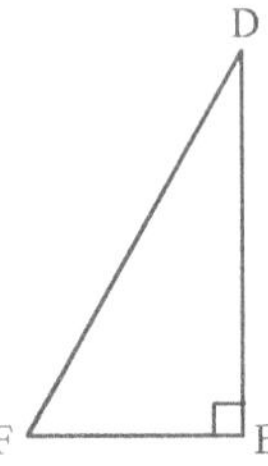

In $\triangle ABC$ and $\triangle DEF$, if

$$\angle B = \angle E \qquad [= 90°]$$

$$\frac{AC}{DF} = \frac{AB}{DE}$$

Then $\triangle ABC \sim \triangle DEF$ [By RHS similarity]

Exercise

1. The centroid, circumcenter, orthocenter in a triangle–
   (a) are always coincident.
   (b) are always collinear.
   (c) are always the inside the triangular area.
   (d) always coincide in a equilateral triangle and otherwise collinear.

2. Two equal circles of radius 4 cm intersect each other such that each passes through the centre of the other. The length of common chord is.
   (a) $2\sqrt{3}$ cm (b) $4\sqrt{3}$ cm
   (c) $2\sqrt{2}$ cm (d) 8 cm

3. E and F are points on the sides PQ and PR respectively of a ΔPQR. In which of the following options is EF $\|$ QR?
   (a) PE = 3.9 cm, EQ = 3 cm, PF = 3.6 cm, FR = 2.4 cm
   (b) PE = 4 cm, EQ = 4.5 cm, PF = 8 cm, FR = 9 cm
   (c) PQ = 1.28 cm, PR = 2.56 cm, PE = 0.8 cm, PF = 0.52 cm
   (d) Both (b) and (c)

4. In the figure, triangle ABC is similar to triangle EDC :

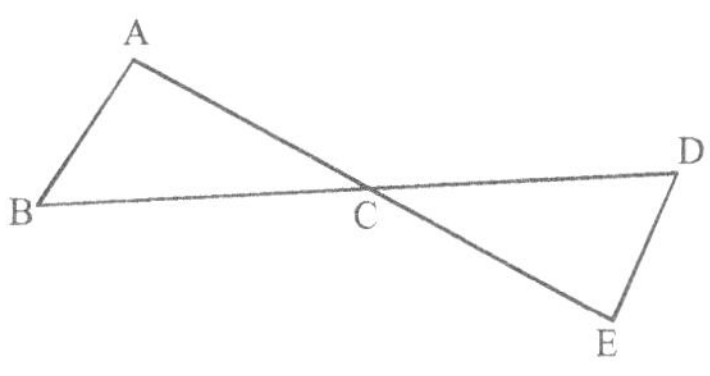

   If we have AB = 4 cm, ED = 3 cm, CE = 4-2 cm and CD = 4-8 cm, then the values of CA and CB respectively are
   (a) 6 cm, 6.6 cm
   (b) 4.8 cm, 6.6 cm
   (c) 5.4 cm, 6.4 cm
   (d) 5.6 cm, 6.4 cm

5. In a ΔXYZ, if the internal bisector of $\angle$X meets YZ at 'P', then ….

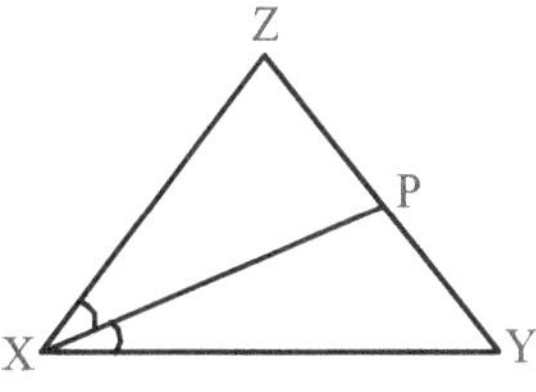

   (a) $\dfrac{XY + XZ}{XZ} = \dfrac{YZ}{PZ}$

   (b) $\dfrac{XY}{PZ} = \dfrac{XZ}{YP}$

   (c) $\dfrac{XY}{XZ} = \dfrac{PZ}{YP}$

   (d) $\dfrac{XZ}{XY} = \dfrac{YP}{YZ}$

6. In the given figure, express x in terms of a, b and c.

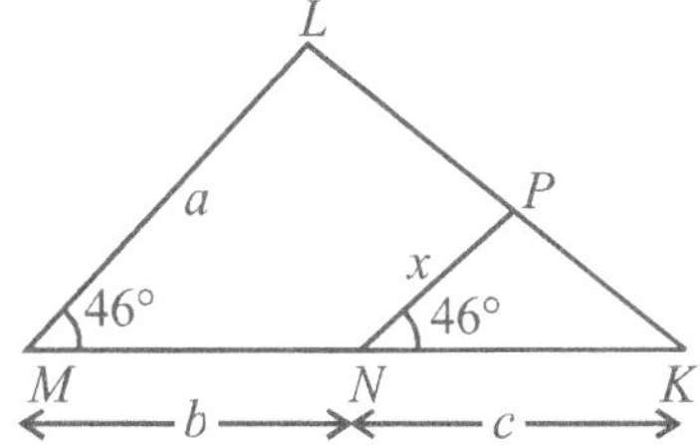

(a) $x = \dfrac{ab}{a+b}$

(b) $x = \dfrac{ac}{b+c}$

(c) $x = \dfrac{bc}{b+c}$

(d) $x = \dfrac{ac}{a+c}$

7. ABC is an isosceles triangle in which AB = AC = 10 cm. BC = 12 cm. PQRS is a rectangle inside the isosceles triangle. Given PQ = SR = y cm. and PS = QR = 2x cm. then x=

(a) $6 - \dfrac{3y}{4}$ (b) $6 + 6y$

(c) $6 + \dfrac{4y}{3}$ (d) $\dfrac{7x+8y}{4}$

8. The internal bisectors of $\angle$B and $\angle$C of $\triangle$ABC meet at O. If $\angle$A = 80° then $\angle$BOC is :

(a) 50°   (b) 160°
(c) 100°   (d) 130°

9. In the figure (not drawn to scale) given below, if $AD = CD = BC$, and $\angle BCE = 96°$, how much is $\angle DBC$?

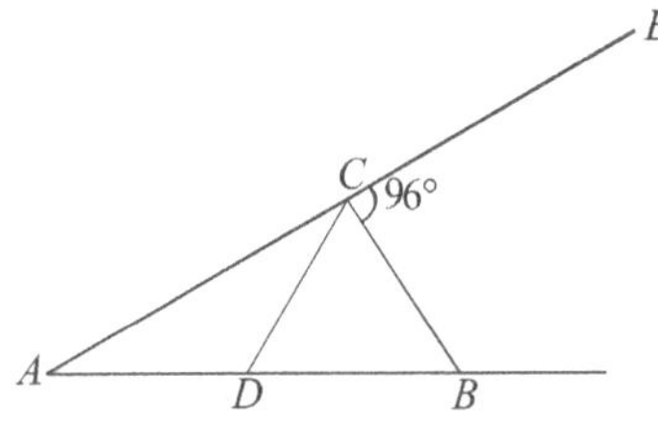

(a) 32°
(b) 84°
(c) 64°
(d) Cannot be determined

10. Two circles inscribed in a right angled triangle have radii 12 cm & 3 cm. Find length of AP.

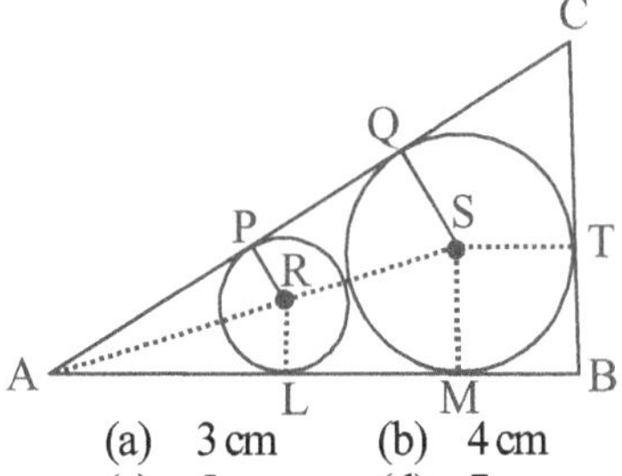

(a) 3 cm   (b) 4 cm
(c) 5 cm   (d) 7 cm

11. In the adjoining figure $\angle$BAC = 60° and BC = a, AC = b and AB = c, then :

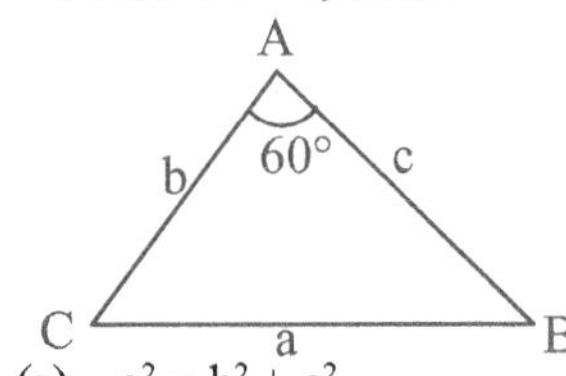

(a) $a^2 = b^2 + c^2$
(b) $a^2 = b^2 + c^2 - bc$
(c) $a^2 = b^2 + c^2 + bc$
(d) $a^2 = b^2 + 2bc$

12. In the figure given below, points P and Q are mid points on the sides AC and BP respectively. Area of each part is shown in the figure, then find the value of $x + y$.

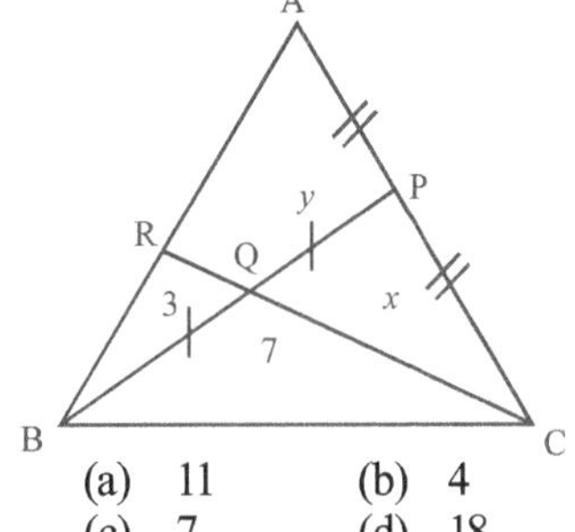

(a) 11   (b) 4
(c) 7   (d) 18

Hints & Solution

1. **(d)** The centroid, circumcenter, orthocenter always coincide in a equilateral triangle and otherwise collinear.

2. **(b)** According to question AB is a common chord. O and O' is the centre of the circle

In $\triangle ODA$

$AO^2 = AD^2 + OD^2$

$(4)^2 = (AD)^2 + (2)^2$

$AD^2 = 12$

$AD = 2\sqrt{3}$

$\therefore AB$

$= 2 \times 2\sqrt{3} = 4\sqrt{3}$

3. **(b)**

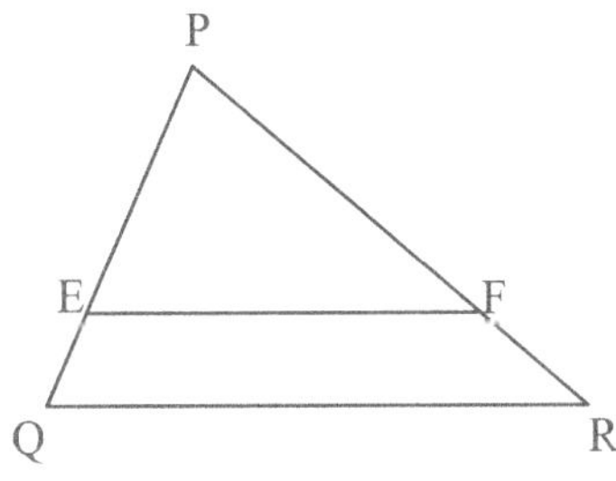

Here, EF $\parallel$ QR

By the converse of basic proportional by

$$\frac{PE}{EQ} = \frac{PF}{FR}$$

Out of all the given options, the following option fulfils the above condition.

(b) PE = 4 cm, QE = 4.5 cm, PF = 8 cm, RF = 9 cm

$$\frac{PE}{EQ} = \frac{4}{4.5} = \frac{8}{9}$$

$$\frac{PF}{FR} = \frac{8}{9}$$

So, $\dfrac{PE}{EQ} = \dfrac{PF}{FR}$

4. **(d)** $\dfrac{AB}{DE} = \dfrac{BC}{DC} = \dfrac{AC}{CE}$

$$\frac{4}{3} = \frac{BC}{4.8} = \frac{AC}{4.2}$$

BC = 6.4 AC = 5.6

5. **(a)** The internal bisector of $\angle X$ meets YZ at P

$$\frac{XY}{XZ} = \frac{YP}{PZ}$$

Add 1 on both the sides

$$\Rightarrow \frac{XY}{XZ} + 1 = \frac{YP}{PZ} + 1$$

$$\Rightarrow \frac{XY + XZ}{XZ} = \frac{YP + PZ}{PZ} = \frac{YZ}{PZ}$$

6. **(b)** In $\triangle KPN$ and $\triangle KLM$, we have

$\angle KNP = \angle KML = 46°$

$\angle K = \angle K$ (Common)

$\therefore \quad \triangle KNP \sim \triangle KML$

(By A-A criterion of similarity)

$$\Rightarrow \frac{KN}{KM} = \frac{NP}{ML} \Rightarrow \frac{c}{b+c} = \frac{x}{a}$$

$$\Rightarrow x = \frac{ac}{b+c}$$

7. **(a)** Using Pythagoras theorem in $\triangle ABL$ we have $AL = 8\,cm$,

Also, $\triangle BPQ \sim \triangle BAL$

$$\therefore \frac{BQ}{PQ} = \frac{BL}{AL} \Rightarrow \frac{6-x}{y} = \frac{6}{8} \text{ or}$$

$$x = 6 - \frac{3}{4}y$$

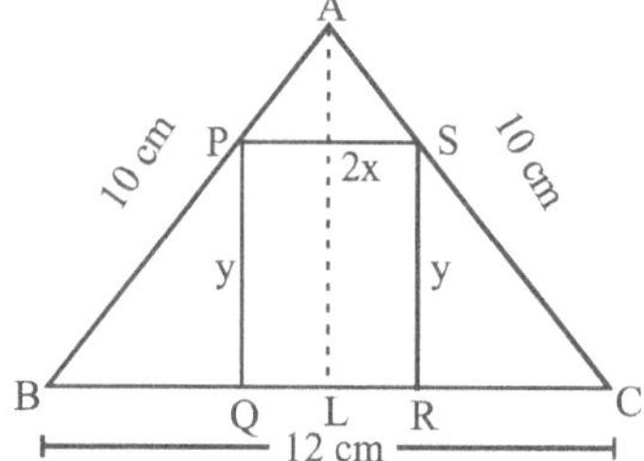

8. **(d)** $\angle BOC = 90° + \dfrac{1}{2}\angle A$

$$= 90° + 40° = 130°$$

9. **(c)**

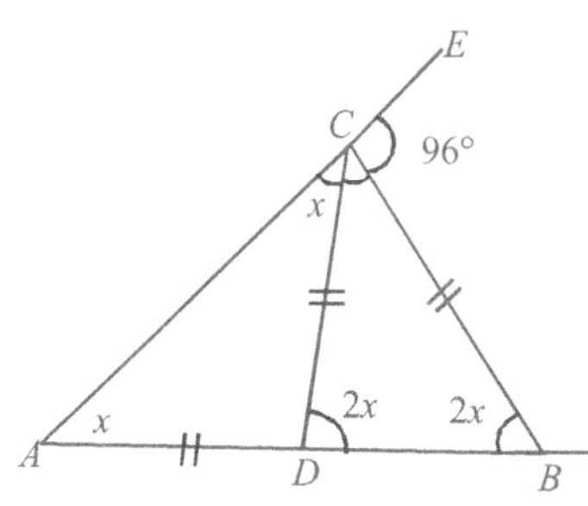

Let $\angle CAD = \angle ACD = x$

At point C,

$x + (180° - 4x) + 96°$

$= 180°$

$\Rightarrow 180° - 3x + 96° = 180°$

$\therefore x = 32°$

Hence, $\angle DBC = 2 \times 32$

$= 64°$

10. **(b)**

$$PQ = \sqrt{(RS)^2 - (QS - PR)^2}$$

$$PQ = \sqrt{(15)^2 - (12 - 3)^2}$$

$$PQ = 12\ cm = LM$$

$\because$ STBM is a square

$MB = BT = ST = SM = 12\,cm.$

In $\triangle APR$ & $\triangle ASQ$,

$$\frac{AP}{AQ} = \frac{PR}{SQ}$$

$$\frac{AP}{AP + PQ} = \frac{3}{12}$$

$$\frac{AP}{AP + 12} = \frac{1}{4}$$

$4AP = AP + 12$

$3AP = 12$

$\therefore \quad AP = 4\,cm.$

11. **(b)** $\cos A = \dfrac{b^2 + c^2 - a^2}{2bc}$

(cosine rules)

$$\frac{1}{2} = \frac{b^2 + c^2 - a^2}{2bc}$$

$(\because \cos 60° = 1/2)$

$\therefore \quad a^2 = b^2 + c^2 - bc$

12. **(d)** We have a theorem which says

If ABC is a triangle in which D is the mid-point of BC and E is the mid-point of AD then area

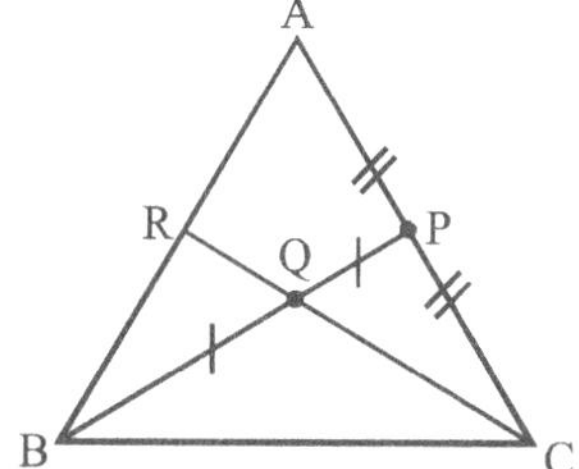

$$(\triangle BED) = \frac{1}{4}$$

area $(\triangle ABC)$

So, by applying this theorem we get

$$ar\,(\triangle PQC) = \frac{1}{4}$$

$$ar\,(\triangle BAC)$$

$$\Rightarrow\ x = \frac{1}{4}(10 + x + y) \Rightarrow 3x = 10 + y$$

$$..(a)$$

Also, $ar\,(\triangle BPC) = ar\,(\triangle BAP)$

($\because$ BP is median)

$$\Rightarrow\quad 7 + x = 3 + y \Rightarrow 4 = y - x\ ...(b)$$

from (a) and (b)

$$3x = 10 + (4 + x)$$

$$\Rightarrow 3x = 14 + x \Rightarrow x = 7$$

and $y = 11$

Thus, $x + y = 7 + 11 = 18$

Coordinate Geometry

The distance between two points $P(x_1, y_1)$ and $Q(x_2, y_2)$
is given by $PQ = \sqrt{(x_2 - x_1)^2 + (y_2 - y_1)^2}$

Distance of point $P(x, y)$ from the origin $= \sqrt{x^2 + y^2}$

1. **If distance between the point (x, 2) and (3, 4) is 2, then find the value of x.**

Sol. $2 = \sqrt{(x-3)^2 + (2-4)^2}$

$\Rightarrow 2 = \sqrt{(x-3)^2 + 4}$

Squaring both sides
$4 = (x-3)^2 + 4 \Rightarrow x - 3 = 0 \Rightarrow x = 3$

2. **Find the distance between the points**
A(– 6, –1) and B(– 6, 11)

Sol. Here the points are A(–6, –1) and B(–6, 11)
By using distance formula, we have

$$AB = \sqrt{\{-6-(-6)\}^2 + \{11-(-1)\}^2} = \sqrt{0^2 + 12^2} = 12$$

Hence, AB = 12 units.

(i) Co-ordinates of a point which divides the line segment joining two points $P(x_1, y_1)$ and $Q(x_2, y_2)$ in the ratio $m_1 : m_2$ are

$$\left(\frac{m_1 x_2 + m_2 x_1}{m_1 + m_2}, \frac{m_1 y_2 + m_2 y_1}{m_1 + m_2} \right)$$

If $m_1 = m_2$, then the point will be the **mid point** of PQ, whose co-ordinates

$$= \left(\frac{x_1 + x_2}{2}, \frac{y_1 + y_2}{2} \right)$$

(ii) When we need to find the ratio in which a point on a line segment divides it, we suppose the required ratio as k : 1 or m/n : 1.

3. **Find the points of trisection of line joining the points A (2, 1) and B (5, 3).**

Sol. (2, 1) $\overset{\longleftarrow 1 \longrightarrow \longleftarrow \quad 2 \quad \longrightarrow}{\underset{A \qquad P_1 \qquad P_2 \qquad B}{\rule{6cm}{0.4pt}}}$ (5, 3)

$$P_1(x_1, y_1) = \left(\frac{1 \times 5 + 2 \times 2}{1 + 2}, \frac{1 \times 3 + 2 \times 1}{1 + 2} \right) = \left(3, \frac{5}{3} \right)$$

$$P_2(x_2, y_2) = \left(\frac{2 \times 5 + 1 \times 2}{2 + 1}, \frac{2 \times 3 + 1 \times 1}{2 + 1} \right) = \left(4, \frac{7}{3} \right)$$

4. **Prove that points A (1, 1), B (–2, 7) and C (3, –3) are collinear.**

Sol. $AB = \left| \sqrt{(1+2)^2 + (1-7)^2} \right| = \left| \sqrt{9+36} \right| = 3\sqrt{5}$

$BC = \left| \sqrt{(-2-3)^2 + (7+3)^2} \right| = \left| \sqrt{25+100} \right| = 5\sqrt{5}$

$CA = \left| \sqrt{(3-1)^2 + (-3-1)^2} \right| = \left| \sqrt{4+16} \right| = 2\sqrt{5}$

Clearly, BC = AB + AC. Hence A, B, C are collinear.

Shortcut Approach - 3

Let A (x_1, y_1), B (x_2, y_2) and C (x_3, y_3) are vertices of any triangle ABC, then Co-ordinates of centroid,

$$G = \left(\frac{x_1 + x_2 + x_3}{3}, \frac{y_1 + y_2 + y_3}{3} \right)$$

5. **The two vertices of a triangle are (6, 3) and (–1, 7) and its centroid is (1, 5). Find the third vertex.**

Sol. Let ABC be a triangle whose vertices are A = (6, 3), B = (–1, 7), C = (x, y) and centroid G = (1, 5)

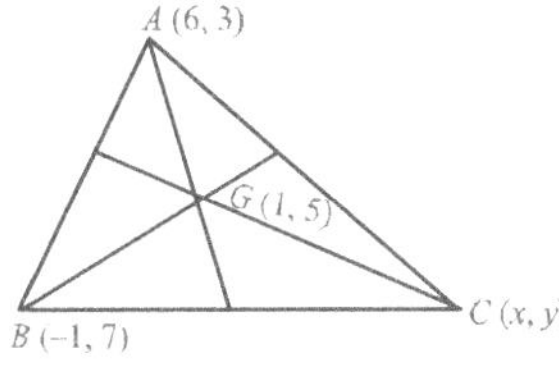

Then using the formula, for the coordinates of centroid; we get

$$1 = \frac{6 + (-1) + x}{3} \text{ and } 5 = \frac{3 + 7 + y}{3} \Rightarrow x = -2 \text{ and } y = 5$$

Hence, the third vertex $C = (-2, 5)$

⊕ Shortcut Approach - 4

Let $A\,(x_1, y_1)$, $B\,(x_2, y_2)$ and $C\,(x_3, y_3)$ are vertices of any triangle ABC, then co-ordinates of incentre,

$$I = \left(\frac{ax_1 + bx_2 + cx_3}{a + b + c}, \frac{ay_1 + by_2 + cy_3}{a + b + c} \right),$$

where a, b, c are length of the sides opposite to vertices A, B, C respectively of triangle ABC.

6. **Find incentre (I) of triangle whose vertices are A (– 36, 7), B (20, 7), C (0, – 8).**

Sol. Using distance formula

$$a = BC = \left| \sqrt{20^2 + (7 + 8)^2} \right| = 25$$

$$b = CA = \left| \sqrt{(-36 - 0)^2 + (7 + 8)^2} \right| = 39$$

$$c = AB = \left| \sqrt{(36 + 20)^2 + (7 - 7)^2} \right| = 56$$

$$I = \left(\frac{25(-36) + 39(20) + 56(0)}{25 + 39 + 56}, \frac{25(7) + 39(7) + 56(-8)}{25 + 39 + 56} \right)$$

$$I = (-1, 0).$$

⊕ Shortcut Approach - 5

Let $A\,(x_1, y_1)$, $B\,(x_2, y_2)$ and $C\,(x_3, y_3)$ are vertices of a triangle, then area of the triangle ABC

$$= \frac{1}{2} \left| x_1(y_2 - y_3) + x_2(y_3 - y_1) + x_3(y_1 - y_2) \right|$$

When one vertex is origin i.e. if the vertices are $(0, 0)$, (x_1, y_1) and (x_2, y_2) then area of the triangle

$$= \frac{1}{2} \left| x_1 y_2 - x_2 y_1 \right|.$$

7. **The area of a triangle is 5. Two of its vertices are (2, 1) and (3, –2). The third vertex lies on the line y = x + 3. Find the third vertex.**

Sol. Let the third vertex be (x_3, y_3), Area of the triangle

$$= \frac{1}{2} \left| [x_1(y_2 - y_3) + x_2(y_3 - y_1) + x_3(y_1 - y_2)] \right|$$

As , $x_1 = 2$, $y_1 = 1$, $x_2 = 3$, $y_2 = -2$ and Area of $\Delta = 5$

$$\therefore \quad 5 = \frac{1}{2}\left|2(-2-y_3) + 3(y_3-1) + x_3(1+2)\right|$$

$$\Rightarrow \quad 10 = |3x_3 + y_3 - 7| \Rightarrow 3x_3 + y_3 - 7 = \pm 10$$

Taking positive sign, $3x_3 + y_3 - 7 = 10$

$$\Rightarrow \quad 3x_3 + y_3 = 17 \qquad \qquad \qquad \text{...(1)}$$

Taking negative sign, $3x_3 + y_3 - 7 = -10$

$$\Rightarrow \quad 3x_3 + y_3 = -3 \qquad \qquad \qquad \text{...(2)}$$

Given that (x_3, y_3) lies on $y = x + 3$

So, $-x_3 + y_3 = 3 \qquad \qquad \qquad \text{...(3)}$

Solving eqs. (1) and (3), $x_3 = \dfrac{7}{2}, y_3 = \dfrac{13}{2}$

Solving eqs. (2) and (3), $x_3 = \dfrac{-3}{2}, y_3 = \dfrac{3}{2}.$

So the third vertex are $\left(\dfrac{7}{2}, \dfrac{13}{2}\right)$ or $\left(\dfrac{-3}{2}, \dfrac{3}{2}\right)$

Exercise

1. The equation of the line passing through $(2, -4)$ and parallel to $X - 2Y - 5 = 0$, is
   (a) $2X + Y + 3 = 0$ (b) $X - 2Y - 10 = 0$
   (c) $X - 2Y + 8 = 0$ (d) $X - 2Y + 13 = 0$

2. For what value of k, the equations $3x - y = 8$ and $9x - ky = 24$ will have infinitely many solutions ?
   (a) 6 (b) 5 (c) 3 (d) 1

3. The two vertices of a triangle are $(3, -5)$ and $(-7, 4)$. If its centroid is $(2, -12)$, find the third vertex.
   (a) $(10, -35)$ (b) $(-2, 10)$
   (c) $(10, 35)$ (d) $(-3, 10)$

4. The vertices of triangle ABC are $A(4, 4), B(6, 3), C(2, -1)$; then angle $\angle ABC$ is equal to
   (a) $45°$ (b) $90°$
   (c) $60°$ (d) None of these

5. If two opposite vertices of a rectangle are $(4, 2)$ and $(10, 6)$ and the equation of other diagonal is $x - 3y + k = 0$. Find the value of k?
   (a) $\dfrac{1}{2}$ (b) 3 (c) 5 (d) 4

6. Let the vertices of a triangle ABC be $(4, 4), (3, 5)$ and $(-1, -1)$, then the triangle is :
   (a) scalene
   (b) equilateral
   (c) right angled
   (d) None of hese

7. Find the co-ordinates of the centroid of a triangle whose vertices are $(0, 6)$ $(8, 12)$ and $(8, 0)$.
   (a) $\left(\dfrac{16}{3}, 6\right)$ (b) $\left(6, \dfrac{16}{3}\right)$
   (c) $(6, 5)$ (d) $(6, 3)$

8. The centroid of the triangle whose vertices are $(3, 10), (7, 7), (-2, 1)$ is
   (a) $(8/3, 6)$ (b) $(6, 8/3)$
   (c) $(-4, -7/3)$ (d) None of these

9. Find the third vertex of the triangle whose two vertices are $(-3, 1)$ and $(0, -2)$ and the centroid is the origin.
   (a) $(2, 3)$
   (b) $\left(\dfrac{-4}{3}, \dfrac{14}{3}\right)$
   (c) $(3, 1)$
   (d) $(6, 4)$

10. The incentre of the triangle with vertices $(1, \sqrt{3}), (0, 0)$ and $(2, 0)$ is
    (a) $\left(1, \dfrac{\sqrt{3}}{2}\right)$
    (b) $\left(\dfrac{2}{3}, \dfrac{1}{\sqrt{3}}\right)$
    (c) $\left(\dfrac{2}{3}, \dfrac{\sqrt{3}}{2}\right)$
    (d) $\left(1, \dfrac{1}{\sqrt{3}}\right)$

11. If $P\left(\dfrac{a}{3}, 4\right)$ is the mid-point of the line segment joining the points $Q(-6, 5)$ and $R(-2, 3)$, then the value of a is

(a) -4

(b) -12

(c) 12

(d) -6

12. The centre and radius of the circumcircle of the triangle whose vertices are $(-2, 3)$, $(2, -1)$, and $(4, 0)$ are

(a) $(3, 5); 5\sqrt{2}$

(b) $(0, 0); \dfrac{5\sqrt{2}}{2}$

(c) $\left(\dfrac{1}{2}, \dfrac{3}{2}\right); \dfrac{\sqrt{2}}{2}$

(d) $\left(\dfrac{3}{2}, \dfrac{5}{2}\right); \dfrac{5\sqrt{2}}{2}$

Coordinate Geometry

Hints & Solution

1. **(b)** Line parallel to $X - 2Y - 5 = 0$ will be $X - 2Y + K = 0$.
Put the point in this equation we have
$2 + 8 + K = 0$
or $K = -10$ or line is $X - 2Y - 10 = 0$

2. **(c)** For infinite solution
$$\frac{3}{9} = \frac{-1}{-k} = \frac{8}{24}$$
$$\Rightarrow \frac{1}{3} = \frac{1}{k} \Rightarrow k = 3$$

3. **(a)** Use Shortcut Approach -3

4. **(d)** Angle ABC is the angle between the lines AB and BC.
Now slope of line $AB =$
$$m_1 = \frac{3-4}{6-4} = -\frac{1}{2}$$
and slope of line $BC = m_2$
$$= \frac{-1-3}{2-6} = \frac{-4}{-4} = 1$$
Now,
$$\tan\theta = \frac{m_1 - m_2}{1 + m_1 m_2} = -1$$
$$\Rightarrow \theta = 135°$$

5. **(c)**

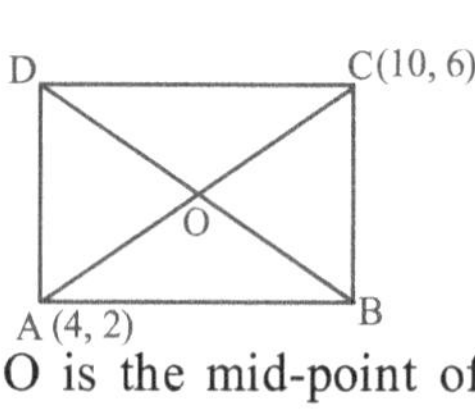

O is the mid-point of diagonal AC and BD
co-ordinate
of $O = \left(\dfrac{4+10}{2}, \dfrac{2+6}{2}\right)$
$= (7, 4)$
Point O is also situated on line
$x - 3y + k = 0$
$\Rightarrow 7 - 3 \times 4 + k = 0 \Rightarrow 7 - 12 + k = 0 \Rightarrow k = 5$

6. **(c)** Use Shortcut Approach -1

7. **(a)** Centroid of a triangle
$$\equiv \left(\frac{x_1 + x_2 + x_3}{3}, \frac{y_1 + y_2 + y_3}{3}\right)$$
$$\equiv \left(\frac{0+8+8}{3}, \frac{6+12+0}{3}\right)$$
$$\equiv \left(\frac{16}{3}, 6\right)$$

8. **(a)** Centroid $=$
$$\left(\frac{3+7-2}{3}, \frac{10+7+1}{3}\right)$$
$$= \left(\frac{8}{3}, 6\right)$$

9. **(c)** Use Shortcut Approach -3

10. **(d)** Clearly, the triangle is equilateral.

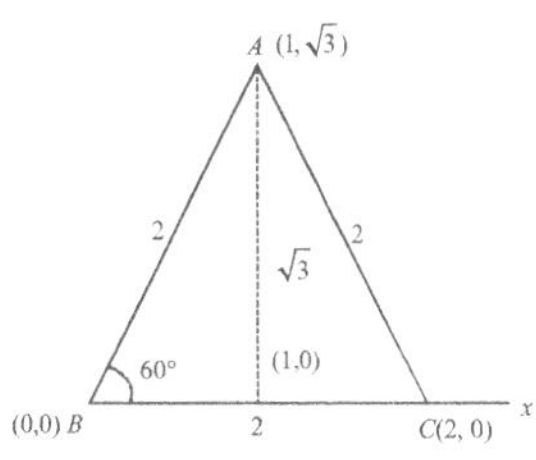

So, the incentre is the same as the centroid.

∴ Incentre

$$= \left(\frac{1+0+2}{3}, \frac{\sqrt{3}+0+0}{3} \right)$$

$$= \left(1, \frac{1}{\sqrt{3}} \right)$$

11. **(b)** As given that $P\left(\dfrac{a}{3}, 4 \right)$ is the mid-point of line segment joining the point Q (–6, 5) and R (–2, 3)

Since, P is the mid-point of QR, then

$$\frac{a}{3} = \left(\frac{-6+(-2)}{2} \right)$$

$$\Rightarrow a = -12$$

12. **(d)** Use Shortcut Approach –4, 5

Mensuration Plane Figures

Shortcut Approach - 1

Side of the largest possible square tiles of equal size so that the tiles exactly fit in the floor of a rectangular room
= HCF of length and breadth of the room.

1. **A room, 39 m 10 cm long and 35 m 70 cm broad, is to be paved with equal square tiles. Find the side of the largest tile so that the tiles exactly fit in the floor of the room.**

Sol. Side of the largest possible tile
= HCF of 39.10 m and 35.70 m = 1.70 m = 1 m 70 cm

Shortcut Approach - 2

When area of the path of uniform width is given, then area of the square garden enclosed by the path

$$= \left[\frac{\text{Area of path} - 4 \times (\text{Width of the path})^2}{4 \times \text{Width of path}} \right]^2$$

2. **A path 3 m wide running all around a square garden has an area of 5300 sq. m. Find the area of the garden enclosed by the path.**

Sol. Area of the square garden

$$= \left[\frac{5300 - 4 \times (3)^2}{4 \times 3} \right]^2 = \left[\frac{5264}{12} \right]^2 = 192428.44 \text{ sq. m.}$$

Shortcut Approach - 3

If from centre of each side of a rectangular field of length 'l' and breadth 'b', a path of width 'w' goes across to the centre of the opposite side, then area of the path
$= w(l + b - w)$

3. **A rectangular field is of measures 29.35 m by 15 m 5 dm. From the centre of each side, a path 2.5 m wide goes across to the centre of the opposite sides. What is the area of the path?**

Sol. Area of the path $= w(l + b - w)$

$$= 2.5 \times (29.35 + 15.5 - 2.5) \text{ sq. m.}$$

$$= 2.5 \times 42.35 \text{ sq. m.} = 105.88 \text{ sq. m.}$$

⊕ Shortcut Approach - 4

Area of a rhombus, length of whose one side and diagonal are given

$$= (\text{diagonal}) \times \sqrt{(\text{side})^2 - \left(\frac{\text{diagonal}}{2}\right)^2}$$

4. Find the area of a rhombus, length of whose one side is 30 cm and length of one diagonal is 42 cm.

Sol. Area

$$= 42 \times \sqrt{(30)^2 - \left(\frac{42}{2}\right)^2}$$

$$= 42 \times \sqrt{900 - 441} = 42 \times \sqrt{449}$$

$$= 42 \times 21.2 = 890.4 \text{ cm}^2$$

⊕ Shortcut Approach - 5

If taking each vertex of an equilateral triangle as centre, a circle is drawn with radius of length half of a side of the equilateral triangle as shown in the figure, then area of the triangle which is not included in the circles (shaded region)

$$= \left(\sqrt{3} - \frac{\pi}{2}\right) (\text{radius})^2$$

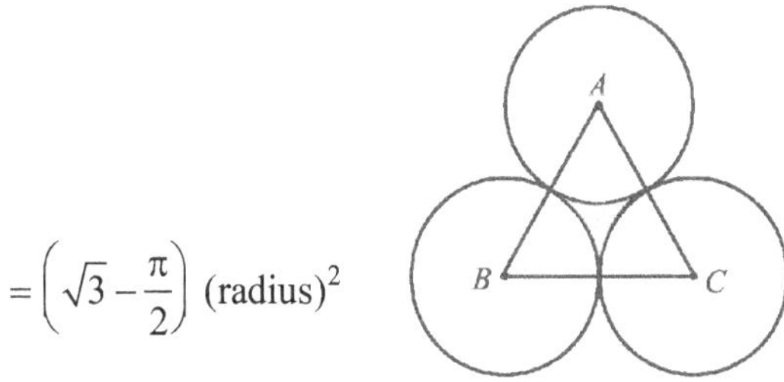

5. There is an equilateral triangle of which length of each side is 4 cm. Taking each vertex of the triangle as centre, a circle of radius 2 cm is drawn. Find the area of the triangle which is not included in the circles.

Sol. Required Area

$$= \left(\sqrt{3} - \frac{\pi}{2} \right) (\text{radius})^2 = \left(1.732 - \frac{22}{14} \right) \times 4$$

$$= (1.732 - 1.571) \times 4 = 0.644 \text{ cm}^2$$

⊕ Shortcut Approach - 6

If taking each vertex of a square as centre, a circle is drawn with radius of length half of a side of the square as shown in the figure (shaded region), then area of the square which is not included in the circles

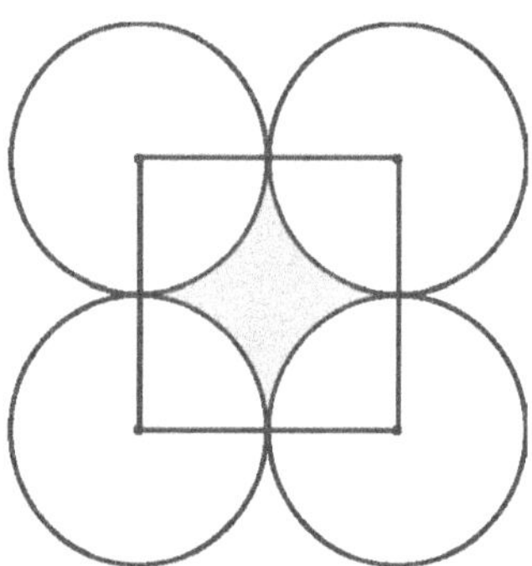

6. **Taking each vertex of a square of side length 6 cm as centre, a circle is drawn with radius of length half of a side of the square. Find the area of the square which is not included in the circles.**

Sol. Required Area

$$= (4 - \pi) \times (\text{radius})^2 = (4 - 3.14) \times (3)^2$$

$$= 0.86 \times 9 = 7.74 \text{ cm}^2$$

⊕ Shortcut Approach - 7

If the sides of a triangle, rectangle, square, circle, rhombus (or any 2-dimensional figure) are increased (or decrease) by x %, then its area is

increased or decrease by $\left(2x + \dfrac{x^2}{100} \right) \%$

7. **If the sides of a rhombus increased by 20%, then find the percentage increase in area of the rhombus.**

Sol. Increase in Area $= \left(2 \times 20 + \dfrac{(20)^2}{100} \right)\% = (40 + 4)\% = 44\%.$

Shortcut Approach - 8

If the length of a rectangle increased by x %, then the percentage decrease in width of the rectangle so that area of the rectangle remains the same

$$= \frac{100x}{100 + x}\%$$

8. **Let the length of a room be 60 cm and width be 40 cm. If the owner wants to increase the length of the room by 20% without changing the area of the room, then find the percentage decrease in the width of the room.**

Sol. Required percentage decrease in width of the room

$$= \frac{100 \times 20}{100 + 20}\% = \frac{100 \times 20}{120}\% = 16.66\%$$

Shortcut Approach - 9

If the length of a rectangle decreased by x %, then the percentage increase in width of the rectangle so that area of the rectangle remains the same

$$= \frac{100x}{100 - x}\%$$

9. **Let the length and width of a runway of an airplane be 1800 m and 100 m respectively. If length of runway is decreased by 10% without changing the area of runway, then find the percentage increase in width of runway.**

Sol. Required percentage increase in width of runway

$$= \frac{100 \times 10}{100 - 10}\% = \frac{100 \times 10}{90}\% = 11.11\%$$

Shortcut Approach - 10

If length and breadth of a rectangle is increased by x and y percent

respectively, then area of the rectangle is increased by $\left(x + y + \dfrac{xy}{100} \right)\%$

10. **If length of a rectangle increases by 20% and breadth of the rectangle is decreases by 16%, then find the % change in area of the rectangle.**

Sol. Percentage change in area

$$= \left(x + y + \frac{xy}{100} \right) \%$$

Here $x = 20$, $y = -16$ (as breadth decreases)

$\therefore$ Percentage change in area

$$= \left[20 + (-16) + \frac{20 \times (-16)}{100} \right] \%$$

$$= \left(4 - \frac{16}{5} \right) \% = 0.8\%$$

Positive sign of 0.8% means increase in area.

⊕ Shortcut Approach - 11

If the area of a square is x cm^2, then area of the circle formed by the same perimeter

$$= \frac{4x}{\pi} \text{ cm}^2$$

11. A wire is in the form of a square enclosing an area of 44 cm^2. If the same cord is bent into a circle, then find the area of that circle.

Sol. Area of the circle

$$= \frac{4x}{\pi} = \frac{4 \times 44 \times 7}{22} = 56 \text{ cm}^2$$

⊕ Shortcut Approach - 12

If r be the radius of a circle, then the area of a square inscribed in a circle is $2r^2$.

12. Find the area of a square inscribed in a circle of radius 10 cm.

Sol. Area of the square

$$= 2r^2 = 2 \times (10)^2 = 200 \text{ cm}^2$$

⊕ Shortcut Approach - 13

Area of the largest triangle inscribed in a semi-circle of radius r cm is r^2 cm^2.

13. Find the area of the largest triangle inscribed in semi-circle of radius 8 cm.

Sol. Area of the largest triangle $= r^2 = (8)^2 = 64 \text{ cm}^2$

Exercise

1. One diagonal of a rhombus is 24 cm whose side is 13 cm. Find the area of the rhombus.
   (a) 25 sq. cm
   (b) 312 sq. cm.
   (c) 125 sq. cm.
   (d) 120 sq. cm.

2. The area of a square field is 576 km^2. How long will it take for a horse to run around at the speed of 12 km/h ?
   (a) 12 h   (b) 10 h
   (c) 8 h   (d) 6 h

3. The length and breadth of a square are increased by 60% and 40% respectively. The area of the resulting rectangle exceeds the area of the square by :
   (a) 224%   (b) 24%
   (c) 124%   (d) 100%

4. The perimeter of the figure given below (correct to one decimal place) is :

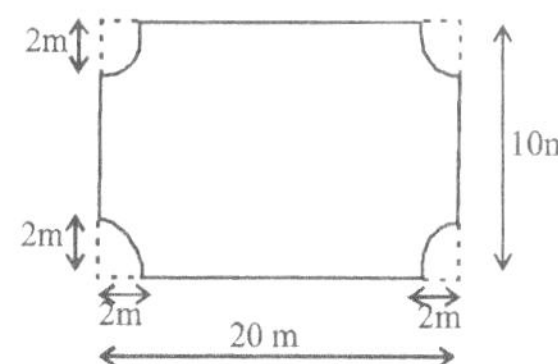

   (a) 56 m   (b) 56.6 m   (c) 57.2 m   (d) 57.9 m

5. A circle and a rectangle have the same perimeter. The sides of the rectangle are 18 cm and 26 cm. What is the area of the circle ?
   (a) 88 cm^2
   (b) 154 cm^2
   (c) 1250 cm^2
   (d) 616 cm^2

6. If every side of a triangle is doubled, then increase in area of the triangle is :
   (a) 200%
   (b) 300%
   (c) 400%
   (d) None of these

7. ABCD is a square in which $\triangle OBC$ is an equilateral triangle then find $\angle DOA$.

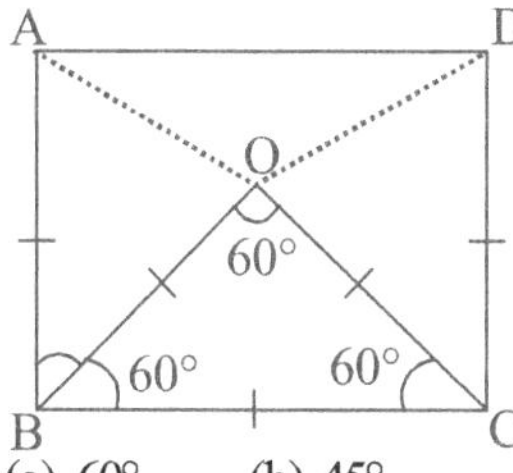

   (a) $60°$ (b) $45°$
   (c) $150°$ (d) $90°$

8. In the given figure, AB is a line of length 2a, with M as mid-point. Semi–circles are drawn on one side with AM, and AB as diameters. A circle with centre O and radius r is drawn such that this circle touches all the three semi-circles. What is the value of r?

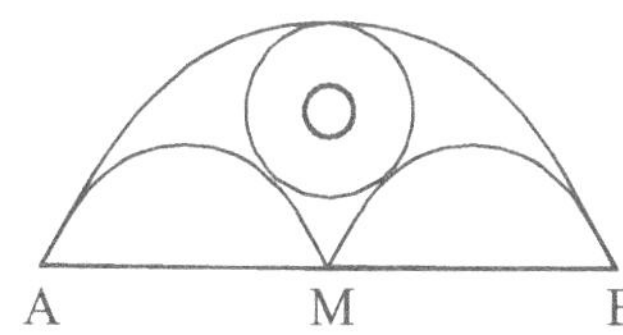

(a) $\dfrac{2a}{3}$ (b) $\dfrac{a}{2}$

(c) $\dfrac{a}{3}$ (d) $\dfrac{a}{4}$

9. Three circles with centres A, B and C and with unit radii touch each other at O, P and Q. Find the area of the shaded region.

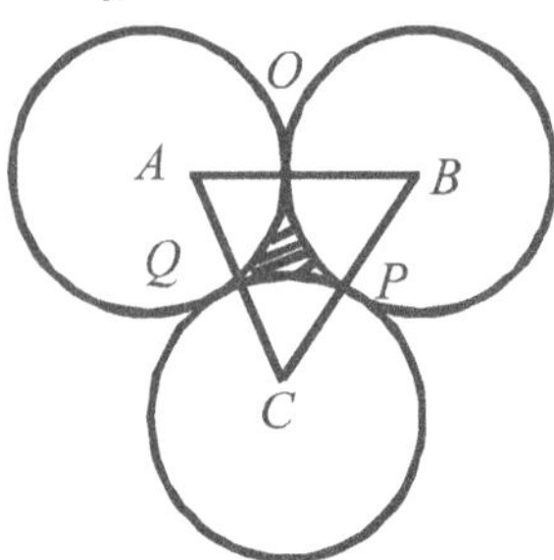

(a) 0.16 sq. units
(b) 1.21 sq. units
(c) 0.03 sq. units
(d) 0.32 sq. units

10. ABCD is a square, 4 equal circles are just touching each other whose centres are the vertices A, B, C, D of the square. What is the ratio of the shaded to the unshaded area within square?

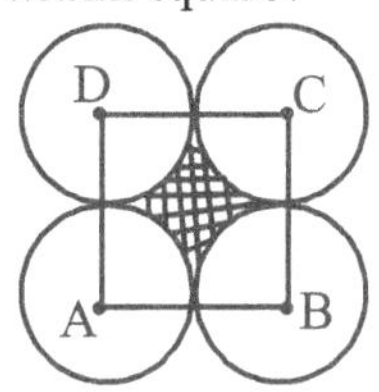

(a) $\dfrac{8}{11}$ (b) $\dfrac{3}{11}$

(c) $\dfrac{5}{11}$ (d) $\dfrac{6}{11}$

11. ABCDEF is a regular hexagon of side 6 cm. What is the area of triangle BDF?

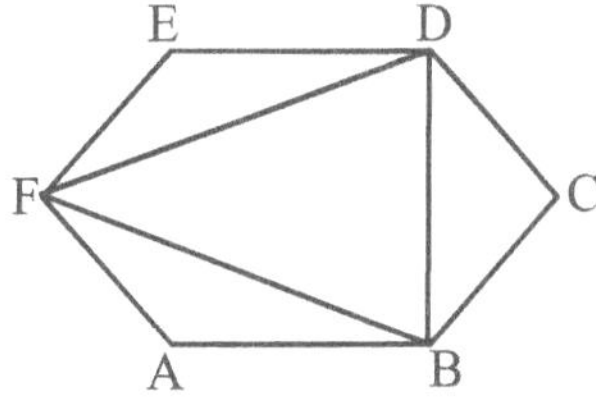

(a) $32\sqrt{3}$ cm^2

(b) $27\sqrt{3}$ cm^2

(c) 24 cm^2

(d) None of these

12. A circle is inscribed in an equilateral triangle of side a. What is the area of any square inscribed in this circle?

(a) $\dfrac{a^2}{3}$ (b) $\dfrac{a^2}{4}$

(c) $\dfrac{a^2}{6}$ (d) $\dfrac{a^2}{8}$

Hints & Solution

1. **(d)** Use Short Approach -4

2. **(c)** Area of field $= 576 \text{ km}^2$.
Then,
each side of field $=$
$\sqrt{576} = 24$ km
Distance covered by the horse
$=$ Perimeter of square field $= 24 \times 4 = 96$ km
$\therefore$ Time taken by horse
$$= \frac{\text{distance}}{\text{speed}} = \frac{96}{12}$$
$$= 8 \text{ h}$$

3. **(c)** Use Short Approach -10

4. **(b)** Required perimeter
$$= 4 \times \left(\frac{2 \times 22 \times 2}{4 \times 7} \right) + 2(16 + 6) = 56.57 \text{ m}$$

5. **(d)** Perimeter of the circle $=$
$$2\pi r = 2(18 + 26)$$
$$\Rightarrow 2 \times \frac{22}{7} \times r = 88$$
$$\Rightarrow r = 14$$
$\therefore$ Area of the circle
$$= \pi r^2 = \frac{22}{7} \times 14 \times 14 = 616 \text{ cm}^2.$$

6. **(b)** Use Short Approach -7

7. **(c)**
$$360 - (75 + 75 + 60)$$
$$= 150°$$

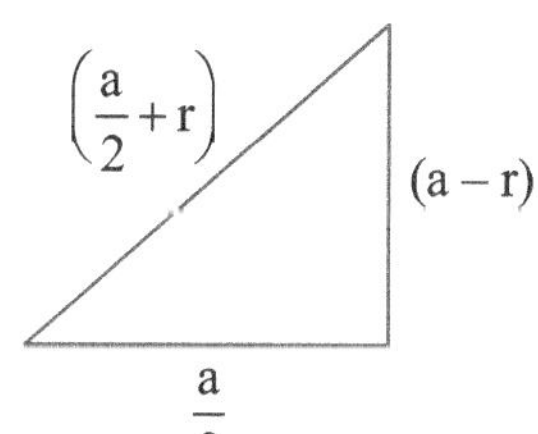

$$90° - 60° = 30°$$

$$AB = BO$$
$$\angle BAO = \angle BOA = \frac{180 - 30}{2} = 75°$$
$$\angle AOB = \angle DOC = 75°$$
$$\angle AOD = 360° - [\angle AOB + \angle DOC + \angle BOC]$$
$$= 360° - 210° = 150°.$$

8. **(c)**

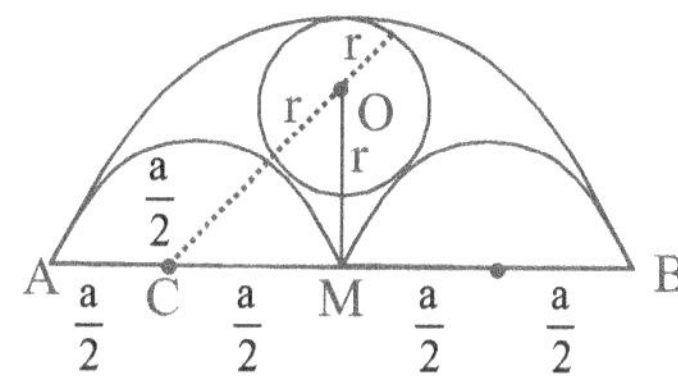

$$\left(\frac{a}{2} + r \right)^2 = \left(\frac{a}{2} \right)^2 + (a - r)^2$$
$$\Rightarrow$$
$$\frac{a^2}{4} + r^2 + ar = \frac{a^2}{4} + a^2 + r^2 - 2ar$$

$$\Rightarrow 3ar = a^2 \Rightarrow r = \frac{a^2}{3a} \Rightarrow$$
$$r = \frac{a}{3}$$

9. **(a)** Use Short Approach -5
10. **(b)** Use Short Approach -6
11. **(b)**

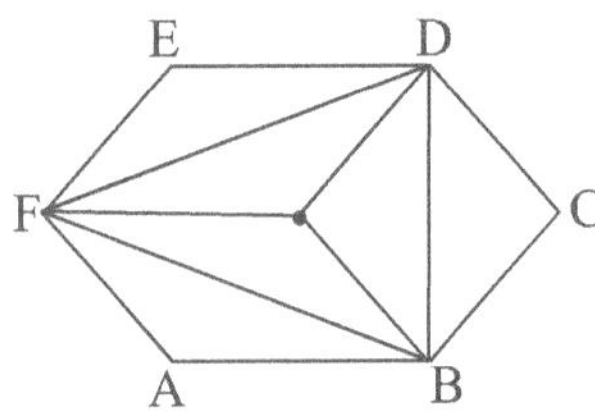

$$\frac{\text{Area of } \Delta BDF}{\text{Area of hexagon}} = \frac{1}{2}$$

As there is a perfect symmetricity.

$\therefore$ Area of hexagon

$$= \frac{3\sqrt{3}}{2} \times (6)^2 = 54\sqrt{3} \text{ cm}^2$$

$\therefore$ Area of

$$\Delta BDF = 27\sqrt{3} \text{ cm}^2$$

Alternatively:

Subtract the areas of three triangles DEF, BAF, BCD from the area of hexagon.

Area of

$$\Delta DEF = \frac{1}{2} \times 6 \times 6 \sin 120°$$

$$= 9\sqrt{3} \text{ cm}^2$$

$\therefore$ Area of all the three triangles $= 27\sqrt{3}$ cm

$\therefore$ Required area of

$$\Delta BDF = 54\sqrt{3} - 27\sqrt{3}$$

$$= 27\sqrt{3} \text{ cm}^2$$

12. (c)

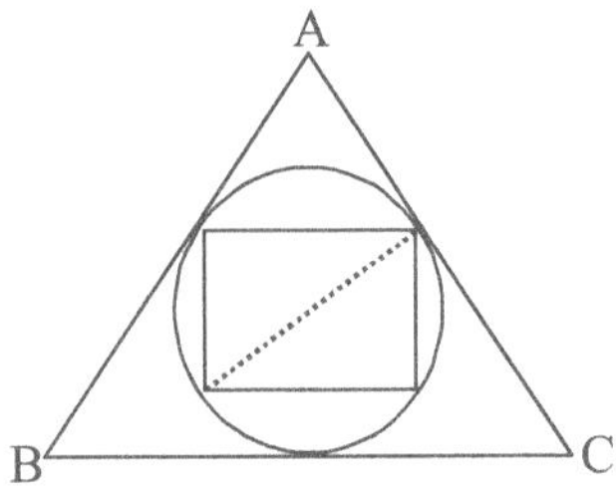

Altitude of equilateral

$$\text{triangle} = \frac{\sqrt{3}}{2} a$$

Radius of incircle

$$= \frac{\sqrt{3}}{2} a . \frac{1}{3} = \frac{a}{2\sqrt{3}}$$

Diameter of incircle
= Diagonal of square

$$\text{Diameter} = \frac{a}{2\sqrt{3}} \times 2 = \frac{a}{\sqrt{3}}$$

$$\text{Diagonal of square} = \frac{a}{\sqrt{3}}$$

$$\text{Area} = \frac{(\text{Diagonal})^2}{2} = \frac{\left(\frac{a}{\sqrt{3}}\right)^2}{2}$$

$$= \frac{a^2}{6}.$$

Mensuration -Solid Figures

If length, breadth and height of a cuboid are changed by $x\%$, $y\%$ and $z\%$ respectively, then its volume is increased by

$$\left[x + y + z + \frac{xy + yz + zx}{100} + \frac{xyz}{(100)^2}\right]\%$$

1. **If length, breadth and height of a cuboid increases by 15%, 10% and 20% respectively, then find the percentage increase in the volume of the cuboid.**

Sol. Percentage increase in volume

$$= \left[x + y + z + \frac{xy + yz + zx}{100} + \frac{xyz}{(100)^2}\right]\%$$

$$= \left[45 + \frac{150 + 200 + 300}{100} + \frac{15 \times 10 \times 20}{(100)^2}\right]\%$$

$$= [45 + 6.5 + 0.3]\% = 51.8\%.$$

If side of a cube or radius (or diameter) of sphere is increased by $x\%$, then its volume increases by

$$\left[\left(1 + \frac{x}{100}\right)^3 - 1\right] \times 100\%$$

2. **Diameter of a sphere is increased by 20%. Find the increase in volume of the sphere.**

Sol. Percentage increase in volume

$$= \left[\left(1 + \frac{20}{100}\right)^3 - 1\right] \times 100\%$$

$$= \left[\left(\frac{6}{5}\right)^3 - 1\right] \times 100\% = 72.8\%.$$

⊕ Shortcut Approach - 3

Three cubes of metal whose sides are x, y and z respectively are melted to form a new cube, if there is no loss of weight in this process. Then side of the new cube will be

$$\sqrt[3]{x^3 + y^3 + z^3}$$

3. The sides of three cubes of metal are 30 cm, 40 cm and 50 cm respectively. Find the side of a resulting cube formed by melting these cubes together.

Sol. Side of resulting cube

$$= \sqrt[3]{(30)^3 + (40)^3 + (50)^3}$$

$$= \sqrt[3]{27000 + 64000 + 125000} = \sqrt[3]{216000} = 60 \text{ cm}$$

⊕ Shortcut Approach - 4

If in a cylinder or cone, height and radius both change by $x\%$, then its volume changes by

$$\left[\left(1 + \frac{x}{100}\right)^3 - 1\right] \times 100\%.$$

4. Both height and radius of a cone are increased by 50%. Find the percentage increase in its volume.

Sol. Percentage increase in volume

$$= \left[\left(1 + \frac{x}{100}\right)^3 - 1\right] \times 100\%$$

$$= \left[\left(1 + \frac{50}{100}\right)^3 - 1\right] \times 100\%$$

$$= \left[\left(\frac{3}{2}\right)^3 - 1\right] \times 100\% = 237.5\%.$$

⊕ Shortcut Approach - 5

If radius of a cylinder or cone is changed by $x\,\%$ and height is changed by $y\,\%$, then volume is changes by

$$\left[2x + y + \frac{x^2 + 2xy}{100} + \frac{x^2 y}{100^2}\right]\%$$

5. **Radius and height of a cylinder are increased by 10% and 20% respectively. Find the percentage increased in volume.**

Sol. Percentage increase in volume

$$= \left[20 + 20 + \frac{100 + 400}{100} + \frac{2000}{10000} \right] \%$$

$$= \left(45 + \frac{1}{5} \right) \% = 45.2\%$$

Shortcut Approach - 6

If radius of a cylinder changes by $x\%$ and height remains the same, then volume of the cylinder changes by

$$\left[\left(1 + \frac{x}{100} \right)^2 - 1 \right] \times 100\%.$$

6. **Find the percentage change in volume of a cylinder if its radius changes by 20% but height remain the same.**

Sol. Percentage change in volume

$$= \left[\left(1 + \frac{x}{100} \right)^2 - 1 \right] \times 100\%$$

$$= \left[\left(1 + \frac{20}{100} \right)^2 - 1 \right] \times 100\%$$

$$= \frac{36 - 25}{25} \times 100\% = 44\%.$$

Exercise

1. The edge of a cube is increased by 100%, the surface area of the cube is increased by :
   (a) 100% (b) 200%
   (c) 300% (d) 400%

2. A rectangular block has length 10 cm, breadth 8 cm and height 2 cm. From this block, a cubical hole of side 2 cm is drilled out. Find the volume and the surface area of the remaining solid :
   (a) $152\ cm^3, 512\ cm^2$
   (b) $125\ cm^3, 215\ cm^2$
   (c) $152\ cm^3, 240\ cm^2$
   (d) $125\ cm^3, 512\ cm^2$

3. The length, breadth and height of a cuboid are in the ratio $1:2:3$. The length, breadth and height of the cuboid are increased by 100%, 200% and 200%, respectively. Then, the increase in the volume of the cuboid will be

   (a) 5 times (b) 6 times
   (c) 12 times (d) 17 times

4. If h, s, V be the height, curved surface area and volume of a cone respectively, then $(3\pi Vh^3 + 9V^2 - s^2h^2)$ is equal to:
   (a) 0 (b) π

   (c) $\dfrac{V}{sh}$ (d) $\dfrac{36}{V}$

5. If P, R, T are the area of a parallelogram, a rhombus and a triangle standing on the same base and between the same parallels, which of the following is true?
   (a) $R < P < T$
   (b) $P > R > T$
   (c) $R = P = T$
   (d) $R = P = 2T$

6. If the radius of a sphere is diminished by 10%, the volume is diminished by
   (a) 31.2% (b) 20.4%
   (c) 27.1% (d) 25%

7. The length of a cold storage is double its breadth. Its height is 3 metres. The area of its four walls (including the doors) is $108\ m^2$. Find its volume.
   (a) $215\ m^3$ (b) $216\ m^3$
   (c) $217\ m^3$ (d) $218\ m^3$

8. A square of side 3 cm is cut off from each corner of a rectangular sheet of length 24 cm and breadth 18 cm and the remaining sheet is folded to form an open rectangular box. The surface area of the box is
   (a) $423\ cm^2$ (b) $468\ cm^2$
   (c) $396\ cm^2$ (d) $612\ cm^2$

9. If length, breadth and height of a cuboid is increased by $x\%$, $y\%$ and $z\%$ respectively then its volume is increased by

(a) $\left[x+y+z+\dfrac{xy+xz+yz}{100} + \dfrac{xyz}{(100)^2} \right]\%$

(b) $\left[x+y+z+\dfrac{xy+xz+yz}{100} \right]\%$

(c) $\left[x+y+z+\dfrac{xyz}{(100)^2} \right]\%$

(d)   None of these

10. Three cubes each of edge 3 cm long are placed together as shown in the adjoining figure. Find the surface area of the cuboid so formed :

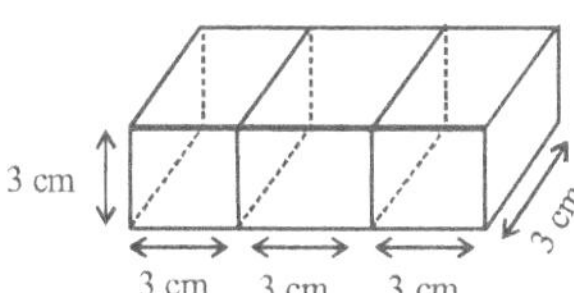

(a) 182 sq. cm

(b) 162 sq. cm

(c) 126 sq. cm

(d) None of these

11. A hemispherical bowl is filled to the brim with a beverage. The contents of the bowl are transfered into a cylindrical vessel whose radius is 50% more than its height. If the diameter is same for both the bowl and the cylinder, the volume of the beverage in the cylindrical vessel is:

(a) $66\dfrac{2}{3}\%$

(b) $78\dfrac{1}{2}\%$

(c) 100%

(d) More than 100%

12. The ratio of the surface area of a sphere to the curved surface area of the cylinder circumscribing the sphere is:

(a) $1:2$ (b) $1:1$

(c) $2:1$ (d) $2:3$

Hints & Solution

1. **(c)** Let each edge of smaller cube $= 1$ m

∴ Each edge of larger cube $= 2$ m

and Surface area of smaller cube $= 6 \times (1)^2 = 6\,m^2$

∴ Surface area of larger cube $= 6 \times (2)^2 = 24\,m^2$

∴ % increase in surface area

$$= \frac{24 - 6}{6} \times 100 = 300\%$$

Alternatively :

$$\frac{S_2}{S_1} = \left(\frac{e_2}{e_1}\right)^2 \Rightarrow \frac{S_2}{S_1} = \frac{4}{1}$$

where S = surface area, e = edge of cube.

∴ Percentage increase in surface area

$$= \frac{4 - 1}{1} \times 100 = 300\%$$

2. **(c)** Net volume $= (10 \times 8 \times 2) - (2 \times 2 \times 2)$

$$= 152\,cm^3$$

Net surface area

$$= 2\,(10 \times 8 + 8 \times 2 + 2 \times 10)$$
$$+ 4\,(2 \times 2) - 2\,(2 \times 2)$$
$$= 240\,cm^2$$

3. **(d)** Use Short Approach -1

4. **(a)** $3\pi Vh^3 + 9V^2 - s^2h^2$

$$= 3\pi\left(\frac{1}{3}\pi r^2 h\right)h^3$$

$$+ 9\left(\frac{1}{3}\pi r^2 h\right)^2$$

$$- \pi^2 r^2 \, (r^2 + h^2)h^2$$
$$= (\pi r h^2)^2 + (\pi r^2 h)^2$$
$$- (\pi r h)^2 (r^2 + h^2)$$
$$= (\pi r h)^2 (r^2 + h^2) -$$
$$(\pi r h)^2 (r^2 + h^2) = 0$$

5. **(d)** Parallelogram Area $= 1 \times b$

Rhombus area $= 1 \times b$

Triangle area $= \dfrac{l \times b}{2}$

Therefore R $=$ P $=$ 2T.

6. **(c)** Use Short Approach -2

7. **(b)** Let L be the length and B be the breadth of cold storage.

$L = 2B, H = 3$ metres

Area of four walls $= 2[L \times H + B \times H] = 108$

$\Rightarrow$ $6BH = 108 \Rightarrow B = 6$ ∴ $L = 12, B = 6, H = 3$ Volume $= 12 \times 6 \times 3 = 216\,m^3$

8. **(c)**

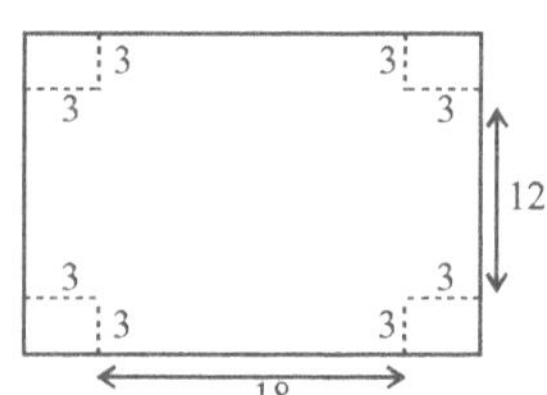

$\ell = 18$ cm, $b = 12$ cm, $h = 3$ cm

$S = 2(\ell h + bh) + \ell b$

{Box is open from upper side}

$= 2\,(54 + 36) + 216$

$= 396$ cm^2

9. **(a)** Use Short Approach -1

10. **(c)** Required surface area

$= 2\,(9 \times 3 + 3 \times 3 + 3 \times 9)$

$= 126$ cm^2

11. **(d)** Let the height of the cylinder be h then its

radius $= h + \dfrac{50h}{100} = 1.5h$

Volume of cylinder

$= \pi r^2 . h$

$= \pi (1.5h)^2 . h = 2.25\,\pi h^3$

ATQ,

Radius of hemisphere

$=$ Radius of cylinder

$= 1.5\,h$

$\therefore$ Volume of hemisphere

$= \dfrac{2}{3}\pi (1.5h)^3 = 2.25\pi h^3$

Thus, volume of cylinder $=$ Volume of hemisphere. so, the cylindrical vassel contains 100% volume of beverage.

12. **(b)**

Height of the cylinder $=$ Diameter of sphere.

$CSA = 2\pi rh = 2\pi r . 2r = 4\pi r^2$

Total surface area of the sphere $= 4\pi r^2$

Required ratio $= 4\pi r^2 : 4\pi r^2$

$= 1 : 1$

Set Theory

$A' = U - A = \{x : x \in U \text{ but } x \notin A\}$

1. If $U = \{1, 2, 3, 4, 5, 6, 7, 8\}$ and $A = \{2, 4, 6, 8\}$ then $A' = ?$
    (a) $\{1, 2, 3, 4\}$ (b) $\{3, 4, 5, 7\}$
    (c) $\{1, 3, 5, 7\}$ (d)   None of these

Sol. (c) $A' = U - A = \{1, 3, 5, 7\}$

$A - B = \{x : x \in A \text{ but } x \notin B\}$

2. If $A = \{2, 4, 6, 8\}$, $B = \{2, 6, 10\}$ them $A - B = ?$

    (a) $\{2\}$ (b) ϕ (c) $\{4, 6\}$ (d) $\{4, 8\}$

Sol. (d) $A - B = \{4, 8\}$

Number of Subsets of a set having n elements $= 2^n$

3. **Find the number of subsets of A where A = {1, 3, 5, 7, 9}**
    (a) 16   (b) 10   (c) 32   (d) 64

Sol. (c)   Number of subsets of $A = 2^n = 2^5 = 32$

$A \cup B = \{x : x \in A \text{ or } x \in B \text{ or } x \in A \text{ and } B\}$

4. **If A = {x : x is an odd number less than 100} and B = {x : x is a even number less than 100} then what is A $\cup$ B ?**
    (a) $\{x : x$ is a prime number less than 100$\}$
    (b) $\{x : x$ is whole number less than 100$\}$
    (c) $\{x : x$ is a natural number less than 100$\}$
    (d) None of these

Sol. (c)

Shortcut Approach - 5

$A \cap B = \{x : x \in A \text{ and } x \in B\}$

5. If $(A) = \{1, 2, 3, 4, 5, 6, 7, 8, 9\}$ and $B = \{1, 3, 5, 7, 9\}$ them $A \cap B = ?$
   (a) $\{1, 3, 5, 7, 9\}$ (b) $\{2, 4, 6, 8\}$
   (c) $\{1, 2, 3, 4, 5\}$ (d) None of these

Sol. (a) $A \cap B = \{1, 3, 5, 7, 9\}$

Shortcut Approach - 6

If A and B are disjoint sets them $A \cap B = \phi$

6. If $A = \{x : x \text{ is a number less than } 100\}$ and $B = \{x : x \text{ is a even number less than } 100\}$ then $A \cap B = ?$
   (a) $\{1, 3, 5, ---- 99\}$ (b) $\{2, 4, 6, 8 ---- 98\}$
   (c) ϕ (d) None of these

Sol. (c)   There A is a set of add number less than 100 and B is a set of even number less than 100

   therefore, $A \cap B = \phi$

Shortcut Approach - 7

If A and B are two finite sets then

$$n(A \cup B) = n(A) + n(B) - n(A \cap B)$$

7. If in a class, 20 students play cricket 40 students play football and 10 students play both cricket and football then find the is number of students in the class?
   (a) 40   (b) 60   (c) 70   (d) 50

Sol. (d) $n(C \cup F) = n(C) + n(F) - n(C \cap F) = 20 + 40 - 10 = 50$

Shortcut Approach - 8

If A, B and C are three finite sets, then

$$n(A \cup B \cup C) = n(A) + n(B) + n(C) - n(A \cap B) - n(B \cap C)$$
$$- n(C \cap A) + n(A \cap B \cap C)$$

8. In a group 60 persons can speak in English, 70 can speak in Hindi and 40 can speak in Bangla. 10 persons can speak in all three languages. 20 persons can speak in Hindi and English, 10 persons

can speak in Hindi and Bangla and 30 persons can speak in English and Bangla then find the number of persons in the group.

(a)   100   (b) 110   (c) 120   (d) 125

8.   **(c)**   Required number of persons

$$n(E \cup H \cup B) = n(E) + n(H) + n(B) - n(E \cap H)$$

$$-n(H \cap B) - n(B \cap E) + n(E \cap H \cap B)$$
$$= 60 + 70 + 40 - 20 - 10 - 30 + 10 = 120.$$

Exercise

1. If X and Y are two sets such that $n(X) = 17$, $n(Y) = 23$ and $n(X \cup Y) = 38$, then $n(X \cap Y)$
   (a) 2   (b) 1
   (c) 3   (d) 4

2. In a certain office, 72% of the workers prefer tea and 44% prefer coffee. If each of them prefers tea or coffee and 40 like both, the total number of workers in the office is :
   (a) 200   (b) 240
   (c) 250   (d) 320

3. A survey show that 63% of the Indians like cheese whereas 76% like apples. If $x\%$ of the Indians like both cheese and apples, then find the range of x.
   (a) $0 \le x \le 23\%$
   (b) $0 \le x \le 39\%$
   (c) $4 \le x \le 35\%$
   (d) $6 \le x \le 33\%$

4. In a town three newspapers A, B and C are published. 42% of the people in that town read A, 68% read B, 51% read C, 30% read A and B, 28% read B and C, 36% A and C and 18% do not read any paper. Find the % of population of town that reads all the three.
   (a) 15%   (b) 25%
   (c) 20%   (d) 35%

5. In an examination out of 100 students, 75 passed in English 60 passed in Mathematics and 45 passed in both English and Mathematics. What is the number of students passed in exactly one of the two subjects?
   (a) 45   (b) 60
   (c) 75   (d) 90

6. In a car agency one day 120 cars were decorated with three different accessories *viz.*, power window, AC and music system. 80 cars were decorated with power windows, 84 cars were decorated with AC and 80 cars were decorated with music systems. What is the minimum and maximum number of cars which were decorated with all of three accessories?
   (a) 10, 61
   (b) 10, 45
   (c) 25, 35
   (d) None of these

7. In an examination 70% of the candidates passed in English, 65% in Mathematics, 27 % failed in both the subjects. If 248 candidates passed in both the subjects, then find the total number of candidates.
   (a) 200   (b) 400
   (c) 300   (d) 100

8. Out of 800 boys in a school, 224 played cricket, 240 played hockey and 336 played basketball. Of the total 64 played both basketball and hockey, 80 played cricket and basketball and 40 played cricket and hockey, 24 played all the three games. The number of boys who did not play any game is:
(a)   128   (b)   216
(c)   240   (d)   160

9. From 50 students taking examination in Mathematics, Physics and Chemistry, each of the students has passed in at least one of the subject, 37 passed Mathematics, 24 Physics and 43 Chemistry. Atmost 19 passed Mathematics and Physics, atmost 29 Mathematics and Chemistry and atmost 20 Physics and Chemistry. Then, the largest numbers that could have passed all three examinations, are
(a)   12   (b)   14
(c)   15   (d)   16

10. A market research group conducted a survey of 2000 consumers and reported that 1720 consumers like product P_1 and 1450 consumers like product P_2. What is the least number that must have liked both the products?
(a)   1150   (b)   2000
(c)   1170   (d)   2500

11. In a town of 10000 families, it was found that 40% families buy newspaper A, 20% families buy newspaper B and 10% families buy newspaper C, 5% buy A and B, 3% buy B and C and 4% buy A and C. If 2% families buy all of three newspapers, then the number of families which buy A only, is
(a)   4400   (b)   3300
(c)   2000   (d)   500

12. A survey of 500 television viewers produced the following information, 285 watch football, 195 watch hockey, 115 watch basket-ball, 45 watch football and basket ball, 70 watch football and hockey, 50 watch hockey and basket ball, 50 do not watch any of the three games. The number of viewers, who watch exactly one of the three games are
(a)   325   (b)   310
(c)   405   (d)   372

Hints & Solution

1.	**(a)**	Use Shortcut Approach -7	**8.**	**(d)**	Use Shortcut Approach -8
2.	**(c)**	Use Shortcut Approach -7	**9.**	**(b)**	Use Shortcut Approach -8
3.	**(b)**	Use Shortcut Approach -7	**10.**	**(c)**	Use Shortcut Approach -7
4.	**(a)**	Use Shortcut Approach -8	**11.**	**(b)**	Use Shortcut Approach -8
5.	**(a)**	Use Shortcut Approach -7	**12.**	**(a)**	Use Shortcut Approach -8
6.	**(d)**	Use Shortcut Approach -8			
7.	**(b)**	Use Shortcut Approach -7			

25 Chapter

Trigonometry

Shortcut Approach - 1

A vertical tower stands on a horizontal ground and is surmounted by a flagstaff. If height of the top of the flagstaff is H metre and angle of elevation of top and bottom of the flagstaff at a point on the ground are θ_1 and θ_2, then height of the tower

$$= H\left(1 - \frac{\tan\theta_2}{\tan\theta_1}\right)$$

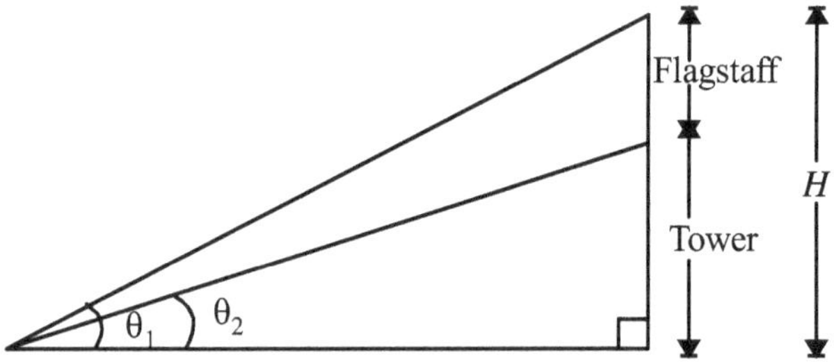

1. An aeroplane when 1500 m high passes vertically above another aeroplane at an instant when the angle of elevation of the planes at the same observing point are 60° and 30° respectively. How many metres lower is one plane than the other?

Sol. Required distance $= H\left(1 - \frac{\tan\theta_2}{\tan\theta_1}\right)$

$$= 1500\left(1 - \frac{\tan 30^\circ}{\tan 60^\circ}\right)$$

$$= 1500\left(1 - \frac{\frac{1}{\sqrt{3}}}{\sqrt{3}}\right) = 1000 \text{ m}$$

Shortcut Approach - 2

Angle of elevation of a lamp post changes from θ_1 to θ_2 when a man walks towards it. If the height of the lamp post is H metres, then the distance travelled by the man is given by

$$\frac{H(\tan\theta_2 - \tan\theta_1)}{\tan\theta_1 \cdot \tan\theta_2} \text{ metres}$$

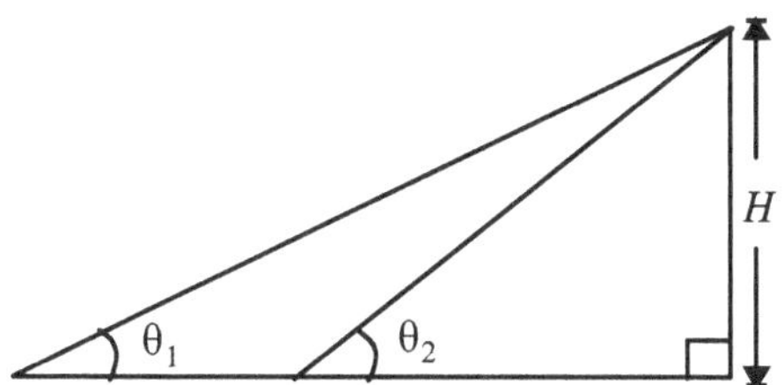

2. **The pilot of a helicopter, at an altitude of 1200 m finds that the two ships sailing towards it in the same direction. The angle of depression of the ships as observed from the helicopter are 30° and 45° respectively. Find the distance between the two ships.**

Sol.

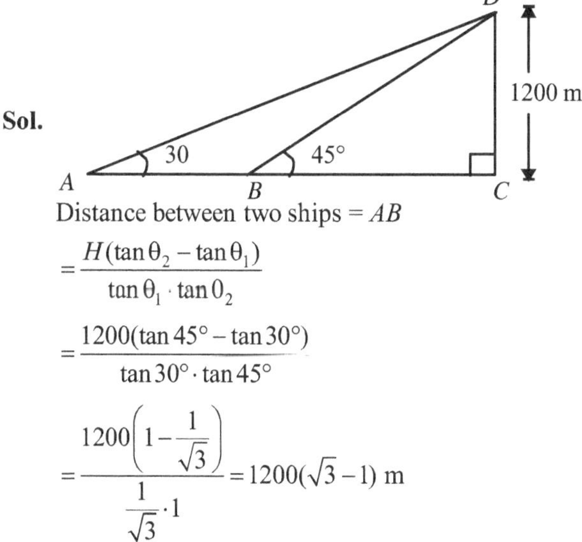

Distance between two ships $= AB$

$$= \frac{H(\tan\theta_2 - \tan\theta_1)}{\tan\theta_1 \cdot \tan 0_2}$$

$$= \frac{1200(\tan 45° - \tan 30°)}{\tan 30° \cdot \tan 45°}$$

$$= \frac{1200\left(1 - \dfrac{1}{\sqrt{3}}\right)}{\dfrac{1}{\sqrt{3}} \cdot 1} = 1200(\sqrt{3} - 1) \text{ m}$$

Shortcut Approach - 3

A lamp post is stands on a horizontal plane. At a point on this plane a man finds that the angle of elevation of the top of the flagstaff is θ_1. On walking x units towards the tower, he find that the angle of elevation of the top of the flagstaff is θ_2, then height of the tower $= \dfrac{x \tan\theta_1 \cdot \tan\theta_2}{\tan\theta_2 - \tan\theta_1}$ units

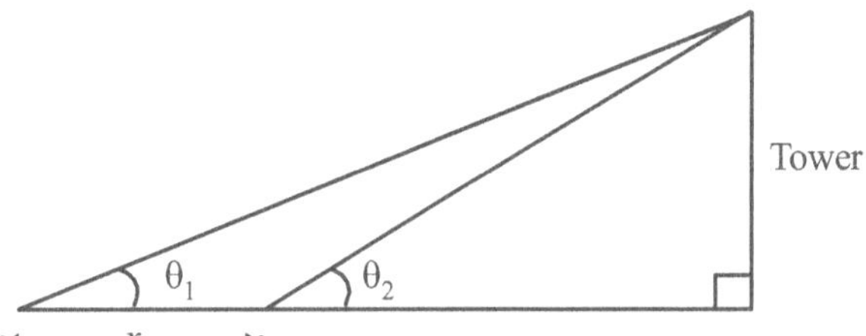

3. **The angle of elevation of top of a tower changes from 30° to 60° when a man walks 60 m towards it. What is the height of the tower.**

Sol. Height of the tower

$$= \frac{x \cdot \tan\theta_1 \cdot \tan\theta_2}{\tan\theta_2 - \tan\theta_1}$$

$$= \frac{60 \cdot \tan 30° \cdot \tan 60°}{\tan 60° - \tan 30°} = \frac{60 \times \dfrac{1}{\sqrt{3}} \times \sqrt{3}}{\sqrt{3} - \dfrac{1}{\sqrt{3}}}$$

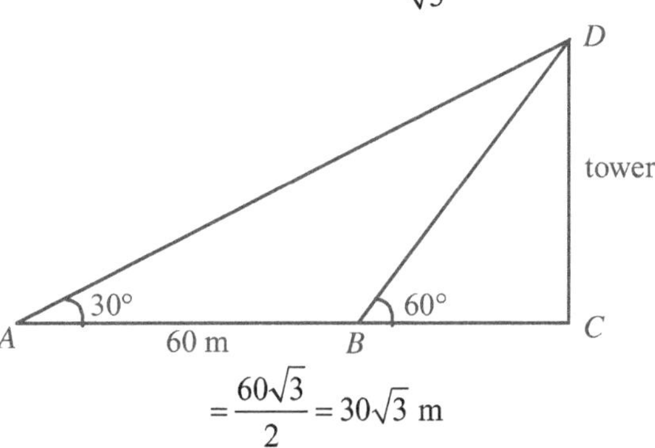

$$= \frac{60\sqrt{3}}{2} = 30\sqrt{3} \text{ m}$$

⊕ Shortcut Approach - 4

The horizontal distance between two towers is x unit. The angle of depression of the first tower when seen from the top of the second tower is $\theta°$.

(i)   If the height of the second tower is y_1 units then the height of the first tower $= (y_1 - x \tan\theta)$ units.

(ii)   If the height of the first tower is given as y_2 units, then the height of the second tower $= (y_2 + x \tan\theta)$ units.

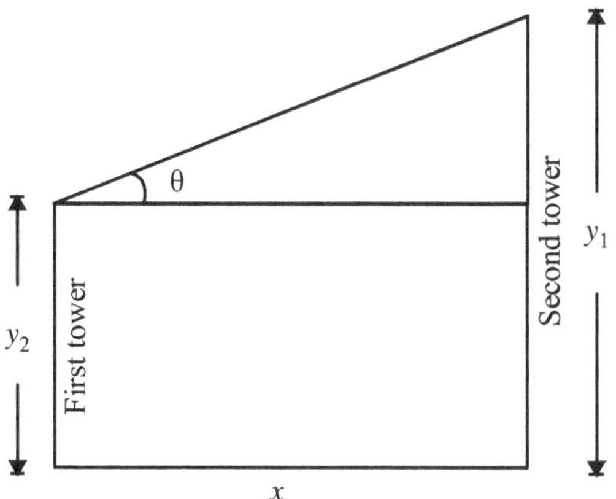

4. Distance between base of the two towers is $60\sqrt{3}$ m. The angle of depression of the first tower when seen from the top of the second tower is 30o. If the height of the second tower is 180 m, find the height of the first tower.

Sol. Height of the first tower $= y_1 - x\tan\theta$

$$= 180 - 60\sqrt{3}\times\tan 30°$$

$$= 180 - 60\sqrt{3}\times\frac{1}{\sqrt{3}} = 120 \text{ m}$$

⊕ Shortcut Approach - 5

Two poles of equal heights stand on either sides of a roadway which is x units wides. At a point P on the road way between the poles AB and CD, the elevation of the tops of the pole are θ_1° and θ_2°, then the

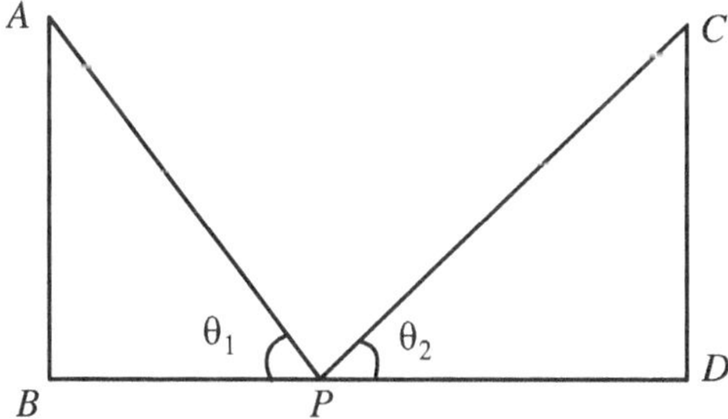

(i) Height of the pole $= \dfrac{x\tan\theta_1\cdot\tan\theta_2}{\tan\theta_1 + \tan\theta_2}$ units.

(ii) (a) Distance of the point P from B $= \left(\dfrac{x\tan\theta_2}{\tan\theta_1 + \tan\theta_2}\right)$ units

(b) Distance of the point P from $D = \left(\dfrac{x \tan \theta_1}{\tan \theta_1 + \tan \theta_2} \right)$ units

5. Two poles of equal heights stand on either side of a roadway which is 30 m wide. At a point on a roadway between the poles, the elevation of the top of the poles are 45° and 30°. Find the height of the poles.

Sol. Height of the pole $= \dfrac{x \tan \theta_1 \cdot \tan \theta_2}{\tan \theta_1 + \tan \theta_2}$

$$= \frac{30 \cdot \tan 45^\circ \cdot \tan 30^\circ}{\tan 45^\circ + \tan 30^\circ} = \frac{30 \cdot \dfrac{1}{\sqrt{3}}}{1 + \dfrac{1}{\sqrt{3}}} = \frac{30}{\sqrt{3} + 1} \text{ m}$$

⊕ Shortcut Approach - 6

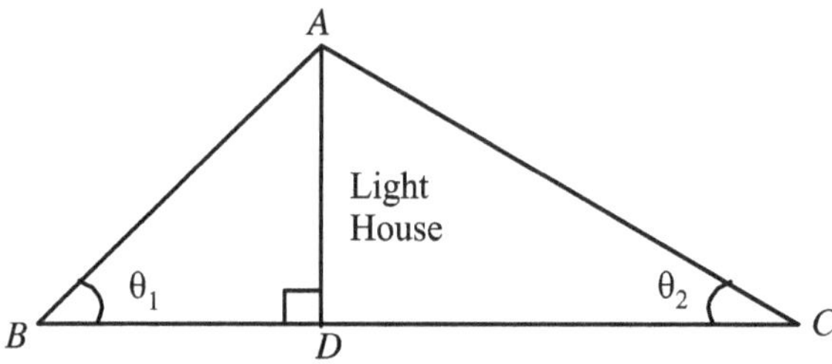

The angle of depression of two ships at B and C from the top A of a light house AD are $\overset{\circ}{\theta_1}$ and $\overset{\circ}{\theta_2}$. If the ships are x units apart, then

(i) The height of the light house $= \dfrac{x \tan \theta_1 \cdot \tan \theta_2}{\tan \theta_1 + \tan \theta_2}$ units

(ii) Distance of the ship at B from the foot of the light house

$$= \frac{x \tan \theta_2}{\tan \theta_1 + \tan \theta_2}$$

(iii) Distance of the ship at C from the foot of the light house

$$= \frac{x \tan \theta_1}{\tan \theta_1 + \tan \theta_2}$$

6. Two boats approach a light house in mid-see from opposite directions. The angle of elevation of the top of the light house from the two boats are 30° and 45° respectively. If the distance between the two boats is 200 m, then
(i) Find the height of the light house.
(ii) Find the distance of the first boat from light house.

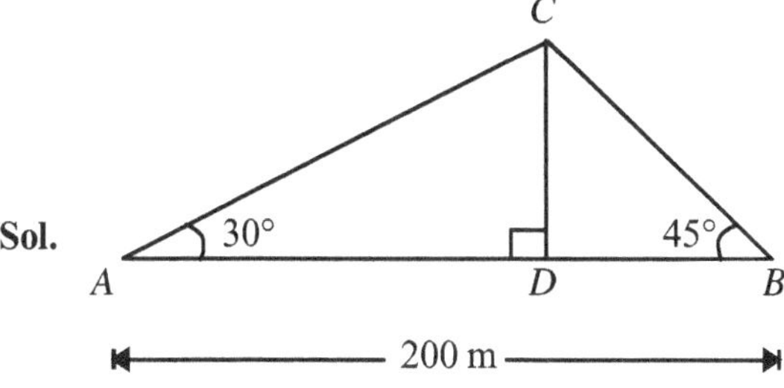

Sol.

(i) Height of the light house

$$= \frac{x\tan\theta_1 \cdot \tan\theta_2}{\tan\theta_1 + \tan\theta_2} = \frac{200\tan 30^\circ \cdot \tan 45^\circ}{\tan 30^\circ + \tan 45^\circ}$$

$$= \frac{200 \times \dfrac{1}{\sqrt{3}} \times 1}{\dfrac{1}{\sqrt{3}} + 1} = \frac{200}{\sqrt{3}+1}\ \text{m}$$

(ii) Distance of the first boat from light house

$$= \frac{x\tan\theta_2}{\tan\theta_1 + \tan\theta_2} = \frac{200\tan 45^\circ}{\tan 30^\circ + \tan 45^\circ}$$

$$= \frac{200 \times 1}{\dfrac{1}{\sqrt{3}} + 1} = \frac{200\sqrt{3}}{\sqrt{3}+1}\ \text{m}$$

⊕ Shortcut Approach - 7

Angle of elevation of top of a tower from top and bottom of a building of height h units are θ_1° and θ_2° respectively, then

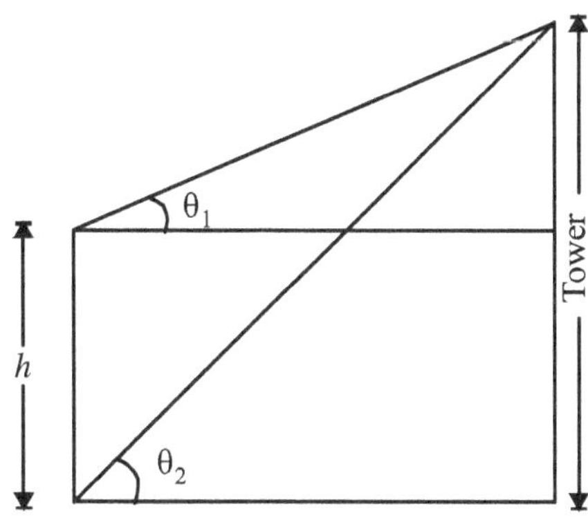

(i)   Height of the tower $=\dfrac{h\cdot\tan\theta_2}{\tan\theta_2-\tan\theta_1}$ units

(ii)   Distance between the building and the tower

$$=\dfrac{h}{\tan\theta_2-\tan\theta_1}\text{ units}$$

7.   **Angle of elevation of a tower from top and bottom of a building of height 80 m are 30° and 45° respectively. Find the**
    (i)   Height of the tower.
    (ii)   Distance between the building and the tower.

Sol.   (i)   Height of the tower $=\dfrac{h\tan\theta_2}{\tan\theta_2-\tan\theta_1}$

$$=\dfrac{80\tan45°}{\tan45°-\tan30°}$$

$$=\dfrac{80\times1}{1-\dfrac{1}{\sqrt3}}=\dfrac{80\sqrt3}{\sqrt3-1}\text{ m}$$

   (ii)   Distance between the building and the tower

$$=\dfrac{h}{\tan\theta_2-\tan\theta_1}=\dfrac{80}{\tan45°-\tan30°}$$

$$=\dfrac{80}{1-\dfrac{1}{\sqrt3}}=\dfrac{80\sqrt3}{\sqrt3-1}\text{ m}$$

⊕ Shortcut Approach - 8

The angles of elevation of the top of a tower from two points at distances m and n metres are complementary. If the two points and the base of the tower are on the same straight line, then the height of the tower is $\sqrt{mn}$.

8.   **The angle of elevation of the top of a tower standing on a horizontal plane from two points on a line passing through the foot of the tower at a distance 16 m and 25 m respectively are complementary angles. Then height of the tower is**

Sol.   Height of the tower $=\sqrt{m.n}$

    here m $= 16$ m, n $= 25$ m.

    $\therefore$ Height of the tower $=\sqrt{16*25}$

$$=4*5=20\text{ m}.$$

Exercise

1. The angle of elevation of the top of a tower at point on the ground is $30°$. If on walking 20 metres towards the tower, the angle of elevation become $60°$, then the height of the tower is
   (a) 10 metre
   (b) $\dfrac{10}{\sqrt{3}}$ metre
   (c) $10\sqrt{3}$ metre
   (d) None of these

2. If $\cos^4 \theta - \sin^4\theta = \dfrac{2}{3}$, then the value of $2\cos^2\theta - 1$ is:
   (a) 0   (b) 1
   (c) $\dfrac{2}{3}$ (d) $\dfrac{3}{2}$

3. If $\sin \theta + \sin^2 \theta = 1$. Find the value of $\cos^2 \theta + \cos^4 \theta$
   (a) 0   (b) 2
   (c) 1   (d) 3

4. If the length of the shadow of a tower is $\sqrt{3}$ times that of its height, then the angle of elevation of the sun is
   (a) $15°$ (b) $30°$
   (c) $45°$ (d) $60°$

5. The value of $\tan 4°. \tan 43°. \tan 47°. \tan 86°$ is
   (a) 0   (b) 1
   (c) $\sqrt{3}$ (d) $\dfrac{1}{\sqrt{3}}$

6. A person, standing on the bank of a river, observes that the angle subtended by a tree on the opposite bank is $60°$; when he reaches 20 m far (away) from the bank, he finds the angle to be $30°$. The height of the tree and the breadth of the river are :
   (a) $10\sqrt{3}$ m, 10 m
   (b) $10, 10\sqrt{3}$ m
   (c) 20 m, 30 m
   (d) None of these

7. If $a \cos \theta + b \sin \theta = m$ and $a \sin \theta - b \cos \theta = n$, then $a^2 + b^2 =$
   (a) $m^2 - n^2$ (b) $m^2 n^2$
   (c) $n^2 - m^2$ (d) $m^2 + n^2$

8. In a triangle, the angles are in the ratio $2 : 5 : 3$. What is the value of the least angle in the radian ?
   (a) $\dfrac{\pi}{20}$ (b) $\dfrac{\pi}{10}$
   (c) $\dfrac{2\pi}{5}$ (d) $\dfrac{\pi}{5}$

9. Find the minimum & maximum value of $\sin^6\theta + \cos^6\theta$.
   (a) $\dfrac{1}{4}, 1$ (b) $\dfrac{1}{4}, \dfrac{1}{2}$
   (c) $\dfrac{3}{4}, 1$ (d) $\dfrac{1}{4}, \dfrac{3}{4}$

10. The angles of elevation of the top of a tower standing on a horizontal plane from two points on a line passing through the foot of the tower at a distance 9 ft and 16 ft respectively are complementary angles. Then the height of the tower is

(a) 9 ft   (b) 12 ft

(c) 16 ft   (d) 144 ft

11. An aeroplane flying horizontally 1 km. above the ground is observed at an elevation of $60°$ and after 10 seconds the elevation is observed to be $30°$. The uniform speed of the aeroplane in km/h is

(a) 240

(b) $240\sqrt{3}$

(c) $60\sqrt{3}$

(d) None of these

12. The angles of elevation of the top of a tower from two points at distances $4m$ and $9m$ metres are complementary. If the two points and the base of the tower are on the same straight line, then the height of the tower is

(a) $6\,m$

(b) $36\,m$

(c) $\dfrac{9}{4}\,m$

(d) None of these

Hints & Solution

1. (c) Use Shortcut Approach -3

2. (c) $\cos^4\theta - \sin^4\theta = \dfrac{2}{3}$

$$\left(\cos^2\theta\right)^2 - \left(\sin^2\theta\right)^2 = \dfrac{2}{3}$$

$$\Rightarrow \left(\cos^2\theta + \sin^2\theta\right)\left(\cos^2\theta - \sin^2\theta\right) = \dfrac{2}{3}$$

$$\Rightarrow \cos^2\theta - \sin^2\theta = \dfrac{2}{3}$$

$$\Rightarrow \cos^2\theta - \left(1 - \cos^2\theta\right) = \dfrac{2}{3}$$

$$\Rightarrow \cos^2\theta - 1 + \cos^2\theta = \dfrac{2}{3}$$

$$\Rightarrow 2\cos^2\theta - 1 = \dfrac{2}{3}$$

3. (c) $\sin\theta + \sin^2\theta = 1 \Rightarrow \sin\theta = 1 - \sin^2\theta$
$\Rightarrow \sin\theta = \cos^2\theta$ Now,
$\cos^2\theta + \cos^4\theta = \cos^2\theta + (\cos^2\theta)^2$
$= \sin\theta + \sin^2\theta = 1.$

4. (b)

A

h

θ

B $\sqrt{3}\,$h C

Let AB is a tower height h and BC is its image

then BC $= \sqrt{3}\,$h.

Again, let angle of elevation of the sun is θ.

then, $\tan\theta = \dfrac{AB}{BC} = \dfrac{h}{\sqrt{3}.h}$

$\tan\theta = \dfrac{1}{\sqrt{3}}$

$\Rightarrow \tan\theta = \tan 30°$

$\therefore \quad \theta = 30°$

5. (b) $\tan 4°.\tan 43°.\tan 47°.$
$\tan 86°$
$= \tan 4°.\tan 43°.\tan$
$(90° - 43°)\tan(90° - 4°)$
$= \tan 4°.\tan 43°.\cot 43°$
$\cot 4°$
$[\because \tan(90 - \theta) = \cot\theta]$
$= \tan 4° \times \tan 43° \times$

$$\dfrac{1}{\tan 43°} \times \dfrac{1}{\tan 4°}$$

$$\left[\because \cot\theta = \dfrac{1}{\tan\theta}\right]$$

6. (a) Use Shortcut Approach -2, 3

7. (d) $(a\cos\theta + b\sin\theta)^2 + (a\sin\theta - b\cos\theta)^2$
$= m^2 + n^2.$
$a^2\cos^2\theta + b^2\sin^2\theta +$
$2ab\cos\theta.\sin\theta + a^2\sin^2\theta$
$+ b^2\cos^2\theta - 2\,ab\sin\theta.$
$\cos\theta$
$= m^2 + n^2.$
or $\quad a^2(\cos^2\theta + \sin^2\theta) + b^2$
$(\sin^2\theta + \cos^2\theta)$
$= m^2 + n^2.$
or $\quad a^2 + b^2 = m^2 + n^2$

8. (d) Let angles are $2x$, $5x$ and $3x$.

$2x + 5x + 3x = 180°$

(sum of interior angle of triangles is 180°)

$10x = 180°$

$x = 18°$

$\therefore$ Least angle in degree

$= 2x = 2 \times 18 = 36°$

In radian

$= \dfrac{\pi}{180°} \times 36° = \dfrac{\pi}{5}$

9. (a) $\sin^6\theta + \cos^6\theta$

$= (\sin^2\theta)^3 + (\cos^2\theta)^3$

$= (\sin^2\theta + \cos^2\theta)^3 - 3\sin^2\theta . \cos^2\theta (\sin^2\theta + \cos^2\theta)$

$= 1 - 3\sin^2\theta \cos^2\theta$

$= 1 - \dfrac{3}{4} \times 4\sin^2\theta . \cos^2\theta$

$= 1 - \dfrac{3}{4}(2\sin\theta . \cos\theta)^2$

$= 1 - \dfrac{3}{4}(\sin 2\theta)^2$

Min $\sin 2\theta = 0$

So, Max $(\sin^6\theta + \cos^6\theta) = 1 - \dfrac{3}{4}(0)$

$= 1 - 0 = 1$

Max $\sin 2\theta = 1$

So, min $(\sin^6\theta + \cos^6\theta)$

$= 1 - \dfrac{3}{4}(1) = \dfrac{1}{4}$

10. (b) Use Shortcut Approach -8

11. (b) $d = H \cot 30° - H \cot 60°$

Time taken $= 10$ second

speed $=$

$\dfrac{\cot 30° - \cot 60°}{10}$

$\times 60 \times 60 = 240\sqrt{3}$

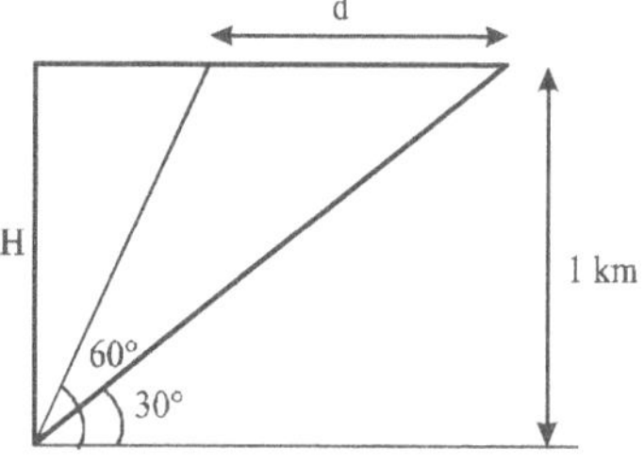

12. (a) Use Shortcut Approach -8

Logarithm

If $\log_a b = x$ then $a^x = b$.

1. Find the value of x, if $\log_{3\sqrt{3}}\left(\dfrac{1}{729}\right) = x$.

Sol. $\log_{3\sqrt{3}}\left(\dfrac{1}{729}\right) = x \Rightarrow (3\sqrt{3})^x = \dfrac{1}{729}$

$\Rightarrow (3)^{\frac{3}{2}x} = (3)^{-6} \Rightarrow x = -4$

2. Find the value of x, if $\log_3 [\log_2 (\log_5 x)] = 0$.

Sol. $\log_3[\log_2(\log_5 x)] = 0$

$\Rightarrow \log_2(\log_5 x) = 1 \qquad\qquad [\because \log_a(1) = 0]$

$\Rightarrow \log_5 x = 2 \Rightarrow x = (5)^2 = 25.$

$a^{\log_a x} = x$

3. Find the value of $7^{\log_7 6}$.

Sol. $7^{\log_7 6} = 6.$

4. Find the value of $5^{3 - \log_{625} 125 + \log_5 25}$.

Sol. $5^{3 - \log_{625} 125 + \log_5 25} = 5^3 \times 5^{-\log_{625} 125} \times 5^{\log_5 25}$

$= 5^3 \times 5^{-x} \times 25 \qquad\qquad [\text{let } x = \log_{625} 125]$

$= 5^5 \times 5^{-x}$

Now, $x = \log_{625} 125 = \dfrac{\log_5 125}{\log_5 625} = \dfrac{\log_5 (5)^3}{\log_5 (5)^4} = \dfrac{3}{4}$

$\therefore 5^{3 - \log_{625} 125 + \log_5 25} = 5^5 \times 5^{-\frac{3}{4}} = 5^{5 - \frac{3}{4}} = 5^{\frac{17}{4}}$

⊕ Shortcut Approach - 3

$$\log_{b^y} a^x = \frac{x}{y}(\log_b a)$$

5.   **Find the value of $\log_{25} 125 - \log_8 4$.**

Sol. $\log_{25}(125) - \log_8(4) = \log_{5^2}(5)^3 - \log_{2^3}(2)^2 = \dfrac{3}{2} - \dfrac{2}{3} = \dfrac{5}{6}.$

6.   **If $\log_8 x + \log_4 x + \log_2 x = 11$, then find the value of x.**

Sol. $\log_8 x + \log_4 x + \log_2 x = 11$

$$\Rightarrow \log_{2^3} x^1 + \log_{2^2} x^1 + \log_2 x = 11$$

$$\Rightarrow \frac{1}{3}\log_2 x + \frac{1}{2}\log_2 x + \log_2 x = 11$$

$$\Rightarrow \left(\frac{1}{3} + \frac{1}{2} + 1\right)\log_2 x = 11$$

$$\Rightarrow \frac{11}{6}\log_2 x = 11 \Rightarrow \log_2 x = 6$$

$$\therefore x = (2)^6 = 64.$$

⊕ Shortcut Approach - 4

Number of digits in a^b = [Integral part of $(b\log_{10} a)$] + 1

7.   **Find the number of digits in 2^{52}. (Given that $\log_{10} 2 = 0.3010$).**

Sol.   Number of digits in 2^{52}

$= $ [Integral part of $52\log_{10}2$] $+ 1$

$= $ [Integral part of 52×0.3010] $+ 1$

$= $ [Integral part of 15.652] $+ 1$

$= 15 + 1 = 16.$

Exercise

1. Find the value of
$\log_{10}100 + \log_{10}1000 + \log_{10}10000$.
   (a) 2
   (b) 9
   (c) 24
   (d) 100

2. Find the value of
$\log_5 10 \times \log_{10} 15 \times \log_{15} 20 \times \log_{20} 25$.
   (a) 5/2
   (b) 5
   (c) 2
   (d) $\log\left(\dfrac{5}{2}\right)$

3. If $a = \log_8 225$ and $b = \log_2 15$, then a, in terms of b, is :
   (a) $b/2$
   (b) $2b/3$
   (c) b
   (d) $3b/2$

4. If $\log_5\left[\log_3\left(\log_2 x\right)\right] = 1$,
   then x is
   (a) 2^{234}
   (b) 243
   (c) 2^{243}
   (d) None of these

5. If $\log_{10}2 = a$ and $\log_{10}3 = b$, then $\log_5 12$ equals:
   (a) $\left(a+b\right)/\left(1+a\right)$
   (b) $\left(2a+b\right)/\left(1+a\right)$
   (c) $\left(a+2b\right)/\left(1+a\right)$
   (d) $\left(2a+b\right)/\left(1-a\right)$

6. Find the value of
$\log_{20}100 + \log_{20}1000 + \log_{20}10000$
[Assume that log 2 = 0.3]
   (a) 90/13
   (b) 80/13
   (c) 110/13
   (d) 70/13

7. $\log_{\sqrt{a}}b^2 \times \log_{\sqrt{b}} c^2$
$\dots \times \log_{\sqrt{y}} z^2 \times \log_{\sqrt{z}} a^2$ is
   (a) 2^{27}
   (b) 2^{52}
   (c) 2^{54}
   (d) 2^{26}

8. The value of $(\log_2 8 + \log_3 9 + \log_5 25)$ is :
   (a) 5
   (b) 6
   (c) 7
   (d) None of these

9. If $p = \log_{12} 18$, $q = \log_{24} 54$ then the value of $pq + 5(p - q)$ is
   (a) 0
   (b) 4
   (c) 1
   (d) 9

10. Find the value of
$3 \log\dfrac{81}{80} + 5\log\dfrac{25}{24} + 7\log\dfrac{16}{15}$
   (a) log 2
   (b) log 3
   (c) 1
   (d) None of these

11. If $3^{x+1} = 6^{\log_2 3}$, then x is
   (a) 2
   (b) 3
   (c) $\log_3 2$
   (d) $\log_2 3$

12. The value of
$$\left[\frac{1}{\log_{xy}(xyz)} + \frac{1}{\log_{yz}(xyz)} + \frac{1}{\log_{zx}(xyz)} \right]$$
is equal to
   (a) 1
   (b) 2
   (c) 3
   (d) 4

Hints & Solution

1. **(b)** $\text{Log}_{10}100 + \text{Log}_{10}100 + \text{Log}_{10}10000$

$= \text{Log}_{10}10^2 + \text{Log}_{10}10^3 + \text{Log}_{10}10^4$

$= 2 + 3 + 4 = 9$

2. **(c)** $\log_5 10 \times \log_{10} 15 \times \log_{15} 20 \times \log_{20} 25.$

$= (\log 10/\log 5) \times (\log 15/\log 10) \times (\log 20/\log 15) \times (\log 25/\log 20)$

$= \log 25/\log 5 = 2\log 5/\log 5 = 2.$

3. **(b)** Use Shortcut Approach-3

4. **(c)** $\log_5 \left[\log_3 \left(\log_2 x \right) \right]$

$= 1 = \log_5 5$

$\Rightarrow \log_3 \left(\log_2 x \right) = 5 = \log_3 3^5$

$\Rightarrow \log_2 x = 3^5 = 243$

$\Rightarrow 2^{243} = x$

5. **(d)** $\log_5 12 = \log_5(3 \times 4)$

$= \log_5 3 + \log_5 4$

$= \log_5 3 + 2\log_5 2$

$= \{(\log_{10}3)/(\log_{10}5)\} + \{(2\log_{10}2)/(\log_{10}5)\}$

$= [(\log_{10}3)/\{(\log_{10}10) - (\log_{10}2)\}] + [(2\,\log_{10}2)/\{(\log_{10}10) - (\log_{10}2)\}]$

$= \{b/(1-a)\} + \{2a/(1-a)\}$

$= (2a + b)/(1-a)$

6. **(a)** Use Shortcut Approach-3

7. **(b)** Since

$$\log_{\sqrt{a}} b^2 = 4\log_a b = \frac{4\log b}{\log a}$$

Similarly $\log_{\sqrt{b}} c^2 = \dfrac{4\log c}{\log b}$

Hence given expression is equal to

$4^{26} \times \dfrac{\log b}{\log a} \times \dfrac{\log c}{\log b} \times \dfrac{\log d}{\log c} \times \ldots$

$\times \dfrac{\log z}{\log y} \times \dfrac{\log a}{\log z} = 4^{26} = 2^{52}$

8. **(c)** Use Shortcut Approach-3

9. **(c)** We have

$$p = \log_{12} 18 = \frac{\log_2 18}{\log_2 12}$$

$$= \frac{1 + 2\log_2 3}{2 + \log_2 3}$$

$$q = \log_{24} 54 = \frac{\log_2 54}{\log_2 54}$$

$$= \frac{1 + 3\log_2 3}{3 + \log_2 3}$$

Putting $x = \log_2 3$, we have

$pq + 5(p - q) =$

$$\frac{1 + 2x}{2 + x} \cdot \frac{1 + 3x}{3 + x} + 5\left\{ \frac{1 + 2x}{2 + x} - \frac{1 + 3x}{3 + x} \right\}$$

$$= \frac{6x^2 + 5x + 1 + 5\left(-x^2 + 1\right)}{(x + 2)(x + 3)}$$

$$= \frac{x^2 + 5x + 6}{(x + 2)(x + 3)} = 1$$

10. **(a)** Use Shortcut Approach-3

11. **(d)** $3^{x+1} = (3 \times 2)^{\log_2 3}$

$\Rightarrow 3^{x+1} = 3^{\log_2 3} \times 2^{\log_2 3}$

$\Rightarrow 3^{x+1} = 3^{\log_2 3} \times 3$

$\Rightarrow 3^x = 3^{\log_2 3}$

$\Rightarrow x = \log_2 3$

12. **(b)** Given expression

$= \log_{xyz} (xy) + \log_{xyz} (yz) + \log_{xyz} (zx)$

$= \log_{xyz} (xy \times yz \times zx)$

$= \log_{xyz} (xyz)^2$

$= 2\log_{xyz} (xyz) = 2 \times 1 = 2$